Photo on page i: Franz Kafka, Albert Ehrenstein,
Otto Pick, and Lise Kaznelson, Vienna, the Prater, 1913

Loser Sons
Politics and Authority

Avital Ronell

University of Illinois Press
Urbana, Chicago, and Springfield

Library of Congress Cataloging-in-Publication Data
Ronell, Avital.
Loser sons : politics and authority / Avital Ronell.
p.   cm.
Includes index.
ISBN 978-0-252-03664-4 (cloth)
ISBN 978-0-252-09370-8 (ebook)
1. Authority in literature.
2. Authority.
3. Fathers and sons in literature.
4. Fathers and sons.
5. Kafka, Franz, 1883–1924—Family.
6. Lyotard, Jean-François, 1924–1998.
I. Title.
PN56.A87R66   2012
809'.93353—dc23   2011047445

While writing this book, I read Percy Bysshe Shelley's *The Cenci: A Tragedy in Five Acts*. Inescapably I began a long-distance relationship with Beatrice Cenci, the young Roman aristocrat brutalized by her father. Imprisoned in 1599 for conspiring to murder the tyrannical father, Beatrice Cenci and her relatives were tortured. The Rome of Pope Clement VIII was greatly invested in upholding paternal authority, and declined to address the storm of violence—sexual, physical, altogether demolishing—visited upon a tormented family by its patriarch. It has been said that Caravaggio witnessed her execution while putting together his ideas for *The Martyrdom of Saint Matthew*. I would like to dedicate this work to her plight and person, remembering the Beatrices among us.

Contents

Preface
Wrestling a Bad Object

This work was long in coming. During the time that I was preparing its elephantine birth—I have stopped counting the years—other works and responsibilities commanded my attention, averted my gaze, and gnawed at me like undeflectable energy vampires. It's hard enough to set apart some sheltering space in order to write. In our age of deficit it is moreover hard but essential to justify the work that we do, to have writing even qualify for a prevalent concept of work or to get filed as part of some labor force. And maybe this is as it should be. Still, it is difficult not to lose courage when so many are underpaid or unemployed, and still others, closer to my own job description, are prevented from publishing and teaching, regardless of how well-trained and talented they prove to be. If I may register a complaint, I can say that in my corner, I give up a lot of energy. Does anyone know how exhausting it is to teach, write evaluations and letters of recommendation, administrate, participate in colloquia, stay close to the artistic pulse, travel, feign a life, push back the false unconscious—maybe I should leave it at that, before I trip into a memoir or pitch myself into a confessional abyss. I look at my colleagues and see brilliant scholars ground down by the institutional praxeology, turned over to the bureaucracy of teaching, its unending evaluations and businesslike downgrades, as if "results" could be yielded in the traumatic precincts of learning. This type of consistent demotion to a result-oriented quotient belongs to the subject (and hell) I would want to raise here. I cannot seem to break away from the feeling that so much wracks the committed scholar, the artist, poet, and the burnt-out student body these days. I certainly do not want to ring up an inventory of excuses. I am well aware that others are truly compromised, dragged down by material inequities, insult, distress, and they don't even get to the starter's position, much less to the purported finishing line.

Of course, many people wouldn't want this job—its implication of searing solitude, the haranguing drills of a sole sentence's fate, and the inescapability of relentless autocritique. It may be pointless to indicate at the beginning of a work what a grandiose hassle it all was when the rhetoric of these things dictates that one should speak of its urgency and ineluctability, its sense of mission or accomplishment. Whom does that sort of opening statement reassure or convince—that you, too, could barely make it? When following Nietzsche's style sheet, you don't take the laurels for having initiated a work, but say it seized or befell you, you were just in some outfield of thought when it came at you. You leave out the part about struggling with your radical passivity, somehow sustaining the crushing overload that has one bowed in receptive anticipation. Let's just say it the way I started off: this work was long in coming. In some respects, it sat out the Bush years over which it was watching. Stupefied yet receiving signals and taking hits, it was benched.

Many friends and colleagues urged me to get the book out before the Bush-Cheney years were over, so that I could make a timely contribution to political thought. This perspective had its merits and scored some bullet points with me. Yet I decided (permit me the illusion of decision here) that in this case I would not produce a chiefly reactive text, but keep my vigil, absorb the damages, wait it out. Those years are not over. The damages are colossal, the indignities still to a great extent uncounted. Even in the palpable sigh of relief that we call Obama, the corruption of historical narrative, the material poverty of means, and corrosion of constitutional integrity cannot be easily repaired, much less recounted. Maybe I am bringing up the rear (like all latecomers, I am fated to rear-end history); maybe I'm speaking from a lookout point in the future, from the event of returns and revenants that have always borne down on my texts. Please allow me the ambiguous situation of staying close to a troubled past that swings over to the future, demanding that a serious analysis be attached to its stealthy gait.

Some points hang in suspension, awaiting their time, or they are allowed to vanish into the thin air of a speculative leap. Some leaps are calculated to land in something like an ungroundable *anahistory* that requires a different kind of approach—an alternative universe of writing, probing, and piercing. Anahistory, holding us as firmly as history and its tally of traumatic punch-outs, calls for a different tenor of the *cri/écrit*, the nocturnal expanse of a thinker's anguish. Partnered to history, it introduces different registers of thought that accumulate around inoccurrence and the subterranean maneuvers of eventfulness. It is not only a matter of discerning disavowed

horrors, though anahistory hunkers down with such unearthable narratives, but also requires us to scour something like the national unconscious, even when this turns out to be a "false unconscious." Both Freud and Lacan make allowances for the *false unconscious,* a repository of traces that shadow unconscious receptors and create their own mess of jumbled surges.

All this backlog of indeterminacy is hanging over our heads today. You can choose not to go with it, keeping yourself from plunging into the depths of near unintelligibility. In my case it's not a matter of choice. I have to go in where things get messy, or sometimes I see myself walking through the unyielding frankness of deserted fields, scanning the wreckage, maybe on the lookout for a sign of life, a breeze, or an unexpected sound.

❂ ❂ ❂

An ongoing provocation, the thought on authority was pressed into these pages by several considerations and not a few urgencies. To the extent that I felt compelled by the themes constituting this work, I was stalled and undermined by the sway of their worldly cast, the anxious pinch of timeliness to which they bear witness. As it happens, I am a creature of the untimely, coached by Nietzschean temporal leaps yet put through my paces by obligatory relapses into what one might call "tradition." This is the only way in which I might be considered conservative, or a conservationist—by adhering to the demands of traditional narratives and their often-silenced partners. That is to say, in part, that I am in my comfort zone when ferreting out the heavily sedated traces and repressed remnants of historical eventfulness. Trained on the sidelines of the master discourses, I advocate a kind of untimely activism, driven home by the joint closure of the philosophical and the political. The long conversation within the philosophical and political partnership has reached in many ways, and by necessity, a lull. Yet, powerful inroads persist, together with a store of untapped reserves. If something has not been accounted for, I want it. The least probable cause, the darkest and most unavailable docket, sparks my curiosity (*curiosity:* itself a philosophically devalued motor for investigation). I scour the peripheries, the often-abandoned sites of ethical reconnaissance.

Given these constraints and the way I curb the so-called object of contemplation, I like to stay away from the dominant trends and approved protocols for reading politics. Especially where "politics" becomes censorious and inevitable, unconditional (or as Arendt puts it, "total") and thus, in terms of the way discursive containers are regulated and managed, kind of DOA, as so-called contemplative objects go. (Well, I suppose anything submitted to contemplation shows up de facto DOA. Let me clarify. I mean more mangled or disfigured, more subject to *Entstellung*, disturbed by displacement, than even language habitually demands—barely recognizable or plainly obsolesced in terms of its presentation. That's when it comes my way.)

I honor and read my colleagues, those known to me and those unfamiliar, some of whom have sat on panels with me or have run the other way, who make it their life's work to put unceasing pressure on the elaboration of social formations, and bravely continue to work through the mires of a relentlessly agonistic politics. But, for me, whether by default or theoretical perversion, there's another way of going about things, another hand that can be played when it comes to the domination of the political and the necessity of sizing up its implications. I start off by conducting nano-analyses, following minor or minoritarian tracks that may lead nowhere or, suddenly, they may flip into "the big picture" to function as the rush of canaries in a political coal mine.

Growing into small spaces in order to bear hard upon big issues has its advantages, and I'm not the first to try this scholarly diet. Still, there are pitfalls and dramatic dissolutions. At the same time as one may be motivated by Kafkan velocities to interrogate the fate of a speck—at the same time as one senses the surprising advance of nano-traces, evicted conceptual shells or the itineraries of imperceptible systemic disruption—one is also arrested by the magnitude of oversized concerns that bind to existence. One is compelled to return to the fundamental structures that keep us going, if only in the mode of stationary mobility and according to archeophiliac determination—meaning that one is magnetized by the return of and driven by the return to ancient objects, concepts, formulae when piecing together the remnants of world.

Even if one may favor the miniaturized portion of heavy-hitting problems, one sometimes crashes against the wall of their magnitude. Though preferring the speck to the spectacular, I must take my questions—well, they are not really questions, they are *calls*—I take these calls, given a choice (though it is not a matter of choice, but let us go on); they should, these calls, in order to be worthy of presentation, light up only when and if they arrive beyond themselves, from where they loom—big, barely manageable, yet nondialectically allied with the speck. The calls may seem marginal, yet they require sizable backup from the tradition, the books, textual fronts, historical feints, and referential pretenses that increase their expanses. By chasing down the motif of the loser son—where big meets little, constantly exchanging attributes—I am attacking a cluster of issues that has been heckling me from the philosophical bleachers and that asks, in a way that won't let up, these questions: Where does the political pose problems? How is the very possibility of peaceful coexistence undermined by apparently unbreachable structures?

These prods have brought me to a register of concern that makes me wonder in what way the victory of patriarchy is still something to contend with. What happened when metaphysics elevated the "paternal metaphor" to the status of authority? To what extent is the son's failure-to-be bound up with claims made for authority's rule? Riding on this putative authority, how does the impossible figure of the father, whether split or faux unitary, still hold sway? Freud himself, zeroing in on problems of filial remorse and the construction of legacy, has remarked that we cannot point to the authority that bolsters the father, except to the extent that this very stature remains an effect of "the victory of patriarchy."[1] Unauthorized yet pumping meaning, the values associated with Father continue to mark the limit where politics meets psychoanalysis and generates questions of power. At once phantomal and commanding, the paternal, like Hamlet's father, directs the way the whole house comes down, falling apart around a shared name that seals the demise of a split son.

Similar scenes, though less eloquently equipped to handle the historical blow, occur in many households where paternity retains a trace of sovereign right. This trace is what interests me here—archaic, nearly effaced, although vibrant in an ineluctable yet dreary kind of way. Thus I am also trying to create a chart for the largely unmarked and phantomal spread of paternal residue, to see where its seepage begins in the glacializing spaces of cruel bureaucracies, among implacable administrators, in terms of religious gridlock, alongside the regulatory state, and other rule-productive structural oppressions that take off from Father's tracks.

The figure of father, as ordinary as it sits, also enthrones the unfathomable and is riddled by an enigmatic grid. Even the unfathomable has a history, boasts a lineage. It is very likely that the persistence of the paternal incursion, its often stealth logic, has created a legacy of mutant breakdown—a fissuring of a special stripe. Irrevocably connected, these calls, or bullet points, bring into view the particularly modern phenomenon of a loser inheritance. I'll try to make this contention intelligible by keying into a number of telling texts and crucial idioms that speak to the pervasive sense of our impoverished political existence, even where the political brings hope and assuming the political and existence still match up credible prints. In any case, I will examine the edges of archaic contamination and draw up a map of prevalent forms of aggressive coexistence.

Although recognizably modern in its articulation, there is nothing as such *new* about the mark of humiliation borne by the drummed-out or di-

---

1. Sigmund Freud, *Moses and Monotheism: Three Essays*, Standard Edition of the Complete Psychological Works of Sigmund Freud (London: Hogarth Press, 1975), 23:118.

vested son. Isaac would fill in as biblical ancestor to such a figure—benched before he could be sacrificed, counted out in the squabble between two representatives of killer paternity, the submissive and the dominant versions, both murderous. Spared but forgotten, left to dwindle in the desert solitude of a discarded filiation, he is at once elected and faded, chosen for the journey to Mount Moriah, on a mission that must be aborted, taken up only to be put down in the hollow of paternal testing grounds. That is one way to run the narrative, by casting light on the emptiness that followed upon the failed sacrifice: he lost out on the transcendental leap, receded from history into a mold of inoccurrence. This inoccurrence still speaks to and imprints us, however.

Another type, if not archetype, to fill in the blank of what I am trying to draw out would be represented by Faust, the celebrity *Streber* or striver, who inherited the burden of a deficient father, a doctor who by lazy but persistent acts of malpractice was responsible for dozens of deaths. An embarrassment to Nietzsche and nearly everyone else in the reader's circle, Faust, after the embrace that he holds with Mephistopheles, must be saved in the end of Goethe's rendition by the intercession of a divine father, redeemed from a more terrestrial struggle with his inherited nullity. Stripped of the mantel of authority, or unable to grow under the pressure of aberrant assertions of paternity (though aberration may be the rule), Isaac and Faust, in differing but related ways, are set on autodestruct, losing a legacy—maybe only at the end of their stories, but also from the get-go—when they try to break through to historical narrative. In the end, they are bound by a restraining order from which they cannot cut loose, or to which they remain blindly stuck and submissive. In itself, this would not be a bad thing.

The unconscious billing system that attacks the world and relentlessly escalates aggression causes the trouble that I want to track. Poetic or scriptural "dummies" such as Isaac and Faust help us think through the default of the political—which, given problems of grounding or founding or of merely shallow depths, remains wholly indistinct if not rhetorically depleted, philosophically flamed out. At the same time, despite considerable theoretical obstacles, political rigor and vigilance require an ongoing critique of models, motifs, and ideologies that have served to indicate how coexistence is mapped and regulated. Many of these models come from totalitarian vocabularies that still stand in their rooted if wobbly monumental ways, or are frankly resuscitated with no apologies offered. There are ways to get past some of these abiding theoretical insults, even where they tend continually to rerun through history's more deliberate projections.

Key motifs upon which I call, whether deployed or parked on the side, come from undervalued psychoanalytic probes that should help us produce a road map, even where we part ways with some of the insistent tendencies that have informed current theories and politologies. Like literature, psychoanalysis offers significant access to political undercurrents and untapped tropological reservoirs. I thus want to treat texts and supporting fictions where there is no traceable movement from the structures of narcissism to those of identification, a movement that for Freud signals the start of the political. The Freudian science, Philippe Lacoue-Labarthe and Jean-Luc Nancy remind us in "La panique politique," is "by rights a science of culture, and consequently a political science." Even and precisely if it turns out, they continue, "that this right gives rise to the greatest difficulties, indeed to the greatest disorder, and to the threat, as we will see, of a theoretical panic."[2] The panic and avoidance strategies nailed by the Freudian science belong to the vocabularies and reflections that we are trying to build on, understanding that one still seeks *a political solution* to inhumanity. This is why one has to return with obsessional acuity to that which, in institutions or in hermeneutic circles, among professionals or amateur commentators, off and on the medial screen, on some level of consciousness, whether avowed or dismissed, provokes panic—or critical narcolepsy, the other side of panic. To the extent that narcissism serves as a controlling cipher for our era, backed by capital and other state-subventioned tyrannies, including technological addiction, narcissism's run calls for inquiry, for a real sense of how it instates the negation of all relation, beginning with the Freudian investigation. Let us however hold off on an analysis of the politics of narcissistic refusal until all the players are on the field.

To what extent does the fate of such loser types mirror the predicament or warp of authority today? How can they be put in contact with specific forms of tyranny that torture and thrive in what may well be a postpolitical age, where the political achieves closure and completion? These boys, after all, had something that we no longer lay claim to in any serious way, though the death rattle of the divine can be heard thumping in the background of our modernity. These sons, whether they emerge from the pages of *Totem and Taboo*, or take up residence in biblical drama and Bildungsroman, were driven, if only into the ground, by divine law and higher prompts of authority.

2. Philippe Lacoue-Labarthe and Jean-Luc Nancy, "La panique politique," in *Retreating the Political*, ed. Simon Sparks (London and New York: Routledge, 1997), 9.

We late moderns, left only with the emptying-out of divine spaces, we're stuck with what is now known as Father in his legacy of failure, dumping and thumping in ungodly war zones on those without cover of sanctioned transcendence. Isaac and Faust, and those bound to them in nearly archetypal kinship, had the alibi of commandment and divine ordinance watching their backs, even as they vanished or sealed deals with paternal surrogates. Persuaded by these shadows, I'll try to make the plight of the loser son as clear as possible, giving it where possible theoretical buoyancy and punch so that it can take its place in the columns of political anxiety of the day. I enter these areas, not always sanctioned by cognition, with the understanding that I lack the authority to do much more than protect a question or visit with an unoccupiable concept. Maybe I can allow myself to gather a cluster of motifs, mostly emptied and abandoned, in order to examine what passes for the political. Maybe I'll manage to overturn some contestable models that block our path, but this, too, is not sure, given the way the political has exhausted philosophy. The point is to stick with the blockage and look at it without flinching. In a similar context Lacoue-Labarthe has noted, when exploring the practical deprivation of philosophy as regards its own authority, it is as if the political has "remained, paradoxically, the blind spot of the philosophical." In other words, when facing the political, or the philosophical essence of the political, philosophy immediately "finds itself implicated as a political practice relieved of its own authority: not simply of its possible social or political power, but relieved of the authority of the theoretical or the philosophical as such (however one determines such a practice: critique, back to basics, thinking and distorting re-appropriation [*Verwindung*], step backwards, deconstruction, etc.)."[3] The deflation of critical power in the face of political anxiety invites further reflection at this time.

❂ ❂ ❂

If some of the questions raised by what follows offer a sense of contemporaneity with issues of the day, alongside the backdrop of dislodged transcendence, then a few words might help to situate my intentions here and create distance from similarly calibrated projects that try to address the "fate of politics today." Perhaps I should begin by stating what I am not doing, by explaining how I engage the paradoxes of scholarly avoidance, which is not the same as opting out or choosing disengagement. On the contrary. Still,

3. Delivered by Lacoue-Labarthe and Nancy in Paris as the inaugural address to the Centre for Philosophical Research on the Political, 8 December 1980. Now reprinted as "The Centre: Opening Address," in *Retreating the Political*, 112.

I have to deal with the fact that an empirical approach is no longer in any significant way decisive. I can no longer rely heavily on the yields of such an approach, even where they support my cause. At the same time, I cannot simply discard empirical gains or stomp out material traces. It is in any case embarrassing for a philosophical sensibility to think that, empirically encouraged, she may be restricted to taking the pulse of the *Weltgeist*, that she might be on schedule for recognizable events, right on time, cannily capable of arrival and descent—all delusional fractures and misguided hopes as concerns the pressure-point of attentive anxiety that, precisely, always misses its mark, ruins its chances for self-satisfaction. The pull of elided concepts or the long rule of the plainly unintelligible—the pulse of fateful inoccurrence—demand their time, too, which, more likely than not, is on nobody's watch. The tensed attunement of all-too-clamorous topics such as abet the concern for terror, injustice, authority must be regarded with suspicion. Suspicion is our gain, however, fueled by the struggle with hesitation and doubt. The metaphysically laden problems of authority, injustice, terror, teach one continually to beat a retreat and recalibrate. These themes, which break open any containment of the philosophical, invite us to widen the range of critical motion and look for alternative types of cognition.

During the time I was preparing this book—it was, I repeat, an elephantine birthing that occurred in dog-time, so it's a matter of multiplying the years and zoography here—I listened to many lectures and read or attended a lot of different kinds of writing; I exposed myself to theater, cinema, digital invention, dance performance, a thick scale of music and art, a wide range of protest movements. I listened hard and let myself be washed in the works and projections of others. I tried to remain open, which requires a lot of effort on the part of a writer. Normally you go into voluntary lockdown or you try your best to stay tightly sealed in your bubble, building up a narcissistic shield. . . . Do you have any idea how many dissertation chapters, stray manuscripts, reviews, requests, and conscripted reports make daily runs into my no-fly zone and threaten my sanity? How many people come to me with writer's-block stories, despite my interdictions and phobic shooing gestures, fingers in my ears, lalalala'ing? Or how many friends pull me away from my writing desk, if only because they pretend they want to see me "for coffee"? I do not drink coffee. Everyone knows that I do not drink coffee, that it makes me paranoid, OK—*more* paranoid, so why do they taunt me with this pretend-invitation, a total intrusion that, even when politely repelled, ruins my day because then I am stranded in guilty rumination round the clock, loop after loop? There are some people who cannot say "no" without serious psychic consequence and debilitating aftermaths. My friends know that about me—that I am condemned to be a yes-sayer to practically any proposition—and, still, they regularly attack by inviting me out "for coffee." I will not go there now, because I cannot bear the stress of remembering the dossiers of obstacles, as well as the friendless cultural denigrations, that make writing nearly impossible in our day, at least in my day.

One never knows where something like influence sets out to reel you in. I have very determined reading lists and study habits that define my path, and I believe I have given a full disclosure of the greatest hits that I have taken. I suppose that the structure of indebtedness and questions of legacy have an abiding hold on me. I run in the opposite direction of those who want to be known as "original," those who conceal or go so far as to *defame* their sources, obliterate their origins.[4] I, by contrast, am in perpetual gratitude pose. I remember one summer when my friend Christopher Fynsk gave a lecture on Levinas's notion of a "sabbatical existence" and the question of peace. How shall I account for encounters such as the one offered by Chris in the inventory of thought? Did this lecture seize on me in a way similar to a reading that once invaded Freud, traumatically opening psychoanalysis? I am not suggesting an analogy of names and positions, just cutting into an established history of provocation, recalling how a lecture can call you out of your slumber, throw you, nestle somewhere inside and start sprawling without any precise plan or purpose.

4. When I make a pitch for rigorous nonoriginalness, my purpose is not only to open ethical and political dossiers that bind us in every practice of inscription, but also to situate myself close to Emerson's sense of discernment and ethical urgency. Eduardo Cadava reminds me in an email of 7 January 2011 of this relevant quote: "Emerson has a remarkable passage in his essay 'Quotation and Originality,' in which he writes: 'Our debt to tradition through reading and conversation is so massive, our protest or private addition to tradition so rare and insignificant,—and this commonly on the ground of other reading and hearing,—that, in a large sense, one would say there is no pure originality. All minds quote. Old and new make the warp and woof of every moment. There is no thread that is not a twist of these two strands. By necessity, by proclivity and delight, we all quote. We quote not only books and proverbs, but arts, sciences, religions, customs and laws; nay, we quote temples and houses, tables and chairs by imitation. . . . The originals are not original. There is imitation, model and suggestion, to the very archangels, if we knew their history.'" Such a quote has no doubt served as a basis for Willis Goth Regier's *Quotology* (Lincoln and London: University of Nebraska Press, 2010), which houses Emerson and reflects on our relation to an ethics of citationality. Woof.

Sometimes you do not know where a lecture lands, how greatly shaken you have been, dispossessed, or realigned. Fynsk, if I recall correctly, was talking about a terrible responsibility and the assumption of powerlessness, a situation of unconditional surrender to no power. His presentation went so far as to involve the bodily characteristic of powerlessness of Dasein and what it means to have no need of anything. He unfolded the Shabbath as a practice of peace, the exposure of violence deferring itself. I realized that his understanding of affliction was very close to what I wanted mine to be. Maybe it was the same; maybe, for the span of his reading, *we* were the same. I should confess that I often go into identificatory overdrive. Not always, but often. I have been Derrida, I have been Lacoue-Labarthe, Kofman, I have been Pynchon and Rousseau, I am never not Nietzsche, I have been Acker and Kleist, I was Beckett when I turned into Bettina von Arnim and once I was Aretha Franklin, but that's another track (why do you suppose she sings about *r-e-s-p-e-c-t* and "Think: Think!" if it were not for our shared Kant-through-Heidegger homework assignments?). This type of overidentification plays a decisive role in the political stagings I am analyzing.

The face down between narcissism and identification continues to shape a political genealogy, requiring us to reflect on how one breaks out of an original narcissism—something that I go into in the sections on the disappearance of authority. Identification and Mitsein are different ways in which the subject (an abbreviation) breaks down the stranglehold of isolation and becomes politically assigned, ethically outfitted, but also, in ways that we can explore together, defenseless and downsized. I want to return momentarily to the experience of my colleague's lecture in Switzerland. Fynsk was casting a wide net, raising the question of *the human*, weighing how a just relation to the other stands witness to its own possibility. (Derrida somewhere points out how "weighing" is inextricable from thinking, rallying *peser* [to weigh] to the cause of *penser* [to think].) He was dancing around two essential texts, both by Blanchot, "Being Jewish" and "The Indestructible." What I took away—besides the negative essence and grave truth anchored in "Being Jewish," the philosophical essence of Judaism described by Blanchot—was Fynsk's view of our ethical stuckness, so to speak. There is never a changeover—never a moment of being relieved of ourselves, no escape from the predicament of being responsible. The ethical buck stops here because only humans strip one another of their relation to world—it is not a matter of the elements, a divinity, or anything remedial coming around a destinal bend, from a purported outside or projection booth. Violence is irremediably linked to human power. Maybe this could be put into communication with Benjamin's mystical foundations of violence, but I am not heading in this direction for now—one could check with Derrida and others in order to get a grip on the interpretive layers and positing flexes added on to Benjamin's "Critique of Violence." Right now I am traveling the other side of this question, hugging the margins of the Kafkan world reset by Blanchot in which violence occurs without term. The day of his lecture Chris Fynsk emphasized the point of unstoppable impairment—that there is no limit when it comes to destroying: the indestructible delivers man to destruction. Mercilessly. Can it be that mankind has a radical need for affliction, pounding into itself as if wrestling a bad object?

To a certain degree I suppose that a number of us are doing the same work, harvesting the same reading lists, perhaps mirroring each other, relaying echoes from different peaks or groaning from related valleys according to the notations of a scorched solitude. Maybe we take our cues from the teachers who have trained us, in some cases even diapered us intellectually. Together—I should say apart, but here it is the same thing—we try to relate to what is beyond reach, understanding that speech puts us into contact with what is unknown and foreign, inaugurating an original relation. I think it is Levinas who writes that the Saying stays its own violence, each time laying before you a peace offering.

I am pressed by something else that our teachers have urged upon us, and maybe this is what I am looking at in this book, so long in coming—it staggered and stalled so many times, right after Derrida's death (o, it stings to say that, because, pathologically slow and always perplexed, I still won't have it, don't really believe that he's gone, and won't answer such calls or heed the mourning-timer) until today, it just stops still and I feel I can't go on. At the time I talked to him about it, what I thought I was doing, getting at. Then I watched him slowly decathect from his own work and those addressing him. At one point he said that he did not care anymore, and I must have absorbed that like an injunction, or I fell into identification and for a long while stopped caring myself. Now I think that I don't have the right not to care anymore or at least that I have not *earned* that right. So I explore the exigency of another relation. I contemplate something that Fynsk may have said, unless it came from Blanchot or was rerouted through Derrida and gets reprinted by the relays of my friends: that there is no limit to the destruction of man.

Loser Sons

Introduction

Tiers of Childhood
and the Defeat of Politics

History, no doubt, can bear me out on this: to the extent that the world can be gathered into relatable narratives, it exposes us to the unconscious contrivances of those who cannot beat back a more or less covert portfolio of psychically induced flops. Today I want to visit with the blood-soaked losers among us, whether they are still on the take or drawing interest from a more or less forgotten legacy of world-encompassing disturbance. I feel a duty to complicate the very notion of loser, even though there seems to be a fair amount of consensus about the distinguishing features of a loser culture and its various manifestations or salient qualities. They do not necessarily comprise a mathematical majority, the types I want to collar and shake down, but they leave a disproportionately sizable historical mark. Everything they do involves an inerasable losing streak, reverting to an early stall or blockage that has dragged them down from the get-go, held them back—even if they were indulged, pampered, exempted from the implications of an incessant destruction of their being. Whether or not they presented or even saw themselves as miscreants and misfits, as the perpetual avengers of enslaved docility—what Nietzsche famously calibrated as the revenge of slave morality—they came out fighting on one level or another, wanting ragefully to establish a compensatory economy. What draws my interest to this unlikely horde is the reflection on the possibility—it's only a possibility, I may have gotten it all wrong—that we are paying for the world-historical inscriptions, the negative trust funds set up by what I am calling "loser sons," meaning those who, when all is said and done, get off on *defeat*, whether this be construed as defeating their neighboring others or along the lines of various forms of self-defeat and a mock-up suicidal finale. This is fairly dangerous terrain, opening a highly problematic account, and one doesn't want to get it wrong or seem simplistically folded in by the lures of the *Weltgeist*—by what's left of the *Weltgeist* and its loser squatters.

I do not aim to lash out arbitrarily or rummage around for possibly cool, or strikingly uncool, critical themes. Such themes tend to come toward me according to their own particular travel plans. This time, their envoy came to my neighborhood—I should say, at me: they came *at* me, traveling at high velocities through downtown New York; however, they had always been announcing a visit—huddled in Auerbach's Cellar, and staked out in Bush bunkers. Whether it is a question of Faust, who visits the Cellar in Goethe's drama, or the other W. ("W" was the letter that Goethe traced in the air on his deathbed, his last letter as he was signing off), we are facing the ordeal of a disturbed legacy, a kind of counterfeit legacy that signs and seals a portion of Western history. The loser son in fact does not limit itself as concept or civic identity to the West, but marks the point of encounter between the West and its others, at least in terms of recent history, but also encompasses mythological and biblical thematics. It is as if, slapped down and dragged off the field, Isaac one day got up again, humiliated, and decided to do something about it—about having had his game called off, his mediocrity reinstated. Or Cain decided to make his comeback.

I am not saying that there is something like a winner's circle, something like a philosophically reliable and upgraded hermeneutic circle that could close out the losers. Nor would I ever put myself on the side of a purported domain of legitimacy: I would not sign up with a properly held heritage or advocate for anything that claimed alignment with correct lineup or lineage. The loser sons that I convoke are losers even where they win, when they win out, often tilting the scales of justice and warping the political playing fields on which fateful moves are determined.

From Mohammed Atta to W. Bush—to whom we can add so many additional historical as well as prophetic and projected characters, if not some of the prime rock 'n' roll house of famers, the very kings of pop, be these offprints of Elvis or Michael Jackson—the defeated son takes up the slack to respond to an unmarked strain in existence, an oppressive juncture or disjunction that cannot be rerouted or symbolically turned. Atta's rage flew him into the World Trade Center, attacking the outwardly pointed visage of "Western values." I want to look closely at the sore losers. But I will also call up the minority standouts, the noble type of losers. (To others I leave the work of checking on the blaring sublimators, those who turned their grief into so many strains of high-decibel lament—rock music and other noteworthy forms of intrusiveness in technological modernity.)

The best of them, the good losers and blues singers, were dragged down even as they were being raised, as Kafka would say. Reproaching his father for the double movement of his upbringing (his "downbringing"), he inveighs: your method of raising me has served only to cut and bring me down. Everywhere, according to subtle pressures, Kafka charts the frightful ups and downs, the portentous putdowns involved in bringing up Baby. Kafka was perhaps the best of the loser sons in my group portrait, the most conscious and self-controlling. His inscriptions were possibly the least violent—this is not certain—though he, too, took and delivered a lot of beatings, dreamt of an axe in the frozen sea, prepared ceaseless attestations of lasting agonies. Kafka received his father's words as so many hits upside his head. In a way, he found that there was really no exteriority to the pernicious precincts of the paternal domain. This is what differentiates Kafka from the other contenders in the clan of loser sons—he put himself up as a loser and, among other things, he read and understood Freud. Kafka thus mastered the art of being a loser son without fail. Never truly graduating, he relinquishes the triumphal jubilation of checkmating an oversized father. In fact, Kafka struggles exemplarily with his plight, and his diaries count down the improbabilities of flight. He retains the freshness of defeat that others deter or turn aside, even outside, in the mode of disavowal.

What motivates the engagement to which this work attests? I am not out to get some poor existential schlub. I am going after the materially based winners, the depleters and entitled: the impolite, impolitic, and crude crew that overwrites the efforts of those who struggle earnestly over the possible meanings of justice or fairness—those who try to take measure of equality, hanging on to a remnant of the eighteenth-century notion of "dignity." Anyone who knows me can confirm that I love the underclass of clueless, evicted, hapless creatures that populate my inner and outer environments, my most internal ambiance—my friends and fiends, colleagues, the students, the families, the support groups, the armies of well-intentioned dummkopfs; there is room in my inner districts for maliciously ordinary Daseins and their inevitable claims upon my time. I have made clear my alliances and allegiances, my pathological identifications with those whose courage fails them; hating themselves, they go through their lives with zero self-esteem, less than zero tolerance for the injustice and pain allotted to others. This class of losers inhabits and includes me, means me, suits me. They—we—are not at issue, no more so than is required by the daily reviews and revisions to which we are submitted, to the endless evaluations and diminishments that clinch us, to the self-depreciations that subject us.

This time things are different. I am plagued by the intrusive figure of a predialectized "slave," so to speak—the one who merges strangely yet persistently with the master, or at least with the master discourses that keep us down. I cannot be certain that what I am after remains firmly a trope or represents a historical recurrence. On some level of interpretive vigor, if you've read your Freud, most sons are losers. Until they have assumed their castration. By then, like Oedipus, they may be walking around blind in the overlapping fields of truth and privation, "subjectivized" to the extent that they live knowingly in default. Believe it or not, there are still those entitled snivelers who push away the news of barred existence.

❂ ❂ ❂

Despite my hesitations over this topic, over the book's title and irreversible thematic tendencies, it seemed to me worthwhile to venture in this direction, to probe what such a complication in genealogy offers up to reflection: as of a certain date or event—maybe the Gulf war, maybe when one of my colleagues flipped on me, maybe when I incredulously watched some of the Bush-Cheney defamations of history, the systematic spoilage of phrasal regimes and subversion of constitutional law—I was determined to check out the MO of sons who are neither as such illegitimate nor legitimate, who steal something from history because they themselves feel grievously ripped off—a little like Hamlet, but not quite. Though they do manage in the end to take the whole house down. Loser sons are those whose dose of remorse has gone wayward. Having snuffed out superegoical constraints and perverted internal regulatory monitors, they prove incapable of commuting death sentences or sparing life. Empathetic transmitters have been knocked out in their little— or, rather big—heads. They live with phrasal effects of condemnation that ricochet off themselves to explode on externalized targets. Condemned from the start—to ordinariness, insouciance, last place in the projected boasts of familial hierarchy—they visit a heightened sense of condemnation upon a massively constructed enemy. The loser self is pinned outwardly, becoming identifiable as evil or heretical, falling out of strict orthodoxies of the transparent rivalries that are organized around condemnatory phrases. Whether brutalized or merely slighted by childhood's major players, this brand of sissy places the brunt of an inexhaustible need for blaming and shaming revenge on a calculable program of world: the poor, the sick, the designated minority, the immigrant, the refugee, women, children and other foreigners, get rounded up by the small avenger's machine.

Witless, determined, and brutalizing, the world-belittling son is no slacker, though such might be his cover. In fact, the loser horde may reveal,

given its aim and effectiveness, a distinctive type of overachievement. The world libido has been mobilized to write up their ticket. Apart from the contingent and storied profile represented by Kafka and some others along the way, I am referring here to the devastating theaters of megalomaniacal certitudes staged by little Bush, Osama bin Laden, Mohammed Atta, and other tyrannical types who mirror one another within the firm grasp of a reciprocal enmity that sustains their history. Loser sons need and feed on a simplified notion of enmity. They trail around an enemy hit list. Even Kafka required an enemy, as he pointedly states. (The dreadful Carl Schmitt dreamt that Kafka would write a novel called "The Enemy.") But for him there was no question of vanquishing the crushing adversary, no culture of displaced victories.

Mohammed Atta, the man responsible for crashing planes into the World Trade Center, was saddled in life with a Kafkan father. After his son went up in flames, Atta's father claimed that it was impossible for this son to have committed an act of such manly proportions: his son was a cream puff afraid of flying, a mama's boy photographed sitting on his mother's lap well into his teens. When he did have to board a plane, Atta asked his sister, a physician, to supply him with his stash of tranquilizers. His father belittled the son, demasculated him, even after his spectacular demise. This son, it appears, had written up his phobias as a program; he became an architect of decompletion, taking out buildings, collapsing symbolic entrenchments while plunging into the real. This phobia, spilling out as the expulsion of a long-held psychic terror, became the weakling's form of expression. Held hostage by the terror of flying, he took hostages on flight. Taking down the towers, he remastered castration. (I simplify for effect.)

It is perhaps of some significance that Atta was trained as an architect and came to these shores, as a last stopover in his *Bildung,* from Germany. As a missive or missile, he targeted a site that has been explicitly tagged as a locus of satanic excess and capital voracity. Something in any case returned to sender from Germany with accumulated terrorist rage, a kind of range war of unsettled phantasmata.[1]

---

1. I discuss phantasmatic mappings, the air wars of Blitzkrieg, and carpet bombing in "Support Our Tropes," where I read a tropology of enmity and the Gulf war in terms of the psychic setbacks of "GeoBush" in *Finitude's Score: Essays Toward the End of the Millennium* (Lincoln and London: University of Nebraska Press, 1994), 269–91. The status of "radicalized Germans" in the configurations of terror has become a topic of some investigation, though the link from the traumatic residue of WWII remains to be pursued.

If Mohammed Atta was pounded by his father, even after the son's extinction, his boss bin Laden had a similar up(down)bringing that is worth mentioning, if only very briefly. Of the things we know about Osama bin Laden, one detail appears to be noteworthy—he was marked down by the Saudi Arabian family from early on, his mother having been a Syrian woman who in any case was treated, together with her son, as an outcast. He was among the last and lowest of the sons.

As for George Bush, what can be said but that he is cast historically as the loser son of a father who himself gathered up the attributes of loser son, as I have tried to elaborate elsewhere. Cokehead, alcoholic, cretin turned Christian (these terms are etymologically related), language bungler, he came in second after his younger brother Jeb Bush, the prized son groomed by the family for the presidency of the United States. Vaguely recalling biblical brothers who are set in specular opposition to one another, though in this story with only muffled hatred, they advance on the scene with overly sentimentalized family values. Like other sons who spin their wheels in Father's groove, "W" was bound from the start to a fate of return and repetition: he replayed the drama of paternal error in a doomed effort to get it right. Thus Bush's overtaking his father in the killing of Iraqis comprised a double gesture, producing as much a binding homage as a castrating strategy so that when he plays golf with his father while the wars raged, he feminized him, pokes holes and fun at him, calling him "Betsy" when the elder Bush missed a hole. The loser son turns things around on the playing field of projection, reined in by a politics of reversibility and repetition. Everything that was deemed irreversible—hard-won rights, civil liberties—got washed away in the compulsion to drive in reverse turning back progressive clocks. In fact, regression is his middle name, the brutal trace of his disavowed masochism— a symptomatic territory that Kafka, for his part, exemplarily exposed.

Though each loser son that drives by the historical scanner probably has his own repertoire of syndromic habits and idioms, he also ties into his brethren by means of some common traits. It may seem bizarre to place Goethe's Faust in the lineup that permits us preliminarily to identify the loser son. But, precisely because *Faust* establishes the code for determining a key gestalt in the Western thought of self-overcoming, we must not neglect his loser qualities. He was put up by Marlowe, Goethe, Gounod, Thomas Mann, Valéry, and others as a winning force, emblematic of the powerful human drive to know and exceed the limits of finitude's constraints. Faust created the conditions, or at least the language and setup, for technological dominion, which entail allowances made by the team of writers for a theater of drugs, sex, the supernatural, and poetry. Only Nietzsche saw both the

representative and loser profile of the exalted figure. (Nietzsche was mostly embarrassed by the love story and the Christian kidnapping at the end of Goethe's *Faust I*.) Faust skidded on the track marks left by a father in default. There is something like a crime or debt or humiliation of the father that the loser son unconsciously retrieves (on one level Bush, for instance, saw his father as humiliated by Saddam Hussein). At one point Faust alludes to the murderous error that his father, a doctor, had committed. The error went unseen; it was a private and not a politically proclaimed affair. In fact, Faust's father received acclaim for his humanitarian raids during the plague. Little Faust was at his father's side when the homicidal malpractice occurred, but could say nothing. Like Isaac, he followed his father around in mute compliance as the elder mistook his mission. Kafka updates the ordeal when in the "Letter to Father" he appraises the damage incurred by his father, who routinely tyrannized workers at the factory. Kafka expressly sees himself as *liable* for the violations that accrue to his name, indebted to those mistreated under his father's command, feeling that he owes them unending workers' compensation. (It is perhaps no accident that Franz Kafka became one of the most scrupulous insurance lawyers in our time.) Even in the case of *Hamlet* there is the question, raised by Nicolas Abraham and Maria Torok, of whether or not the father has lied—a fault or debt that triggers the son's world-crashing symptoms. It is as if these sons at once deny and carry the father's debt, his castration, that their actions, whether deliberately calibrated or unconsciously minted, do everything to erase.

✿ ✿ ✿

Returning to Faust, it is essential to underscore that his hysterical relation to knowledge, his hyperscientific drive, is motored by the father's unavowable defeat. The other father in *Faust*, who authorizes the devil to deal with Faust, to test the extent of his capacity for deviancy—God will also come up short on the question of fairly paying out Faust's salvation.[2] One of the themes of Faust's supracognitive quest remains largely untouched. It involves the fine print in his transactions with the satanic powers of Mephistopheles, the self-

2. An earlier version of this text used the designations "G-d" and "God" to summon and cite the Almighty. My reasons for doing so, I thought, were manifold and well-calculated. However, in midrashic conversation with Drs. Willis Regier and Hent de Vries, it seemed that my usage might finally encumber the work. Addressing problems associated with politics and authority, one inescapably comes across G-d. My aim was double and contradictory: I did not want to imply an impolite familiarity with divinity (we are estranged and mostly, from what I can tell, cross with each

professed loser son and erstwhile companion of the Lord. Faust famously signs a pact with the devil, a downright obsessional neurotic who stands on ritual and ceremony, and who throughout his dealings with earthling Faust proves susceptible to superstitious anxiety. But before Mephisto offers his services to the overextended Faust, the professor has tried to conjure other spirits, auditioning different kinds of metaphysical interns. These spirits, rarefied elements from secret spheres, overwhelm Faust and in the end repel him. He cannot step up to the plate of spiritual enhancement. Faust, it turns out, is left in the dust by the extra- and intraterrestrial spirits that he, by magic formula and recondite knowledge, has managed to conjure.

When they appear, the otherworldly beings expressly threaten to snuff him out, decimate him. They rail at him with humiliating disdain. Faust exhausts his supernatural account and must relinquish the spirits he has summoned: extrascholarly knowledge exceeds his capacity to sustain the dematerialized object. He is quickly taught that he cannot handle the truth. Only after these accounts and encounters fold, when Faust has lost out to the higher pagan powers, left back and demeaned, has the ground been prepared for a lasting relationship with the lowest form of partnership, the quasi-Christian projection of father-son bonds: the symptom formation called up as the Lord and his devil.

The famous pact with Mephistopheles is a compromise formation, a consolation prize in the spirit lottery. If Mephisto has gambled on Faust's soul, drawn God into a competition for the most striving human, Faust himself

---

other—no symmetry intended, I accept my mortal fate). "G-d" was meant to mark distance, which historically can be taken for reverence or, for historical stragglers such as myself, its opposite—disrespect on some essential level, disbelief, dissension. I wanted to follow the lead in any case of Rabbi Soloveitchik, who used to write "God" on the blackboard and cross it out. Derrida, as Hent reminds me, "in the footsteps of Jean-Luc Marion's 'Dieu sans l'être' and, of course, Heidegger's 'kreuzweise Durchstreichung des Seins' has experimented with the typographic peculiarity of the divine name." Moreover, these two renderings of "G-d" or "God" "in juxtaposition to 'God' crossed out typographically—now [constitute] part of the philosophical idiom or canon, I would say. This should work fine," Hent counsels, "and give more to think than an undifferentiated use of 'God.' Hegel, Kierkegaard, and Nietzsche did or could not tap into these alternative archival and 'semantic-typographical' resources because they were either unfamiliar with them or were counting on an audience that was not. But then, writing 'G-d' or 'God' is giving 'God' a pseudonym, of sorts. And, at least, Kierkegaard might have liked that." In order not to throw the work into a supplementary disequilibrium I have settled for the all-too-familiar "God."

has lost all bets as concerns the spirit world. After all, the devil spirit arrives in the form of a poodle, perhaps, for all we know, as a French poodle. To Faust's great surprise, when the poodle morphs into Mephisto, he demands a signature and contract. No mere verbal contract will do. As Faust remarks, the devil wants everything in writing.

Goethe's *Faust* is organized in one of its facets around the concept of economy. *Faust II* deals in part with the creation of paper money with abstraction, speculation, and other metaphysical payment policies. The production of capital belongs in Goethe's estimation to the precincts of a libidinal economy. Capital is never just a matter of money, as Deleuze and Guattari have also suggested but, as Goethe has outlined, it begins as substitution and redirects libidinal impulses. The desire for money is linked by Goethe to desire and its peculiar relation to privation. Savings and salvation defer absolute expenditure. It is not clear how to class the fact that God enters a bet with the devil. They bet on who will win Faust, use him up, or save his soul. In order to get the economy of their encounter flowing, Faust must first regress to youthfulness. The devil provides the lures of a total makeover. This is where Nietzsche starts throwing up. The idea that Faust's first stop is to get a girl annoyed the philosopher. He was not prone to evaluating Faust's reversion to adolescent fantasies in favorable terms, as part of a generalized libidinal investment. On a thematic level, Nietzsche may be right: who cares about the teenage courtship of Gretchen when a little acceleration on the will to power could get you anywhere and anything—or maybe even Nothing: Not Nietzsche.

What interests me is the fact itself, at least as it is presented in the drama, of God's taking the bet, closing a preliminary pact of almost Heideggerian insinuation with the devil: to place a bet, a more originary bet must have been placed. Or, even without trifling about the theological implications of God's own need for placing bets, the divine gambling habits—raising Abraham, Job, and the rest of them—why does Goethe start the economies of his great text on the wager? The complicities of promise and payment point to the difficult nature of establishing economies of calculable values. Everything, on every level, fluctuates, obeying more or less secret—or unconscious—determinations of value. The notion itself of flow prohibits the apprehension of economy in terms merely of statistics. Other levels of computation need to be taken into account, bringing economy at every point to the brink of crashing. Goethe has much more to say about this subject, particularly in terms of deflecting military spending: at one point he believed that capital would supersede and obsolesce the human need for expanding killing fields. In the future, he thought one could make a killing by substituting abstraction such as money—an arbitrary system of signs—for demanding the material extinction of life. As universal as monetary systems are, they are also ever on the verge of collapse. This propensity, I believe, is what most fascinated Goethe; namely, the way that material economies have operated conceptually and in principle on trust, confident of exchange and the possibility of equivalencies—confident that money will not be prey to its own manner of Babel, bundled only by the splint of untranslatability and the succession of one factor over another. But money begins its course as a translation of something else, as substitute, and trades on arbitrary valuation—what Schlegel called "reelle Sprache." It functions as its own allegory, assembling the irony of lack, understanding that there can be no unitary monetary fund or foundation. Economy banks on its own impossibility, starts itself off by borrowing from elsewhere, taking recourse to a debt that exceeds sheer economic calculation. *Faust* charges itself up on the unbiased economy of wagering. Goethe's God gets talked into cosigning a bet that mirrors the devil's deal with Faust. Both bets frustrate the certitudes on which winning and losing are based, much the same way that Christianity itself turns earthbound losers into winners of another realm, creating different and differing measures of remittance. This disbursement is based on a debt that Nietzsche could not forgive.

In Christianity, as in its literary derivative, *Faust*, God bets on his "children" with such persistence as to render childhood itself the locus of wager. But childhood remains for all that an enigmatic figure. One barely has access to one's childhood—or as Jean-François Lyotard states in *Lectures d'enfance*, we do not really know what a child is. Childhood, which Lyotard elsewhere sees as an unpayable debt, remains a mystery.[3] It comes at you from elsewhere, as always something that will be explained to the child, read, or historicized for the child. Apart from the fact that childhood is a relatively new historical concept, there is also something like a nearly "transcendental childhood" that runs differently than the one or ones clocked by biological infancy. The way that childhood incessantly returns in loser moments will concern us here. All that can be said in the present is that, given childhood's retiring structures (the memory lapses, blanks, stammers, and the specific types of unrepresentable feelings toward which it recedes) and their peculiarly intense returns (the sudden drops and dips into unconscious idioms,

---

3. See Geoffrey Bennington's discussion of the complex thought of childhood in Lyotard's work in "Before," *AfterWords: Essays in Memory of Jean-François Lyotard*, ed. Robert Harvey (Stony Brook: Humanities Institute, State University of Stony Brook, 2000), 3–28.

unstoppable rage, and the whole enchilada of inexpressible grief): it may well be the case, as Lyotard argues, that adulthood is itself a mystification conceived by wishful thinkers. Thus, "the bottom line is that there's no such thing as a grown-up person," he repeatedly quotes his elder, Malraux, as stating.[4] Even such acts as quoting evoke a childlike recitation.

For Lyotard the way we deal with unrepresentable childhood affects all relationships and prefigures one's own ungraspable death. My birth, he notes, "is always only recounted by others, and my death told to me in the stories of the death of others, my stories and others' stories." The relationship with others is, therefore, "essential to this relation with the nothingness of its being that is reported to me (whence I come and where I am going), and also essential to the presence or the absence of which the relationship with others (this presence of others) comes back to me."[5] This aporetic economy of relations opens the dossier of Kafka's dependency on brutal others. In order to account for his failing relations with others, Kafka will tell himself through his father the story of his childhood and unpack the burden of assuming a permanent losing streak. Unlike the more hapless losers we have encountered, Kafka stares the nothingness of the recounting in the face and bounces stories as well as hypothetical remembrances off the figure of the father. So much is shown to revert to what has been reported to him and depends on the stature of the immense scrambling machine that his father profiles. Kafka knew and taught us what it means to serve as a kind of unauthorized code in a system of proliferating language scanners— there is a mechanicity of inheritance with which he struggles, from which he tries to sift and sort a story that might permit him to escape a sphere of language actions over which his father stands as warden. The dependency of childhood itself—doubling the child's dependency—on the aftereffects of stories that get told in an effort to assemble and resemble something like childhood, emphasizes the precarious nature of that which counts on others for its original reconstitution. The fact of such searing dependency undermines the child's existence at every step of the way. World can slip away at any moment. The child, for Lyotard, is always "a creature living on reprieve from annihilation."[6]

If childhood depends on a concatenation of organized fictions, the traumatic addressee of Kafka's attempt to recall his childhood itself lacks stability.

---

4. Jean-François Lyotard, "The Survivor," in *Toward the Postmodern* (Lancaster: Humanity Books, 1998), 148–49.

5. Ibid.

6. Ibid.

This is one of the dilemmas that faces Kafka as he tries to fix the famously missed appointment with Father. Can a father as father be addressed? Such a question accompanies Lacan's thoughts on the dream of the burning child. Here Lacan introduces the latent complexity of Freud's commentary regarding what it would mean to constitute the father as a witness to the child's address. The question expands into the domain of the father's desire, worrying the issue of whether the father also needs the address of the child to get a close-up of his own desire. Still, as Lacan's reading of the scene indicates, the paternal as such resists consciousness, fails to present itself, for Lacan at one moment writes that "only the father as father—that is to say, no conscious being" can in this case say what the death of a child is.[7]

Kafka's missive missed its target, leaving us to size the failure of the letter to arrive at its destination. Without rehashing the dispute between Lacan and Derrida on this point of *adestination*, it should be possible to realign their conversation along the axis of *The Four Fundamental Concepts of Psychoanalysis*, where the father fades when positioned as essential addressee. In other words, it may not be an accident or simply aleatory when Kafka's letter becomes a dead letter en route to the father as conscious being. The letter may be written to—or even *from*—the paternal unconscious, as Kafka's text in more than one way insinuates. (We shall see how the end of the letter, like the beginning, issues from the "father" whom Kafka mimes and quotes, ventrilocating the condemnation that is said to issue from the other but comes from Kafka's pen. Or the other way around, making it all spill from his father's dictations, franchised out by Franz Kafka.) The killer or death sentence may be written into the very fact of the missive that aims at the interruptive field of the unconscious or at a locus of transmission that can no longer be seen to belong either to son or father exclusively.

There is another, more deadly, communication at play that Kafka tries to diffuse by preparing the unsendable dispatch. The letter traverses a field of absolute destruction, ever pointing beyond where the father can receive it. By making certain that his father will *not* receive the letter—the wager is on the mother not to hand over the letter entrusted to her custody—by managing the deflection via the maternal workstation, Kafka also arranges

7. Jacques Lacan, "Tuché and Automaton," trans. Alan Sheridan, in *Four Fundamental Concepts of Psychoanalysis* (New York: W. W. Norton, 1978). See also Christopher Fynsk, *Infant Figures* (Stanford, Calif.: Stanford University Press, 2000), 113; Cathy Caruth, *Unclaimed Experience*; and Giorgio Agamben, *Enfance et histoire: Dépérissement de l'experiénce et origine de l'histoire*, trans. Yves Hersant (Paris: Éditions Payot), 1989.

to reprieve and *save his father*. The letter will have become a ballistic launch whose success depends on its failure to reach the purportedly assigned target. There remains yet another possibility: that Father was always only fronting for the destination of Mother—the ultimate father. Kafka will allow for such an interpretive turn within the logic of the letter, but he does not stay with its implications and instead returns the letter to Father. The letter returns to Father, but only on the condition that it aim toward where he is *not*.

In a sense, any address to the father, to an inescapably absconding father, must ask, "Father, why have you abandoned me?" Whether the letter is conceived as missive or missile, it is both launched from and aimed at the site where, in default, the father is a nonappearing or dead father. This may offer another reason that Kafka, for his part, more or less deflected the missile where others crashed into the signifier. As we read the sign-off that Kafka gave his father we should bear in mind the photograph, now a well-circulated postcard, that shows Kafka and his friends mounted on an airplane, smiling broadly, sealing an experience of cheer offered by an amusement park. Still, the *envoi* sent by the one who professes to be the child of the father structurally comes from a dead child, a child martyred by the address. The *envoi* or letter survives the sender, serves a testamentary purpose, reports from the dead. (Another reason for Kafka's deflection: to ward off the suicidal circuitry of the letter, to evade, perhaps vainly, the poisoned tip that Hamlet sends himself by return mail.)

Fused at the site of a double death, the son and father divert disaster only to the extent that the abandonment sustains itself, that it does not overturn into a fusion with the greater father, be it Allah, Yahweh, or one among the rest of them. When Mohamed Atta crashed into the World Trade Center, he effected a jump shot into the embrace of the transcendentalized father. If Kafka's letter had met its target, had struck the addressee named as Father, its destiny and destination would have been altogether other. The "father" might have been reached if only to be breached. Not receiving the letter addressed to him, Kafka's disturbing father rigorously remains at most "Herrmann," Mr. Man, The Man. This is an affair among men, a secular colloquy at the level of mortal wounding. The writer is sent to the children's corner to wait it out. What this means is that the writer after Kafka, ever an inaction hero and failing custodian of the real, rigorously desists from exploding into the space of disaster to which writing remains responsible.

❁ ❁ ❁

Let me go back to something that was stated earlier. In his remarks on Hannah Arendt's "banality of evil" (she also wrote of the "stupidity of evil," but that's another story), Lyotard locates the child as that which is "more threatened" by annihilation.[8] The child reflects and localizes the accelerated velocities of threatened being. The child's response to threat, varied but volatile, has everything to do with the war games that mire modernity. For Lyotard the child comes closer to the experience of annihilation than we have wanted to recognize in quotidian discursive sprints or where childhood is erased in philosophical inquiry. Since Hegel, philosophy was explicitly a matter for adults. It is as if the losses tabulated in the column of childhood can under no circumstances be recuperated.

Lyotard's rendering of childhood will concern us in the pages to follow, if only to enable us to listen closely to the politically pitched repertoire of stammers that punctuates the being of the loser child: Kafka makes a good deal out of his syncopated speech when trying to speak to Hermann Kafka. He draws us into a realm designated by Lyotard in which despair leads skepticism (which is permanent), "knowing that there is nothing to do or say, no valid entity even which *is*, acts, all the same, as though there were one."[9] Validity, legitimacy, and authority build threats that tower over the child from day one. These figures, along with their collective bolsters, encroach unbeatably, yet the child senses that the wave of menace comes from nowhere, out of the blue, characterized by a largely invalid yet relentless force. Childhood preenrolls us in the domain indicated by Kant, no doubt for many other reasons and purposes, of the *as if*: the little one "knows all about *as if*, all about the pain of impotence and the complaint of being too small, of being there late (compared to others) and (as to its strength) of having arrived early, prematurely—childhood that knows all about broken promises, bitter disappointments, failings and abandonment."[10] This child profiled by Lyotard shows a different face than the one who will have started off our reflections, the one called up by Goethe and Jean Paul, who created the basic outlines of the child's portrait for the eighteenth and nineteenth centuries.

8. Lyotard, "Survivor."

9. Quoted in Christopher Fynsk, "Jean-François's Infancy," *Jean-François Lyotard: Time and Judgment, Yale French Studies* 99 (2001): 56.

10. Jean-François Lyotard, *Lectures d'enfance* (Paris: Gallilée, 1991), 65. This passage is quoted and translated by Geoffrey Bennington in his discussion of the fantasy of virile filiation. Bennington links the latent relation between Lyotard's work on "mainmise" and the essay on the "jews" in *Heidegger et "les juifs"* (Paris: Galilée, 1988). In "Childish Things" in *Minima Memoria: In the Wake of Jean-François Lyotard*, ed. Claire Nouvet, Zrinka Stahuljak, and Kent Still (Stanford, Calif.: Stanford University Press, 2007), 201.

It is now evident that I have begun to put together an album of children and the ways in which they cringe, lose out, smart, avenge themselves, or drop out of range when summoned by the call. My children's album comprises the work of a highly determined collectivity ranging from Goethe and Hegel (who largely recoups the losses, at least for the parents through the child, in order to spare the child the consequences of superceding the parents), to Blanchot, Lacan, Lyotard, Lacoue-Labarthe, and many others. One might want to ask why the members of this collectivity have *needed* the kindergarten in order to advance theoretical claims, how the child serves a particular philosophical angle. For my part, the tabulations and reflections that I present will run into the place where the empiricists recruited the "ideot childe." The disabled child—in theoretical work, all children are disabled as part of their *Grundstruktur*—encourages philosophy to scope prehistories of understanding as it looks for the clean slate where language start-ups and memory can be investigated.

There are many other early, if partially coerced, photos to paste into this album as we tally the damages and monitor an overstimulated death drive that has seized some of these children, no matter what their age. These children, even where they play hide-and-go-seek, have taken their place as world leaders, as repeat fabricators of disavowal, and they stand as the source of calamitous configurations of power. With regard to some of the portraitures I have labeled, the view historically taken of children hinges on an understanding of what it means to promise. For Goethe the child itself embodies promise; for Lyotard, the child emerges as the being chronically deprived of any promise possibly tendered. Hegel places his bets on reversal and *Aufhebung*, but even here acts of promising lose their authority, and in any case always fake and play validity, raising the stakes on consciousness. To the degree that promise also entails the very possibility of future, one is bound to revisit time and again the sites of failed acts or conditions of promising in order to comb the historical consequences of such constitutive collapses.

In this work I closely audition childhood's losing streak, the annihilating qualities that it bears. I am motivated by many considerations, some of which can be inferred from the pages that follow. Perhaps I can state up front one motivating factor for this study, however. America habitually infantilizes itself, feigning the felicities of sunshine and theme park, turning inside out the sadistic impulse with warping ideologies of "pro-life" and related death-denial operations. You cannot get away from it. Childhood and the tropological train that it trails of "family values," even among the good guys, queers, trannies, solitaires, is required reading in this country if one has any sense at all of civic duty. So I pick up the dark side of what calls me, staying close, by necessity, to Freud's reflections on the death drive and the ever-mutating forms of destructive *jouissance.* There is another side to childhood that Lyotard, in all fairness, commemorates, turning it into a kind of philosophical daybreak. Childhood, according to his report, "also knows all about dreaming, memory, question, invention, obstinacy, listening to the heart, love, and real openness to stories."[11] I'll grant this possibility.

○ ○ ○

As we shall come to recognize in our subsequent visitations and readings, childhood cannot be restricted to a historical phase in human development—it returns every time one is tortured by nonrepresentable feelings or one is stalled, stuttering, stuck in a place without recourse or comprehension. "Childhood is the state of the soul inhabited by something to which no answer is ever given," Lyotard continues. "It is led in its undertakings by an arrogant loyalty to this unknown guest to which it feels itself a hostage." Taking a decidedly Kantian term, Lyotard steers the hostage by means of a notion of *respect*: "I understand childhood here as obedience to a debt (which we can call a debt of life, of time, of event; a debt of being there in spite of everything), a debt for which only the persistent feeling of respect can save the adult from being no more than a survivor, a creature living on reprieve from annihilation."[12] When offering a definition for childhood, Lyotard appears to mesh its chief characteristic—"obedience" to a debt—with adulthood. Heeding an essential debt—to life, time, or event—gives the child a leg up on existence. Whether tinged by negativity or upgraded to the respectful stance—one starts out not on one's own, but owing to the other, on an early-bird ego reduction plan—the relation to what is owed or borrowed or inherited decides how the reprieve will be lived out. In another context that may prove illuminating to us, Freud births psychoanalysis in terms of a relay of highly determined debts. Freud's stated debt to Goethe takes a turn via Shakespeare in order to name what is "owed to Nature." Freud here creates the childhood of psychoanalysis, significantly allowing space for two fathers, when acknowledging or setting up an economy of indebtedness. In Lyotard this is the only bet to take. If something like adulthood could loosen the shackles of childhood or exceed a state of mere survival, this could come about only by a type of feeling elicited by the acknowledgment of a debt. Lyotard rallies to a difficult concept of *feeling* when introducing

11. Lyotard, *Lectures d'enfance,* 57.
12. Ibid.

respect as a key source of reprieve. The sense and sentiment of originary debt is something that Heidegger emphasizes as well in his considerations of *Urschuld*—that which starts us off and never relinquishes its grip.

As we continue to review the dossier on what I am tracking as the syndromic effects of loser sons, we must bear in mind that Christianity sent down a version of just such a filial configuration and familial design, thus repealing and revealing a godly core.

Chapter 1
What Was Authority?

Aggressive coexistence. Neither powered up by a solid sense of (or even desire for) legitimacy, nor a control freak with regard to the possibilities of comprehension, I abide with the weaker neighborhoods of thought, where things do not always work out or offer the narcissistic comfort of landing in the vicinity of secured sense. This time, in order to get a running start on the motif of the loser son, a pervasive world-denting irritant, I am going after *authority*, a problem that has attracted relatively weak bolsters and, for the most part, only tentative interventions. Yet, the problem before us has preoccupied at least two strongly poised generations whose membership has tried very hard, and in vital ways, to stare down authority, question authority, mime, repel, usurp, diminish, lend, or command authority. I want these types and tendencies to approach the bench. They require and deserve a hearing, whether or not they have proven to be rebellious or in egregious complicity with the outer limits of the authoritarian imposition.

To get a provisional grip on what continues to elude while claiming thought—why is there injustice? what holds authority? where does it hurt?—I like to travel different kinds of reflective zones that share with philosophy a sense of vigorous probing but often, despite all good intentions, come with outdated passes or with papers that appear to be even more de-authorized by current practices than philosophy itself.

A running start. At first glance, every attempt to get ahold of authority's meaning and historical rootedness in institutional practice seems encumbered by the poverty of means to arrive at its essential qualities or range. Theorists of a modern cast, including Alexandre Kojève and Theodor

Adorno, take recourse to scales and charts and other computational hazards in order to get the point across that one remains susceptible to and in need of authority; from Hannah Arendt to Giorgio Agamben, the Roman scaffolding is brought back into view in order to expose what authority almost was, or is still about to be. Descriptions flood the arena and, for the most part, accrue to the column tallying up reasons for the necessity of authority, rating the calamitous consequence of its deceleration or outright extinction. The grandeur of authority, its nearly auratic claims, appears to have held things together, having pushed away from more violent shores of human governance. The collapse of authority, the successive demotions of the "big Other," God and State and other mostly masculinist idols, put a fracture in being. In consequence, we are still crawling around with the lesions caused by the affronts of a faux authority trailing its miserable representatives. Kojève derives ontic samples of authority from the workable fiction of divine authority. Adorno goes so far as to study the bulk of hives-inducing authoritarian qualities lodged at the very core of American democracy. He demonstrates the dangers posed by high scorers of the F-scale, referring in his study to the *fascisoid markers* consistently lighting up among more or less normal citizens interviewed, Claude Lanzman–style, by his team of researchers. The gap between the character of authority on the one hand, and the "authoritarian character" on the other, is not so wide as it may seem, yet each player in these constellations has a different investment in the modalities of authority, its inevitable breaches or intractable necessity.

Strangely, yet pertinently, the question of authority—supposing it is still or has ever really been a question—takes us back to earliest childhood, to states of hapless dependency and prepolitical need. No one likes to admit it, yet domination by God-the-Father or dad the father, although in close complicity with maternal runs of interference or, in highly determined chronicled spurts, motherly supersession, continues to pump the machine of still unrelenting effects of authority. Whether or not one autobiographically had a daddy-mommy incubator or the signifier hanging over one's head, one had a relation from day one to authority. One counted, before being able to count, on the authority of those wrapping one's tush and filling one's mouth. According to Melanie Klein's assessment of the way things were from the get-go, one feared the authority even of the breast; coming at one, it gave a real sense of a persecutory tankage (from the start, one had to *work* at loving one's mother, at promoting the "good breast").

My opening set of questions, simple at this point, harnesses Nietzschean energy: What became of authority's hold over early childhood (or childhood's way of holding onto authority), whether well rated or poorly dispatched, whether structuring or debilitating and both? How do we score authority in what looks to be a postpolitical world, where we are faced with the essential finitude of the political? Do we need it, or can authority be disposed of by the purposeful anarchy of questioning? Is it the case that the exercise of authority can stave off tyranny, or does its peculiar stamina, on the contrary, prep the tyrannical stranglehold? But authority does not belong to the class of action or syntax of being that can be "exercised," that is, in any significant way flexed, handled. It belongs to an entirely different scale of showing and being. In effect, it comes along silently, with minimal fuss and even less melodrama. It asserts itself with few words and low phenomenological maintenance. Still, how does it show up on our scanners and what kind of bite marks does it continue to leave on our political bodies? In what way does authority, which notoriously withdraws from thought and shuns ostentation, allow an approach?

In order to wrestle with archaic sovereignties and specify those more original formations that have led to the stagnation of something like a politically progressivist momentum, it is helpful at times to visit with what passes for defunct or condemned sites of knowing. It may mean putting one's stakes in recalcitrant areas of thought that come up as irrelevant, difficult, overly problematic, wearying. Who wants to dwell today in sticky marshes that yield so little in a "result"-prodded era? Well, I do. Setting aside the craving for results, rated upwards from business and objectivist concerns, let us stay in the vicinity of this ever-receding shadow of a concept, assuming we have found it.

The literary prompt. Even something as politically inflected and ethically driven as the problem of authority may summon up literature in order to give itself a running start, a wide enough space in which to unfold its many hidden capacities. To the extent that they have felt engaged by the problem, political and sociological theories have by turns considered the parameters and depth of authority's pervasive but elusive grid. Cognitive approaches have yielded information and given some food for thought, some axioms by which to measure the range and pull of authority and its performative aspects. Still other approaches may involve returning to tranquilized textual instances for the purpose of tapping stores of another type of knowledge, without bringing up the noise of know-it-all discursivities and the voracious paradigms from which they are constituted. Sometimes it becomes necessary to explain *again* why literature, running according to a different metronome of being and prone to altogether contrasting dependencies, summons us to

21

examine the recesses of political exigency. Literature, in the form of fiction or as poetic surround, always accompanies the thought of political injury and persecuted otherness. This fact, in good and gallant Nietzschean terms, may attract both good and bad valences to the extent that poetry and art have been viciously appropriated to killer historical causes and acts, but at the same time, with Hölderlinian strokes of innocence, they inescapably play against empirical-historical currents. It is important in any case for me not to succumb to the temptation, increasing by the day, to write in step with objectivizing science or to produce clean-cut effects of some sort of descriptive politology or political science. I don't think that I risk such an identity crossover—yet, we practitioners and shouters and readers, whether coming from the precincts of *Wissenschaft* or its somewhat edgier outskirts, frequently want the same things, decry the same cognitive distortions. One cannot simply deny the good old-fashioned solidarity that binds us, even where methods clash and turf wars stir in the still of the writing night.

Some of my friends remain nonreaders, solid descriptors. They even claim to cling to transparent utterance, rhetorically uncluttered argument— the hard-and-fast reasoning that overrides the literary snafu. In fact they're making a comeback, undeterred by the sense that uninterrogated clarity has proven to fuel the forces of mendaciousness. Theoretical toughness has lost in many areas of contiguous reflection its essential verve. I don't blame anyone, I just strap on my witness consciousness to note that the hard-hitting punch of critical inscription is by the looks of it (though looks can deceive) on the decline. One is beaten down by softer approaches or, rather: a crop of ex-theorists has thrown in the towel, having been in some cases pummeled by the stupefying steadiness of a numbed and dumbing body politic; or, worn down by effects of certain aspects of common technologies, one has given in to the sheer distress of association with a brutal polity. Who has not cringed or cried or lost courage in the face of the American deconstitution, something that continues to erode confidence in the reparability of world? Why should the widespread disregard for complexity, care, and existential holding patterns not intrude upon critical grammars and theoretical practices? On another level my question concerns, as previously recorded, where the political poses problems—a question that takes one beyond thematic deliveries and areas of rhetorical tranquility.

I for my part no longer believe in Kantian intelligibilities (which, I know, had their limits from day one—a cause of Heinrich von Kleist's nervous breakdown and the direct reason for a slew of historical panic attacks). Now, how does pained existence get soothed or primed and prepared for the battle of existence by the literary intercession? How does authorship, dead or alive, feed the machinery of authority? I'll suspend this part of the equation pro-visionally and ask to what extent fiction constellates the unrecognizable advent of that which terrorizes. If I were to say what terror is and fill it up, seal it with content, I would have eluded its unshakable grip, surrendering the essential unknown to determination and cognition. We know a few things that may scare and scar, but such knowledge does not amount to capturing effects of terror. Wanting to get in touch with the particular qualities of a terror base that marks shared being—what Jean-Luc Nancy designates as being-in-common—I was often brought to a halt by the immediacy of the intrusive phenomena toward which I was trying to establish a scholarly distance. Now the government, like the FDA, is telling us how much terror to take and from where, with color-coded signals. What has been packaged as terror can be in fact misleading.

Opening a political crypt. Tyrannical surges coming from left field or from the heart of democratic safety zones have become part of our politi-cal experience, even where politics in the classical sense seems to be on the retreat. Tyranny, authority, and injustice each have impressive columns in the history of thought to back them up and hold them together, even as in related but different speculative milieux, they stand apart when they are not frankly fueling one another. Although the themes of tyranny and injustice share some common ground with that of authority, I am inclining toward authority. Why this particular emphasis? Because authority is the most elusive of terms that inform relations, and yet no politics, no family, no pride of accomplishment can exist without it, according to the few thinkers who have donated their efforts to writing about or around it or its mysti-cal foundation. Not even tyranny and injustice can be confronted without a close examination of authority's sway. Authority slips away as one tries to pin it down. So say Kojève and Arendt; so contended the Romans who instituted its earliest forms as family-bound *auctoritas.* The Greeks it is said barely had a grip on it but put up, in the works especially of Plato and then Aristotle, something that approximated the modern-day understanding of what is meant by authority. Still, to the very extent that it is crucial to any political rhetoric or practice, authority is also decidedly off the radar, a ghost of itself, gone but spectrally imprinted. For Hannah Arendt, authority is an undeletable term, key to any grasp of politics. At the same time, authority has been on the decline together with religion and tradition even as it remains a primal impulse in the cuing of group formation—one can in any case no longer say what authority *is.* One can barely say what it is *not.* For her part,

Arendt opens the discussion on authority as if she were in the company of a specter, opening a political crypt. Something that still holds us hostage, authority has for all intents and purposes disappeared; it has even eaten away at her title, "What Is Authority?" "In order to avoid misunderstanding," she begins her famous essay, "it might have been wiser to ask in the title: What was—and not what is—authority? For it is my contention that we are tempted and entitled to raise this question because authority has vanished from the modern world."[1] For me, the disappearance of authority functions as a figure for democracy in crisis—a way of describing the panic that prevails within the powerful motifs of sociality, alterity, relation. Elsewhere I have argued that it is democracy's character to be in perpetual crisis.[2] The burn-out of authority opens another fold in the thinking of this crisis.

Authority's disappearance in itself calls for a speculative forensics, particularly since the presumed eclipse of authority is not complete but haunts and hounds human relations, holding things together by nothing more substantial than vague historical memory starts. Arendt's approach to the vanishing of authority recalls in some instances Heidegger's thinking of the forgetting of being. Authority's precarious perch over oblivion endangers existence. Writing of the related loss of tradition, she remarks, "We are in danger of forgetting, and such an oblivion—quite apart from the contents themselves that could be lost—would mean that, humanly speaking, we would deprive ourselves of one dimension, the dimension of depth in human existence." But here the injunction against forgetting works in a decidely non-Heideggerian fashion to save the human, together with the uninterrogated metaphor of depth on which the human stands. The loss of authority is seen as the final and decisive phase "of a development which for centuries undermined primarily religion and tradition. Of tradition, religion, and authority, . . . authority has proved to be the most stable element. With the loss of authority, however, the general doubt of the modern age also invaded the political realm. . . . Only now, as it were after the fact, the loss of tradition and of religion have become political events of the first order" (464). Of inestimable political capital, authority sets up and invests the political; thus, whether viewed as exercising its elusive capacities to the max or in recess, it also belongs to a thinking of the destruction

1. Hannah Arendt, "What Is Authority," in *The Portable Hannah Arendt* (New York, NY: Penguin 2000), 462. Subsequent references are cited parenthetically in the text.

2. Avital Ronell, *The Test Drive* (Urbana and Chicago: University of Illinois Press, 2005).

or end of politics. Because authority is slipping, the alarming agitations of planet-struck religion and perished tradition come into view, taking on the quality of prime political events. Kojève, who takes another tack, is quick to point out that while Hegel works out his encounter with the problem in terms of the master/slave dialectic, and the Scholastics in terms of God, Marx completely neglects the trope of authority and therefore comes up short. For Arendt, the problem of authority arises early, close to the origin of Western civilization, when Plato has to bury Socrates in writing. We'll get to the heart of the story shortly, when we attach to the micrological blips in her argument, which show without saying so how Plato struggled. After the execution of his mentor he was bent on conveying the *authority of philosophy* in an effort both to memorialize and to exact revenge for the passing of the martyred philosopher.

It is not only the case that authority has been lost to us, but it was called up in the first place as a mark of an irretrievable fadeout, to fill in for a loss. The verdict on Socrates is responsible for the birth of authority as a stratagem—an outburst of philosophical insurgency—and a recovery operation. Reading the history of authority—the history of incessant forfeiture leading to the *need* for authority—one has the sense that philosophy was shaken to its core by the state murder, by the terse sign of its own fragility for which evermore it had to compensate by inventing the prestige of authority. Authority in this bereaved light becomes the response to state-inflicted terror that acts as an arbitrary authority, primed on brute violence, a kind of ancient video game where the object of relentless pursuit will have been the philosopher. Plato avenges the loss, upgrades the destitute philosopher, turning him into philosopher-king, with the help of the newly fabricated mantel of authority as counter-authority. The elusive paraconcept outbids the strategic finesse of the other offspring of Logos.

I am not going to try either to rehabilitate authority or to tear down bumper stickers that, despite it all, remain firmly in place on what drives the culture of often "liberal" ideals and broad-based interventions: "Question Authority." Authority, even when it was swarmed by identifiable figures and we thought it exhibited some substantial qualities, always provoked acts of questioning. Unlike neighboring syntagms of power such as those attached to tyranny and injustice, about which examples abound, indeed overflow and cramp, authority is difficult to track, impossible to monitor, discouragingly complicated to talk about. It stares down talk, dismissive of every effort to gain on it. Arendt puts authority on the opposing side of any rhetoric of persuasion. Authority disdains the egalitarian order of persuasion, having little use for the petition of strategically aligned language acts. Standing

25

rigorously on its own, it refuses simple power alliances. Thus it contradicts both coercion by force and persuasion through arguments: you can't talk to it, submit it to any logic, or talk your way out of the troubled facticity of a standoff with authority. If it didn't continue to supply the pregivenness of our way of handling private and public spheres of encounter, domestic and foreign affairs—or insist on rendering the most intimate of decisions and determining the mentors we chose—maybe authority, with its receding qualities of disappearance and ghostly effectiveness, would not have to be bothered with. One would breathe a sigh of relief if authority, finally, could be dispensed with, closed down and forgotten. Perhaps, one projects, one could grow out of authority, get over it, and mature like a child who no longer fears the switch (as if childhood did not return with punishing regularity to gag and scar, as Kafka and Lyotard show; presumably adult and ripened, these children consistently crawl out of historical comfort zones into regressive spaces where one remains stunted or is returned to the starting pen in order to face the ongoing torment of worldlessness).

The forgetting of authority, the temptation to confuse its disappearance with a final call or definitive ending of sorts—imagining that the irreversible demise of authority were accomplished—opens the field to the invasion of unmarked terrorism, new forms of disturbance for which no critical apparatus or conceptual framework yet exists. The fear induced by the loss of authority appears to follow a Schmittian pattern: the loss of something often considered as pernicious—in his work, the loss of the enemy—opens up abysses to a radical disfiguration of relations as it unravels threads and impairs boundaries that have kept the world recognizable, even in its grim particulars. Such losses have been tallied in late modernity to great effect. Related to Benjamin's aura, but less flashy, more perniciously undermining, the disappearance of authority may well supersede Carl Schmitt's enemy constellation, the vanishing of which spells historical calamity. How does the loss of authority inflect our being? Where do the remainders of authority still dwell and sing out like sirens? On another level altogether, are the mourners of authority masking another loss for which "authority" would be a cover? What about the frankly authoritarian features of some of Arendt's choices, her reactionary watchwords?

The invention of hell. Plato began to consider the introduction of authority into the exercises of public affairs in the polis: "He knew he was seeking an alternative to the common Greek way of handling domestic affairs, which was persuasion as well as to the common way of handling foreign af-

fairs, which was force and violence" (Arendt, 464). It was not only that Plato was trying to negotiate between rhetoric and violence. He was mourning the death of Socrates, a seismic event which had unmistakably diminished the pull of persuasion: "It was after Socrates' death that Plato began to discount persuasion as insufficient for the guidance of men and to seek for something liable to compel them without using external means of violence" (475). Scanning for authority, Plato was trying to clinch a force that could dispense with the use of force by priming a power that renounces power. Authority starts at home, as the Romans relayed, taking up Plato's dilemma.

For his part, Plato had to leave the earth to build a case for authority. He started up the machinery of rewards and punishments in the hereafter, "a myth which Plato himself neither believed nor wanted the philosophers to believe" (Arendt, 475). The myth of hell at the end of *The Republic* was aimed at those who are not capable of philosophical truth. In the *Laws*, Plato deals with the same level of perplexity that led to his creation of hell, but in the opposite way; here he "proposed a substitute for persuasion, the introduction to the laws in which their intent and purpose are to be explained to the citizens" (476). Going to hell or citing the law provided Plato with ways to locate coercion without violence (we will not for now engage a critique of violence here or take measure of its overflowing borders, asking where violence begins and ends or whether the invention of hell is all that nonviolent: thanks, Plato). The main dilemma of his political philosophy required that Plato find a means of coercion that parts ways with violence and proves stronger than persuasion and argument.

Seeking a legitimate principle of coercion, Plato was motored, Arendt offers, by the hostility of the polis toward philosophy, "which had probably lain dormant for some time before it showed its immediate threat to the life of the philosopher in the trial and death of Socrates. Politically, Plato's philosophy shows the rebellion of the philosopher against the polis" (475). Like the survivor of so many police films, Plato was set off by the murder of his partner. In his case, he had to reroute the philosophical premium, renouncing his partner's softer ways, the patient if shrewd tapping of persuasive energies with which Socrates to this day is associated. This is not the place to get into some of Socrates' bullying tendencies, which count neither for Plato nor Arendt as cornerstones of violence. Philosophy had to put together a survival kit, and fast. (Plato's survival-mourning involved the outbreak of another myth, that of his taking up writing, whipping out the pen that Socrates had declined. Writing up Socrates may belong to the mourning rituals and hardening that Plato endured after the state murder that complicated the ongoing parricidal itineraries that organize philosophical transmission.) The only way for the philosopher to win a hand was to go through hell and fill out the blanks of a generalizable religion. So Plato, for tactical reasons, finds religion. He is not the only one.

Religion, provided with its rent-controlled abode of the damned, trumps the more earthbound rhetoric of persuasion. Hell burns through the combustible hold of a rhetoric that proves fragile in terms of staying power, ever diminishing its influence over the polis. Both Arendt and Kojève find a sticking point for authority in religion, skimming over the trifle of whether or not God exists. His analyses—phenomenological, metaphysical, ontological—require Kojève to make use of the notion of God ("il faudra se servir de la notion de Dieu"), even while admitting that the latter does not exist ("même en admettant que ce dernier n'existe pas"), except as a "myth." For the man of "faith" ("Car l'homme 'croyant'") has always attributed to God the highest authority, and it is thus through him that one can study this phenomenon as if under a microscope. And to the extent that we are dealing with a "myth," Kojève continues under cover of quotation marks (is it a myth or not, why the persistent sprinkle of quotation marks in this place?), the analysis of *divine* Authority in effect is an analysis of *human* Authority: "without being aware of it, man projects on God that which he discovers—more or less unconsciously—in himself to a degree such that one can study him by studying 'his' God."[3] Kojève shrinks the infinite projection to what we might call a "microspective" size, inverting the "mythic" relationship: God accommodates the microscopic gaze as man inflates.

The ontological proof of God's existence, Kojève further contends, rests on the metaphysical placement of divine Authority as the Authority of the Father, who is seen as cause (85). Every variant of human authority is rooted in the Authority of the Father, which feeds the tendency to locate paternal Authority in power and political Authority. God the Father is cast moreover as Author of a Work (*oeuvre*) who exerts Authority over the *Oeuvre* (88). What interests Kojève about this God-the-Father constitution, besides the status of formal cause underlying what has been created ex nihilo, is that man has renounced consciously and voluntarily any and all "reactions" against divine authority. No one goes up against God, not for long, in any case, and not for good, if the graffiti in public bathrooms are an indication ("Nietzsche is dead. God"). Any thoughts of formulating a reaction to divine acts are given up as vain illusions. This puzzle and its political implications fascinate Kojève. What accounts for the unconditional surrender of human reactivity? How

---

3. Alexandre Kojève, *La notion de l'autorité* (Paris: Gallimard, 2004), 54. Subsequent references are cited parenthetically in the text.

does the "recognition" of divine Authority embed itself and brake human drivenness? Authority, which, once again, is not the same as *power* or *force*, prepares the act, if it is an act, of extreme renunciation.

Recognition of authority means giving up any and all reactions to it, and consists in renouncing resistance. This is far from the Hegelian sense of recognition that involved in his analysis and Kojève's commentary the famous fight or flight reflexes in the arena of death's prestige. Kojève, for his part, in the context of nailing authority, goes on to say that God is always the God of our *ancestors* ("Dieu d'Abraham, d'Isaac et de Jacob," 86), which accounts for the sacred character of "tradition" and its binding tendencies. Tradition as such exercises Authority: "one renounces voluntarily and consciously 'reacting' against tradition to the extent that such a 'reaction' would be a reaction against oneself, a kind of suicide" (87). Coming from a philosopher, this is quite a statement. Philosophy is "traditionally" one of the more parricidal entries in the cultural history of behaviors, among the most tradition-eating practices that typically takes on its own tradition in order to demolish it. We cannot get into the possibility of a death drive installed in the very workings of the philosophical order, though one would be right to suppose that a suicidal impulse accompanies these tracks. At the level of the conscious and political mapping toward which Kojève is turned, tradition needs to be held to a certain determinable degree at least. If I had more energy, I would want to investigate what makes it necessary according to the precepts of his argument for Kojève to hold tradition in place, while everything around it, including divine myth, crumbles. The decision on his part to offer a retention package to tradition, in order to maintain its stature, may be related to the fact that he is inching toward the sections of his work that provide some reflections on disruptions in the sense of history and, implicitly also, in history as conveying the possibility and designated tradition of sense. Clearly panicked at the massive tear in tradition, he has his eye on Hitler's advent—the relentless marker of brute force propped on fake and trumped-up tradition; Hitler delivered a blow to and a rupture with authority, breaking identification with any recognizable figure of authoritative establishment and deliberately pushed aside the paternal base.

A legitimate principle of coercion. Kojève prepares the more sustained "Analyse de l'Autorité du Maréchal" (186–94), where paternal authority has stayed intact, unhampered in the arena of intense political strife. The spillover of "l'Autorité du Père" into the realm of politics is one of the problems that Kojève attacks. At the very least, he wants to prompt a

29

shift from Father to Judge as principal figure holding together political and ethical qualities of existence. Kojève's attempts to dislodge Father as figure, imago, and referential complacency in the field of politics, indicate his reach for a tightened sense of constraint. A place must be arranged for the Judge as well as the judiciary branch of any serious map of governance. But such a shift, presented both as possible and highly improbable—the shift from Father to Judge, their incessant collapses and the threat that power signifiers hold over our heads when Father floods the political—is what Kafka tripped over time and again in a way that remains fateful for us today. Kafka at no point makes a clean getaway from Father to Judge as if these were separable entities, or as if one figuration of invasive supremacy were more auspicious than the other. The clean break that Kojève makes for Judge over Father's dead body remains problematic, something that even a warden protecting Kafkan confines would not abide. Perhaps Kojève fixes its severable function in the political realm as a regulative ideal, endowing it with the qualities of a wish fulfillment or drawing delinkage toward a prescriptive shift that must be imagined. Perhaps the dissociation of Father and Judge is meant to cue up the split-off father, the cruel, sadistic usurper of a dominant paternal imago precariously associated with firm but benevolent caretaking. In any case, Kojève does not dwell on the coalescence of the split parts of fatherhood that in the end may fail to account for political brutality, and that may slip from the noose of mendaciousness that marks egregious leadership. He does not as such take up a sense of the perversion and recast of *Führertum* that breaks away from the paternal configuration. For him, even instances of aberrant encroachment have received at least some start-up funding from sources lodged in divine and fatherlike authority.

Plato, in the meanwhile, is still scouring the planet for a legitimate principle of coercion. His attempts have led him to size up a great number of models to unlock existing relations. Following up on Plato's modeling of authority Kojève, too, offers an anthropological inflection to his remarks. He swerves from a more theoretical line of questioning in order to group different kinds of hierarchical holds that can be reviewed. He considers the authority wielded by the teacher over the student, the officer over a soldier or, alas, a husband over a wife. In a sense, Kojève's examples provide an upgrade, or better said, a modernization, of the examples that Plato establishes for the emergence of authority. Plato looks to the relations between shepherd and his sheep, the helmsman of a ship and passengers, physician and patient, or between master and slave. In all the instances put forth by Plato, Arendt observes, "either expert knowledge commands confidence so that neither force nor persuasion are necessary to obtain compliance,

or the ruler and the ruled belong to two altogether different categories of beings, one of which is already by implication subject to the other, as in the cases of the shepherd and his flock or the master and his slaves. All these examples are taken from what to the Greeks was the private sphere of life, and they occur time and again in all the great political dialogues, *The Republic*, the *Statesman*, and the *Laws*" (476). Arendt's gloss, though characteristically clear and altogether comprehensive, moves in a fast, puzzling manner, proceeding without the bump of a doubt, without any disruption of hierarchical assertion. All these examples, meant to establish a middle ground between persuasion and violence, appear however to imply violence and intrusion upon the subjugated parties—or species—as well as breakage in what she appears to cordon off as merely private aspects of political life. The asserted qualities of expertise and confidence remain unquestioned.

If Arendt is precipitous in marking off these hierarchically bound couples, she does remark nonetheless that Plato himself "was not satisfied with these models" and that in order "to establish the 'authority' of the philosopher over the polis, he returned to them time and time again, because only in these instances of glaring inequality could rule be exerted without seizure of power and the possession of means of violence. What he was looking for was a relationship in which the compelling element lies in the relationship itself and is prior to the actual issuance of commands." Arendt tops off her commentary with what appears to be a tautological stumble: "The patient became subject to the physician's authority when he fell ill, and the slave came under the command of the master when he became a slave" (476). One must take a closer look at the bind that tightens around the slave and ask how this tautological event ("the slave came under the command of the master when he became a slave") erases the question of violence. So intent is she on clearing the way for an authority without violence that Arendt refuses to recognize that there is no slavery without violent possession.

One also wonders—this may seem trivial, but argument allows for such limit-grazing watchfulness—where violence begins or what terms of violence get counted out as concerns the downtrodden and our animal companions. Or is the prod of the sheep exempted from such consideration? Perhaps this is so, at least in the wide swath of philosophical fields. But the tabulation of sheep and the ill, the enlistment of slave and other filiations of the untouchable in relation to power, takes a pernicious turn when analogies are allowed to run fast and loose. Following Plato, Arendt clearly wants to attain to the kind of soft coercion associated with reason and the installment of the philosopher-king. She requires for her demonstration prior instances of subjugation that preempt subversion or, indeed, revolution. What remains

31

intact and important, despite the dead or destitute bodies that are run over on the way, is that Plato, like Arendt, looks to authority as something that would allow violence to subside and persuasion to take a rest. Authority establishes relationality as command, promising compliance in the absence of force or argument.

Linked in an essential way to Kafka's parable, "Before the Law," and to the Levinasian thought on passivity, this priority, or *a priority*, seeks out the condition of hostage-being that suspends effects of persecution and injury to which both Kafka and Levinas attest. Such a view of authority that might take on or shake up the other without harm—ceding originary harm in order to avoid *doing* harm—provides us with a map of the nearly impossible reparations that both Kojève and Arendt attempt to achieve in their encounter with the genealogical purge and political provocation of authority. Authority in these cases subsists on borrowed transcendence. When someone commands authority, this figure or person or institution supersedes the realm of ontic squabbles, leaping over the conflict arenas of everyday pathology and warlike aggression. Matters are helped when authority trickles down from the notion of God, suggesting both a higher column and a more secure ground from which commands can be issued (Arendt does not consider internal command systems and Kojève more or less explicitly rules them out; not even the categorical imperative gets in authority's door). I suspect that authority comes close at times to Kant's thinking of *Achtung* (respect) but, so far, respect, whether commanded or in some ways demanded, has not come into the picture or the framework that they maneuver. The exclusion of respect from the discussion of authority may be theoretically motivated, serving as part of a deliberate omission on the part of Arendt, and possibly also Kojève, that keeps authority structurally bare. What is the sense of keeping authority separate from respect, and what kind of theoretical bulwarking does the strategy of seclusion assure? It is necessary to note at this point only that so little is said about how authority secures respect or produces effects of respectful adherence. Let me take a closer look at what may turn out to be a telling angle in the discourse of their divergence, remembering that respect is sometimes "earned," whereas authority, baffling by nature, simply holds sway or, in Arendt's words, "commands confidence," thus bypassing the intricacies of consensual respect.

The estrangement between authority and respect in terms of philosophical and historical trajectories seems peculiar when one considers, among other things, the emphasis Kant places on *distance* when speaking of respect, thus introducing a quality of coldness but also of parity: Kant plays it on level playing fields, relying on the pull of justice. Authority, in all cases an escapee from explicit forms of violence, even that of speech, tries to prepare the ground for political relatedness, softening the space of committed citizenry with the holdout of deliberate asymmetry. Sometimes the weight of asymmetry can give me the shivers; at other times I recognize its grace, the way it announces a humbling divergence of attributes. I will go on. An otherwise hospitable reader of Kant, Arendt reroutes the question of authority around his thought, which in this context she for some reason snubs or plainly avoids, producing an effect of detour that cannot be missed. The dissociation in late modernity of authority from Kantian respect may account for the secret fissuring of contemporary political sites and practices. The point here is to monitor the blanks left by the removal of Kantian respect from political discourse and to consider what kind of underground life-form respect has assumed in its banished afterlife. Whether respect has morphed into considerations of human dignity or reached its effective expiration date, Arendt takes it off the table of commandments that she associates with the phrasal regimen of authority. Kant gets surprisingly left behind by his prize pupil.

On the other hand, the unneighborly bypass with regard to Kant may have another sort of career path: respect may be incorporated in both Kojève and Arendt into the heart of authority but in such a way as to have prompted a severe mutation, nearing the decidedly more sublime regions of human relatedness. Whatever their subsequent choices or poses, whatever their ideological markers or ethical constraints, both Arendt and Kojève make themselves dependent on essential *inequality* in order to recruit and replenish the notion of authority. This makes me uneasy, although the facile erasure of inequality makes me even more uneasy. In their corner, Maurice Blanchot and Emmanuel Levinas rhyme inequality with responsible asymmetry. In these cases, however, the necessity of the unequal disposition comes from an ever-diminishing egological space and is part of the effort to tame tropes of domination.

The conversation of Blanchot and Levinas with Arendt and Kojève may help us clarify a significant dissension among them at the very place where they appear to meet—a dissension Kant may be seen to leverage. Every member in this group sets some store in the quality of asymmetry, yet it is not the *same* asymmetry that comes into play. In fact, the very nearness that they exhibit on this point sets them apart and makes them split off toward differing destinations of thought and commitment. Uncanny proximity and shared terrain serve to disclose nearly opposing dispositions and altogether different measures in terms of relatedness: The nostalgic impulses running through Arendt's elaboration and the restricted economy of Kojève's speculations on authority show that, despite a shared vocabulary aligning them with pivotal moments in the itineraries of Levinas and Blanchot, they come out at another place, with a different ear for the beat of inequality. Kantian respect seems to survive with some dents and a new face in the considerations of Blanchot and Levinas, where distance is now disturbingly bridged and the other can make persecutory gains on one, turning you into a human shield—if we are still accommodated in the realm of the human. Neither respect nor awe, nor even remote features of sublime trembling, appear to survive in the reflections on authority proposed by Arendt and Kojève, who keep their figures very human, if at times inhumane.

Levinas stresses a different pulsation, another tempo, as he unfolds his thought anarchically, receding as he approaches the other both destitute and majestic, difficult to size up or command—a speck and the immeasurably spectacular (though without the spectacle). Arendtian authority goes admittedly elsewhere, preferring not meet the majestic escalade of the absolute other. Averting her gaze from those debilitated or impoverished warpings under authority's weight, her concerns, along with those of Kojève, remain largely tactical, if not unduly intact, by which I mean that structures and strictures pertaining to Rome, humanism, and patriarchy serve as the unquestioned basis for these reflections, even as they are directed by the destruction of the world. This by no means implies that Levinas and Blanchot have cleared the abysses to which their provisional counterparts turn a blind eye—only that they have acknowledged the hits taken by their complicit histories of thought. Being in some essential ways flattened out and dented by the free run of patriarchy, they have had to let go of the presumptions, to some degree ensnaring, of humanism. I am not insane: It would be fairly outrageous to say that Levinas has run down patriarchy, but the points he makes are differently scored and may assert the deliberations of another exposition of patriarchy, also problematic but significantly neutralized, "weakened," to use his term of endearment.

Perhaps the encounter with Levinas and Blanchot has created too harsh a contest for Arendt and Kojève, for the expression of their largely congruent anxieties over the disappearance of authority. Maybe this failure to stick calls for another look, urging an even closer encounter with the vocabularies and concerns we have introduced thus far. Until we get there I'd like to propose that a scene be recalled: Having narrowly escaped internment—she had already been rounded up and subjected to the misery of deportation—Hannah Arendt, momentarily in Paris, attends Kojève's course in the company of Albert Camus. In the same class Jean-Paul Sartre and Simone de Beauvoir, seated nearby, are also taking notes.

Chapter 2
The Household of Authority

Tabulating the university. Before continuing the reflection on authority, it may be useful for me to reintroduce myself at this juncture, if only for the purpose of offering some contextual prompters and a much-needed roadmap. I would have preferred to relegate this portion of my unfolding commentary to a quiet zone. The place from which one writes, however, is not always indifferent to the topic at hand. Authority, as political motif or theoretical axiom, surfaces in these pages neither as an obsession to which I might be considered strangely partisan, nor does it appear as easy intellectual prey. I find, moreover, that I am not held simply to a mood of scholarly detachment as I dedicate myself to deciphering its pull. There is nothing about authority that allows it to separate off from thought with the elegant aloofness observed by a more traditionally inflected "object of contemplation," though I admit that every one of our precursors struggled with the limits of their inquiry or so-called object. As problem and motif, authority does not keep a distance that would protect one from its encroaching effects. Like the paraconcept of stupidity, it goes after you when roused from philosophical sleep. It turns something like a piercing look on you, making a number of particular demands.

For instance, the office of authority now requires that I pull out some identity papers, without fail. I don't feel that I exercise much of a choice on this matter, so I comply. Let me oblige by situating this endeavor with ever more transparency, perhaps adjusting some boundaries. This does not mean that transparency serves to demarcate an ideal horizon. Authority is complicated, evoking ambivalence at every turn, making one want and hate it at once. It has a nasty habit of needling your innermost convictions, including those that rely on metaphors that still support a sense of "innermost" anything. As hard as it is to pin down with theoretical acuity and materialist verve, I'll begin by articulating two basic questions, as if I'd have to account for my investment in this study before going any further: Where does the anxiety over authority's reach come from in my psychic-somatic-intellectual habitat? How does its persistence as question relate to the simultaneous tendencies of dominance and defeat in the political? Let me explain myself, and, then, let me explain why I need to explain myself.

My work typically borders the by-now-traditional university disciplines that hold these terms in check: political theory, philosophy, history, literary criticism, psychoanalysis, and the less-stable coordinates of ethics. At times I slalom in and out of the discursive formations associated with these and similarly regulated disciplinary markers. On other occasions, I travel their peripheries and tap their margins that, since the thought of Derrida, cannot stay put in remote pockets of inscription but, for all we know, may well constitute their core, if such a thing exists; or, these nearly-off-the-grid issues indicate at least the location from which key propositions pulsate.

Sometimes the subject matter with which one engages frustrates the hermeneutic drive. Or it menaces the whole enterprise and plan of judicious approach, undermining all the good intentions mobilized toward creating sensible dialogue or assuring a purposeful probe. A vexed motif, an unauthorized problem set, threatens to capsize you. Be that as it may, I am a child of the university, an entity whose expressions of ambivalence have not yet destroyed me. (But how does one know that one has not been destroyed? I have evidence to the contrary. That is a topic for another occasion. One day I will investigate the tyranny of the university over my own trajectories and dream projects, beginning with the way it has ruled over and overruled my body, beating down any healthy instinct, trampling the least cellule of creativity, but this problem does not move me now, and I know too well that I'm rigged to be grateful for the fact that traumatic invasiveness, with all its identificatory passes, is also in the end structuring.) I mark these coordinates not out of a sense of entitled indulgence or narcissistic complacency, but in order to align myself near the problem areas that this work claims to traverse. The exercise of authority, including the often-covert habits of tyranny and evocations of injustice in the university, remain to be studied even as such investigations tend to downscale other, more manifestly distressed experiences of wrongdoing. The university, itself embattled by the constant threat of repressive regimes, seems in any case small in comparison to frankly pernicious political entities, and in some cases bravely shelters subversive types of cognitive sprees and intellectual diversity, making room for types of behaviors and reflection that receive no pass in other sectors of

dominant if not overbearing cultures of denialism. Nonetheless, whether or not it mirrors larger social tendencies, the university as life-form should not escape review, for it also sponsors unfreedom in a number of ways and appears to exhaust the teaching body under the weight of an ever-increasing bureaucratic prerogative. University offices, like all bureaucracy, dispense their toxic dosage of authoritarian rule, and the struggle over what carries authority or what is poised to make one perish (which is not limited to grammars of authorship and the contingencies of publication) is unceasing.

I have begun this segment of my run by slowing down for an institutional checkpoint that was largely imagined in order to simplify the ordeal of who's watching whom. This happened in part because the experience of the work, be it flagged by distress, disaster, scales of exaltation or even mundanity, must nowadays be faced without the hallmark of truth. Truth was once affiliated with and came after ruin, often depending for its disclosure and light on the staging of someone's or something's ruinous disintegration. Today, by contrast, disaster is without truth, occurring without a sign cast from the luminous concealment of a *beyond*. Deprived of shelter, pitched on the edge of metaphysics, one is thrown back upon minimalist signposts and decidedly modest directives. We are more on our own than ever before, more responsible for locating the incitements of an essentially untraceable call. I am not the only one to have been left behind when the gods absconded. I have heard you cry, I listen to the rumble of remote but unavoidable clashes: the job description of those left behind, without guarantor or reliable transcendence, without the pat on the back telling you to go on, you're doing the right thing, hang in there.

We scour the breakups, size the fissures, staying close to the fragile understructure of falsely grounded knowledge systems. We come in after the break, in the historical and nearly ontological zone that Jean-Luc Nancy designates as "after tragedy," where he analyzes what "venir après" means—what it means to ride in on the wake, to come in afterwards like the very concept of history, like all the *posts* and their chrono-logic that come after Aristotle.[1] I will be considering the links between the destinies of democracy and the loss of tragedy—the destruction of the tragic ethos. Such links have prompted Nancy to underscore the risks of a continued abandonment in the wake of true tragedy. The vanishing gods have left mortals on their own, among themselves in a space where the address is no longer oriented toward gods, offering victims and sacrifice, but toward one another, left to wonder how and where language

1. Jean-Luc Nancy, "Après la tragédie" lecture given at "Lacoue-Labarthe Today: Caesura and Catastrophe" Colloquium, New York University, 9 April 2008.

holds on to former rites of sacrifice—the subterranean residue of a major switchover. Whether or not we try to track the historical release from truth, its often violent unleashing, or the way ancient scenes of disaster bleed, leak, or smear into contemporary politics, it is still the case that, since or rather "after" Kant, one no longer knows what to do with or where to place "human dignity," how to make it stick or stand plump with meaning.

I, for my part, coming after so many and so much, will grow low now, keep small, without the pretenses of any derivative of God or Subject or master signifier on my side—nor any pretenses of having fully unloaded these unavoidable metaphysical bolsters. I don't even have bragging rights or the wherewithal to boast the triumphalist narcissism of being on my own or ownmost—even my being-towards-death is not my own, but that's another philosophical story. The strictures governing utterance are real and the scene of inscription, as Kafka has taught us, has become uncannily local, personal yet emptied of boastful interiorities, measurable achievement. So, for me, it's back to school, strapped into place on academic death row, last seat in the last row, clenched by a history of repeated punishment. It's not bad; I have grown to like it. I wobble in place without the brace of truth, that's my only point here, which is what forces the "I" onto the page, as I offer a clip, a situation without substantial backing but that delivers the split injunction that must go on, I can't go on.

Can't go on. Many cultural protagonists and meaning carriers have demonstrated a complicated relationship to the university, whether the enrollee be Hamlet, Faust, Martin Luther, Victor Frankenstein, Walter Benjamin, Virginia Woolf, or scores of other "fellows," some of them famous dropouts and relentless contesters. In practical terms, Franz Kafka, who was later to become an institution builder, cofounder of the Jewish School become museum, had only two disciplines open to him as a university student: only the professions of law and medicine were open to Jews in Prague. He went for chemistry, together with his friend, Hugo Bergmann, but couldn't hack it; Bergmann stuck it out for a year; Kafka dropped out after two weeks. He was not meant to be a doctor, nor a lawyer, but jammed between a rock and a hard place he reenrolled himself in law. Things may have evolved since then, but the university—and its filtering systems, its historical admissions policies and sorting mechanisms—has not been a neutral place from which to launch oneself to write freely, even if one is permitted day passes to literary and philosophical studies. The university in many cases preps or rather caps the force fields of that by which we feel disciplined and formed. I leave the university as a sidebar, not only bringing it up for reasons of full disclosure but also to mark the authority that it exerts in the group formation of government-level institutions and agencies. There were many dropouts and serious contestations; yet, the drop-in crowd may be the most worrisome. Even a nontheoretical glance can observe the ties of Yale to the presidential office or those of Harvard to executive advisory boards or Princeton's links to the CIA and a cluster of other academic sites of stateside Pentagon suppliers. Supplying such an inventory of state-university complicities is not necessarily my responsibility in the speculative secretariat. Moreover, to be fair, I'd have to investigate the registrars of prep and elementary, if not preschool training grounds, before issuing further pronouncements on the schooling of authority, its early seating arrangements and tireless roll calls, the reporting of grades, and built-in degradations. I will leave the halls of the institution for now, but we'll have to go back to school wherever the problem of authority and its training regimens, its staple enactments of coerced attendance, take hold of our argument.

A phenomenological approach to "this Authority of the Father." Authority, as Kojève makes clear, has less than nothing to do with force or with strategies of implementation; it evades subphenomena of forcible assertion as well, since it repudiates legal types of bullying and disdains the arbitrary throwing of power punches. In fact, authority supersedes and trumps force on all essential counts, separating off from it with a kind of sovereign aloofness. I would want to argue with this view not only to the extent that "force" has proven to be philosophically inappropriable, difficult to pin down as concept or theme (unlike "violence," with which philosophical thought has a long involvement), but also because we are made to confront other decisive shortfalls: Kojève's set of assertions ignores the positing powers of linguistic acts, suppresses the subtle straits of education, and sideswipes psychoanalysis, where figures of potency power up in covert sites and make legal inroads. Still, Kojève's subtle analysis trains its focus on the debilitating consequences of tropological spillovers where politics is run by covert paternal commands. Examining its various forms, he remains attentive to the way authority lends structure to material existence.

Derrida and Benjamin, in another neighborhood altogether, paired up vitally to mark in what ways authority depends on its own representative and performative capacities, impatient to posit its field of determinations and earn the benefits of its own effectuation. How do we locate authority's domain and sort out its different functions in order to identify its wide-ranging conceptual alliances? Whereas Kant removed authority from persons and offices, trouncing some of Martin Luther's calculated maneuvers, and rerouted authority to the law, Derrida notes that law, in terms of the authority it wields, is not merely "a docile instrument, servile and thus exterior to the dominant power," but instead something that can and does "maintain a more internal, more complex relationship with what one calls force, power, or violence."[2] Lacoue-Labarthe, Nancy, and Samuel Weber control other sectors of the authority problem and stress *panic* as a principal concern for political thought and the way it leads to self-authorizing acts and paternal layovers. The three meet over a reading of *Moses and Monotheism*, where Moses serves both as perpetual child and founding father, both as bearer of the law and breaker of that which regulates social narcissism. Kojève, who does not want to see authority bleed into other qualities of statement or act, opposes authority to force and power, basing his observations on paternal paradigms that are spared deconstructive takedowns. In the introduction to the text I am analyzing, the editor, François Terré, writes when broaching "this Authority of the Father, whether hidden or repressed," that "l'apport discuté de la psychanalyse est ici hors du champs de la refléxion."[3] Psychoanalysis is off the table—right at the moment when paternal authority makes its mark and is shown to be repressed. Although it enacts another scene of the slaying of the father, at least it's honest: psychoanalysis has been tagged out as concerns a phenomenological approach to "this Authority of the Father," and will not contribute to the formation of identity organized around group psychology. Will the spliced-out discipline return to punish or to unsettle the household of authority that Kojève sets out to establish? Doesn't psychoanalysis always come back to bite the ass of the phenomenological politology that thinks it can simply discard it? Such questions seem premature and have entered our sphere only to indicate how authority can replicate itself when under investigation, disabling a friendly discourse such as psychoanalysis—well, maybe not so friendly, nor merely discursive, because too close for comfort. Kojève, in any case, proves impatient with the genealogical and Oedipal tracks that psychoanalysis will have laid down—perhaps even with its ex-

2. Jacques Derrida, "Force of Law: The 'Mystical Foundation of Authority,'" trans. Mary Quaintance, in *Deconstruction and the Possibility of Justice*, ed. Drucilla Cornell, Michel Rosenfeld, and David Gray Carlson (New York: Routledge, 1992), 13.

3. François Terré, in Alexandre Kojève, *La notion de l'autorité*, ed. François Terré (Paris: Gallimard, 2004), 28.

orbitant authority over political analyses in especially weighted theoretical settings—and decisively crowds them out.

Psychoanalysis will not grant Kojève the divorce he seeks, but remains loyal to the tendencies it shares with political philosophy. Psychoanalysis and Kojève draw up new itineraries of pleasure and politics in conjunction with a relentless aestheticization of the political, the historical tendency that both Freud and Kojève have exposed, if not ripped apart. Even though he mutes the psychoanalytic program, Kojève relies on the draw of desire—you may say it's Hegelian, I say it's psychoanalysis (and then, depending on the intellectual climate, may whip out a what's-the-difference-nowadays lecture)—in order to push forward with his political analysis. Kojève insinuates *desire* into the actualization of justice: his work brings to light the *pleasure of judging*, a pleasure as acutely felt and specifically rendered as sexual and aesthetic pleasures. The human psyche is invested in and inspired by the Idea of justice and is outfitted with a properly juridical interestedness, which is as personal as it is pervasive (that is why, I'll venture spontaneously, television offers up so may juridical dramas, to prime and parasite the *personal* investment in law, the delight in representations of juridical eventfulness). One would have to roll back to Kant to see how the recharging of desire works here, in the sphere of judgment. Kojève puts the pleasure back in judgment where Kant directed the explicit thrill of judging to the aesthetic domain, calming it down with disinterestedness, abolishing the privative in order properly to "enliven" judgment and to resurrect it from the numbing fields of the two prior critiques. Jump-started in the Third Critique, judgment comes to life but within the limits of a safety zone secured by constant philosophical inspection.

Following the prompts of an altogether different directory that routes the implicit pleasures and susceptibilities of judgment and the effects of contagion to which they point, one must revert to Luther, remembering that the frontier of Lutheranism marks a crucial break in the very concept of the political (if it is a "concept"). Lacoue-Labarthe has argued that "the modern political, in the very difficulty it encounters in instituting itself, does not begin with the French Revolution but, as Heine and Marx suspected, with the Reformation (the radicalization of Christianity) and the Renaissance (the imitation of the ancients)."[4] Modern political identification germi-

---

4. Philippe Lacoue-Labarthe, "The Spirit of National Socialism and Its Destiny," in *Retreating the Political*, ed. Simon Sparks (Routledge: London and New York, 1997), 154.

nates in the severe agonistic playoffs that Luther instituted and of which only one or two facets can be indicated here.[5] When weighing in on the uses of practical justice, Luther put tight restrictions on acts of judgment. Luther's maneuvers arose from the fear of a nearly libidinal problem, that of allowing for the abandon of judgment—the possibility of a kind of orgy of judgment with the prospect of everyone judging everyone, in which case all hell would break loose.

Judgment cut into the field of authority in specific ways: Luther starts out with antiauthoritarian tendencies only to come down hard with another brand of authority. At odds with worldly authority and yet a mark of inwardly bound authority, negotiating the split between these two strains of authority judgment encourages the freeing up of political energies by issuing permits for uprising as well as spiritual *Spaltung*, carving a split in the newly minted self. When Christianity anointed *faith*, which for Luther henceforth trumps *belief*, it was compatible with and depended on an inner domain of authoritative decision: one could decide and judge for oneself, without and even against institutional, cognitive, or empirical guarantees. One could judge for oneself, despite external signs or pressures that appeared to provide irrefutable roadmaps and directives. (Kant will later see the reliance on external authority as a sign of immaturity.) Yet, if one can judge for oneself, one can shake off worldly restraints, start formulating strategies of resistance—Calvin develops the doctrine of the "right to resist"—and, set on the path to assuming one's mastery as subject, one could go so far as to become a conscientious objector, take on other troubleshooting assignments released to the custody of the new authority of self. Conscience was enthroned by Luther, who thus made room for an unprecedented inwardness and set up the fledgling authority of faith. Priming the absolute inwardness of the subject subventioned by the transcendent nature of Christian freedom vis-à-vis worldly authority, Luther initially brandished the necessity of an

5. Another route that I would like to take here is indicated by Werner Hamacher's reflections on the adjoining deaths of God and democracy, "the experience of the death of democracy and its Christian democratic-familial (filial) God" in "Sketches Toward a Lecture on Democracy," trans. Roland Végsö (*theory@buffalo 10: Democracy and Violence*, 2005), 7. Hamacher outlines how political onto-Christology, driven by a Self that knows itself as "consciousness and conscience" must not put its faith in external authority: "As the attestation of the godly inner self and the resistance against its subjugation by the merely external authority of the *ecclesia*, the Christian religion of God present in every individual is essentially Protestantism" (19).

antiauthoritarian attitude or *Einstellung.*[6] The price for opening this new account of inner self was high: The Christian configuration linking justice with equality and love would have to be supplanted with a firm sense of authority. From now on the proximity of justice and judgment is in any case broken and judgment finds itself severely restricted to sovereign enjoyment, anticipating a Hegelian-Lacanian understanding of power and domination.

The whole system of worldly order will fall apart, Luther warns, if we do not accord unconditional recognition to the ruling authorities, and suppress a situation where "everyone would become a judge against the other," and where consequently "no power or authority, no law or order would remain in the world; there would be nothing but murder and bloodshed. . . . For it is not everyone who is competent to punish wickedness, but only the worldly authority which wields the sword."[7] Luther had to put a lid on the political id that he had released. The repressive measures he introduced involved raising the authority of judgment and limiting the rights of its exercise. Judgment, implicated in and tied to punishment, is reserved for the sovereign will, and one (meaning: you peasants) cannot perform acts of judgment, nor should you count on metaphysical retractions to soften the blow. "Mercy is neither here nor there," Luther admonishes in another address to the rebellious peasants.[8] Luther's diction often positions punishment as the place of need and its fulfillment, offering clues for a level of punishing *jouissance* to which judgment is tied: "The donkey needs to feel the whip and the people need to be ruled with force; God knew that well. Hence he put a sword in the hands of the authorities and not a feather duster."[9] The sword-wielding sovereign, appointed by God to lose the feather duster and administer justice, is in any case his own judge. Only the judge can be the plaintiff, can exercise judgment at whim, will—or indeed, at pleasure. All we can say at this point is that Luther established a libidinal account for the exercise of authority that he

6. On world authority, see Herbert Marcuse, *Studien über Autorität und Familie* (Paris: F. Alcan, 1936).

7. Martin Luther, *Admonition to Peace: A Reply to the Twelve Articles of the Peasants in Swabia* (1525), in *Selected Writings*, ed. Theodore G. Tappert (Philadelphia, Penna.: Fortress Press, 1967), 3:325. Marcuse, *Studien über Autorität und Familie*, 17.

8. Martin Luther, *An Open Letter on the Harsh Book against the Peasants* (1525), in *Selected Writings*, 3:371. We find a powerfully literary interpretation of Luther's quarrel with and positing of authority in Kleist's invention of the terrorist, Michael Kohlhaas, who takes down two towers and converses with a fictionalized Martin Luther.

9. Luther, *Admonition to Peace*, 3:376.

focused principally on judgment. The subsequent restrictions that he puts on judgment travel through the works of his successors, whether avowed or presumably off his map—if there is an off-ramp here, something about which one cannot be sure. (From here on out, we are justified in suspecting that Kafka, too, needs to be viewed under the lens of the Lutherian struggle with authority, its various and contradictory impositions, persons, and offices, its paternal anchor.) Luther's restrictions on the promiscuous cast of judgment succeed in contaminating entire fields of articulation. Joining up forces with improbable conjunctions of thought and political practice, the desire assigned to judgment motivates all sorts of flips and contortions that are traceable to Luther's way of nailing the problem of authority. In fact, his entire oeuvre, off and on the page, can be viewed as a "Letter to Father" to the extent that Luther has made everyone pay for the high-stakes bullying of a famously cursed father.

For Luther, as well as for those under study in this work, all authority arises in the echo chamber of parental authority and requires an understanding of the commanding grammars historically invested in the *pater familias*—all temporal rulers, all "'lords' become 'fathers': Where the rule of parents is absent, this would mean the end of the whole world, for without governance it cannot survive."[10] Some of the texts we are looking at try to divert the rule of unrelieved parental supervision to alternate tropological grounds in order to clear the way for a more viable, possibly more just, thought of human relatedness. It is important to bear in mind that, even for the Freudian representation of political philosophy, the authority of the father is shown continually to crash against its own premises. If anything, we are left to wonder what has elevated the father to the status of authority,

10. Martin Luther, *The Large Catechism* (1529), in *Luther's Primary Works*, trans. H. Wace and C. A. Buchheim (London: Hodder and Stoughton, 1896), 58. Citing Max Weber's emphasis on the entry of "calculation into traditional organization's brotherhood" as a decisive feature of the transformation of the family through the penetration of the "capitalist spirit," Marcuse shows how the old relations of piety "decay as soon as things are no longer shared communally within the family but 'settled' along business lines." But the obverse "side of this development is that the primitive, 'naïve' authority of the *pater familias* becomes more and more a planned authority, which is artificially generated and maintained" (*Studien über Autorität und Familie*, 30). See also Max Weber, *General Economic History*, trans. F. K. Knight (Glencoe, Ill.: Free Press, 1930), 356. In terms of kinship networks and other determinations of legitimacy, consider Judith Butler's reflections on authority in *Antigone's Claim* (New York: Columbia University Press, 2000).

even though this figure may only indicate an effect of the making of authority. Still, Freud keeps returning to the politics of the Father (until maybe *Moses*), which still does not explain the factors that make Kojève suppress the Freudian dossier altogether.

For the purposes of political analysis, Kojève closes the gap between pleasure and judgment, so much so that one can almost see the wheels turning in the minds of at least two of his transfer students—Lacan and Bataille. Because judging is prompted by *urge*—hence the rush of and to judgment—the juridical phenomenon requires a third party, an element of thirdness, when two parties go at each other before the law. This third party, impartial and disinterested, can take the form of legislator, judge, or police, but it is only through the office of the judge that the underlying juridical qualities of existence are revealed, according to Kojève.[11] Juridical interest, always up close and personal, is motored by the Idea of justice and can flip over from the *urge to judge* to the consciousness that finds itself *being judged*. This alternation is part of the circuitry of the Hegelian struggle for recognition, which engages the self-consciousness that splits off the juridical dimension from acts of judgment inherent in religion, morality, economy, and politics.

Superstructuring Hegel, Kojève's reading of the premium of judgment nonetheless offers a dimension that cannot easily be assimilated to what we already know or say about the complex areas of inquiry associated with Hegel and rights. If one opens one's pervertible ears, one discovers something that will be drawn out more explicitly by the Kafkan trespasser or the Lacanian screw-up: Kojève underscores the fact that one gets off on being judged, one puts oneself up consistently for intrusive review. Such acts of compulsive submission are part and parcel of the rush of judgment.

Terré notes that both Hegel and Kojève place the Idea at the heart of the philosophy of rights, but whereas Hegel bases his argument on the Idea of freedom, Kojève shifts ground to the Idea of justice (in Luther, the concerns of the Christian-bourgeois doctrine of freedom neutralize the Idea of justice). This move prompts Kojève to review the question of authority, beginning with the authority of being, which he describes as originating in and as "l'Autorité du type 'Père'" (14). I would like to flag some of the salient points that Kojève exploits in order to approach with critical readiness the motifs that concern us in this study. Let me suggest that Kojève sets up the password for the program that runs through this work, opening a number

11. Kojève, *Notion de l'autorité*, 13. Subsequent references are cited parenthetically in the text.

of dossiers without giving final expression to the type of investigation by which I am compelled. That would be asking a lot of a password. But here is what it can do for us, if only owing to the persistence of its restricted focus.

Kojève has a point to make about the conditions of authority and its precarious hold on modernity. His aims are not far from Arendt's probe of the limitations of authority drawn by Plato and Aristotle, who keep things private, homebound, run on a slave economy—which is why she turns toward the Roman citizenry to achieve political currency with this issue. Kojève also needs to scrape the household glue of authority if he wants to make his point hit home. This is how he goes about making his point: The myths and consigns of paternity sap the energy of what still passes for the polis, with all its updates and reconfigured charters. Not only does the family support the paternal signifier while running on empty, but "l'Autorité du type 'Père'" allows for the perversion of politics and the proliferation of fiefdoms, whether organized by religious fiat or economic voracity. The paternal type of authority, when allowed to infiltrate into state structures and take hold of governance, destroys the very possibility of an honorable politics.

Kojève carries out a double move when dealing with the primal principle of social cohesion, for his aim is to separate family and state but also to disable the foundational myth of family. It is of some consequence for Kojève to disjoin paternal authority from the state and lock it solely into familial structures. The family depends on paternal ontology (setting father as cause, author, origin, and source of what is) by something like ontological default. Father, who figures the authority of the past, maintains himself only by means of ontological "inertia." Kojève attempts to off the father, who cannot be easily removed, with a silencer. But no one will note the big bang of paternal jockeying because father mutely survives himself. Father stays the execution to the extent that lassitude has overtaken the family "vote" and nothing energetically moves in to replace or refute him. His imputed authority accrues to a default position. Here again one might patch into Freudian circuits where the sons mobilize for the purpose of bumping off the father. The overthrow of the paternal according to Freudian patterns gives rise even to more intense displays of authority squired by remorse. Kojève is perhaps equally as severe with these playoffs, if less inclined to construe a narrative explication that accounts for the fantasy of paternal demise. The father only held the key to authority by means of a nearly arbitrary shortfall, the type of inert passivity that Kojève ontologizes. Inert and essentially absent (complaints about absent fathers are only empirical derivatives of this essential feature), Father has a lock on the past even though he was ever always on his way out and off the field of familial-social intensities.

The political domain, by contrast, depends on the authority of action (in the present) and consequently on the authority of the project (for the future), which is to say, on types of authority that Kojève designates as "Maître" and "Chef." The family primes the authority of the father, holding fast to the past, as principal authority from which the others are derived: authority of Judge (of "eternity," which insures impartiality), of Leader (who oversees and guides), and of Master (who decides and acts). Father engenders being and secures the perennial cast of a self-identical past.

In the case of the state a different order obtains. The authority of Father (and of Judge) derives from the Maître and Chef, once again differentiating Family and State. Parents, according to Kojève, do not form an entity of friends opposed to a common Enemy. Nor are they the Governed who recognize "l'Autorité du Maître et du Chef des Gouvernants" (*Notion*, 15). Parents love(d) each other. (This is something that Kojève's sketch does not develop but nonetheless hints at: the love for and of family does not transfer to love of country, an aberration arising from considerable tropological confusion. Nor does he go into the unnavigable recesses of love.) If they recognize an Authority (which gives them the appearance of political unity but remains only family unity), it's the "Autorité P de ce 'parent' par excellence qu'ils reconnaissent," and it is this "Autorité P" of *being* as such that is also recognized by members who are not relatives of the Family: by slaves, writes Kojève in a still Hegelian or Roman arena, as well as by servants, cleaning ladies, and, further down the line, by other families. "The familial organization of Family is distinct therefore from the political organization of State: parents and relatives subordinate themselves to relatives (by love or authority, in terms of the filiation that determines their being, but they are not governed by them)."[12] Kojève argues for different orders of subordination that may or may not bind to authority. Aware of identification and spillage from one set to another, he aspires to a tropological separation of family and state, whose confused mergers and inevitable contaminations hold, he indicates, dire historical consequences. Bound by such consequences, he does not get very far into the metaphysical and ontological studies toward which he aims his thought. Yet he achieves at least one of his major objectives, which consists in making claims for the necessary and vital independence of the judiciary branch of government. The integrity and stabilizing platform of the domain of the Judge is of great importance to Kojève's argument, particularly in light of the fact that everyone wants to get in on acts of judging and thus needs to

12. Alexandre Kojève, *Esquisse d'une phénoménologie du droit. Exposé provisoire* (Paris: Gallimard, 1981), 498.

be restrained from serving judgment—it is as if the entire populace must be kept off the corrupting tendencies to which judgment leads. One could say that judging, from Plato to Luther and Kant through Lyotard and Kafka, is not only crucial to the often-agonistic claims of justice but front-loads desire and acquires addictive qualities: it is hard *not* to judge, and thus judging suffers from overdemocratization, so to speak, with all sorts of stations and interests vying with each other to formulate judgment: whether on the home front or in television series, on the field or in school, at a photo shoot or art opening, at court or on the streets, in the mirror or under scrutiny at work, they are constantly passing judgment. Arendt, for other and equally emphatic reasons, points to the judiciary as a place for renewing foundational acts and vitalizing democracy beyond its representative pitfalls (which relegate democracy to professional politicians, carrying it away from the *demos*).

Distinct hierarchies of authority. For Kojève, family and State obey distinct hierarchies of authority to which they are deemed answerable. They belong to different transversals of time, their overlaps largely illusory. Still, derivations and signals sent across the divide of regularly disbanding typologies are not uncommon. Father mixes in where he was evicted or merely tolerated, and memory traces of early identifications abound. Kojève brings his work on authority to bear on the historical predicament with which he is faced. While covering transhistorical terrain and appearing to provide atemporal schemata, the analysis of authority is itself historically if not materially pitched, locally anchored. It bears a signature and stamps a date, entering the text into the registers of its own historicity. The *Esquisse d'une phénoménologie du droit* is signed "Marseille, 1943." The last page of the manuscript titled *La Notion de l'Autorité* bears the signature *in fine*: "A. Kojevnikoff, Marseille, 16/V 42."[13] Five months later the Allies land in North Africa (November 9) and German forces occupy la Zone "libre."

Something remains to be said about the proving circumstances in which the work on authority was conceived by Kojève, and why these very circumstances and conditionalities—philosophy, in principle, is supposed to be unconditional—apply pressure on us today. On every level of his delivery, from the grander scheme of historical clashes to the demagnified quandary of an abbreviated name-of-the-father, Kojève wrestles with the losses

13. Terré, in Kojève, *Notion de l'autorité*, 16. This is a book that was never finished by Kojève himself. Terré is responsible for putting it together and supplying an introduction as well as commentary.

and compensatory controls that accrue to authority. Something foreboding is coming down the pike, the brute menace against which the revival of authority is meant to fortify. This encroaching menace may account for Kojève's somewhat simplistic temporal scheme that tries to hold in place past-present-future dimensions of existence without allowing for the inundation and standstill of time—the arrests, slumps, and lurches, even the dialectical glitching, the always *après*, the internal collapses, the ticking of remote time bombs, the stalls and formal deadbeats—toward which catastrophe points. He uses the notion of authority as a brace against the wages of an inassimilable history, as something that could override the blanking out of representation, where only a neutral gleam can be detected. Authority is called up to stabilize a relation to disabled time. In a sense we are asked to examine the haunting qualities of a history that cannot be integrated, qualities that resist being simply absorbed, narrated, and quieted down.

Still, one would have wanted Kojève to take a stab at Father Time, to tell what brings time down upon us in terrifying ways, what makes the past recur and stand before us as the foreboding sign of what's ahead, and so on and so back and forth, with childhood crawling through the temporal cracks at moments of extreme vulnerability to said authority. The figuring of time has traditionally been paternalized, but this is outside Kojève's domain, perhaps for good reason, given his materialist rap sheet—and understandably so, if he wants to manifest an intention and plan without formal or aprioristic or ontological weights. Anyone—that is, everyone—subjected to time, bound to the temporal destiny on which Hölderlin broke, is scorched by a "notion of" finitude and left bedazzled by the conspiracy, or authority, of father and time. Let us simply establish a separate dossier for this area of speculative inquiry and wonder how Father Time ticks and tocks to make his offspring lose out to the authority and dissolution of time—an undoubtedly common fate given over to the persecutory invasiveness that Kojève seeks to contain. Hence the revised schedules under which one labors in excess of his program—timetables of compensatory aggression, the itineraries of historical payback, the beat of totalitarian return, whether subtle or overt, that I hope to review.

Among the possibilities and shades of authoritarian markers that present themselves, the *malleability* of authority invites further consideration, particularly since it can turn up as beneficial or—depending on circumstances and philosophical texture—as desolating and inhibitive. One would want to scan the fissuring capacity of authority that falls into good *and* bad holding categories or, as some of the passages in Arendt and Kojève suggest, that are distributed among types of legitimacy that travel beyond good and evil, where Father and God back up a hidden will to power with provisional yet credible fictions. To what extent, and why, are Kojève and Arendt invested in retrieving the prestige of authority? To what end? Is it at all serious to pronounce oneself "for" or particularly "against" authority? Given the theoretical mobilization meant to justify the uses of authority, can one even remotely position oneself *against authority* when it is shown to ward off the most egregious surges of genocidal rage? To stop extreme forms of ethical breach and violation, one sometimes needs to summon the ultimate signatory force, maybe asking God to sign or establish a trust. The Declaration of Independence, according to Derrida, called upon God's signature to seal the deal of the historical break-off. But Kojève wants to cut down on mystical foundations of authority, its possible enforcement or crackdowns.

Kojève finds himself both fighting for a transcendental authority without transcendence and marking down authority because it lacks the necessary transcendental guarantees—a loss for which he shows no nostalgia, but with which he must contend. Authority also turns Arendt toward the vacant lot of divine abandonment, where humankind is left to fend for itself in the draft of monotheistic withdrawal. The gods have fled and the one deity left for us has bailed or retreated into mute indifference. Somehow, authority is summoned to fill in the blanks of an ontotheological arrangement of replacement parts, whether viewed as a form of liberal democracy or as one profile of the secular totalitarianisms. For both Arendt and Kojève, the distress of losing authority convenes core survival issues that need inventive arbitration as well as, in some essential ways, recall.

If one could migrate with this work into truly generous speculative expanses and simultaneously roll back to a micrological operation on the poetically relevant crisis of the name, one would want to read the urgent claims being made to disjoin Family from State with the turn that the proper name Kojenikoff is about to take as he engages this topic, severing the name of the father and pulling away from the site, divested or newly invested, diverting the course of determinations from which such a name originates. Let me pause here to consider the political-autobiographical stakes involved in tossing around and remolding one's own name—a situation that would not necessarily make it through to other discursive boards handling this case.

Kojève charts the course of authority's demise according to two different mappings, one global and the other at the level of his own name, which he decides to prune and integrate. According to the more globally inflected side of things, he finds that the depletion of authority's accounts occurs with remarkable persistence in America and appears to rebound in Japan, where the reign of authority has been historically heightened. With regard to his own account, the author that he has wanted to become has deposed

Mr. Kojenikoff, disturbing something like the proper(ty) of naming. Maybe he wanted to get away from his own father's name after knocking down key monuments of paternity. Maybe he was motivated to Gallicize his name, to move in and up to a better neighborhood, a more suitable address. Maybe he thought that henceforth he would carry a name that bore more authority than his family name could offer.

In his work, Kojève will have emphasized the Godlike authority of the author over the *Oeuvre*. Such a powerful acknowledgment may have jinxed him to the extent that he was unable to finish this book, almost as if God-the-author couldn't hack it after the fourth day or the words didn't flow or the statement lost velocity and no one could offer, "And it was good." Nonetheless, he manages a power move on the periphery of his oeuvre. Cutting off the "koff" or, more precisely, the "nikoff," he gets to be his own father, engender his name, paring down the name of the father. These maneuvers cannot simply remain extraneous to the stakes articulated in the work on authority. Still, I do not want to divert our course by means of a Midrashic rhythm of debate, only to put up a red flag on the metamorphosis of the name signing these reflections on authority's demise. To make these points stick, I would have to put together a group of highly specialized operatives of the genealogical order. I am not sure that I can get the licensure for such a fishing expedition. Such a procedure would have to begin by establishing links among a theory of name change, legal procedure, and parricidal narrative.

An entire history of minorities is bound up in the coerced acquisition or surrender of a name, whether transacted on Ellis Island, on the plantation, in transit from an annihilating past or more or less belonging to self-induced social amelioration as culmination of a history of shaming: remove that telling mark, change the name that exposes your foreignness or overdrawn native belonging, a stinging story. At a critical moment in the "Letter to Father," Kafka switches names to get out from under an impossible heritage. Rerouting the name of the father, by breaking it down and rejecting its endless insinuations, he encourages the diversion of a destiny toward futurity. Let us just note a proliferation of letters at this point and post them, adding "K" to the entries that govern our reflections on authority, ranging from Kleist to Kohlhaas to Kafka to Klein to Kojevnikoff, to Kojève, to the fateful "K" that has been collaring and haunts . . . Amerika.

Turning back to the journeys of Arendt and Kojève, we find the two protagonists struggling around the flagging trope of authority, showing themselves to be unusually timid, if one can say so, at least in terms of a normed rhetoric of assertion. Sometimes hedging is called for. Yet it is not so much a matter of hesitation, uncertainty, or lack of conviction that distracts their aims. One could say that there is *too much* conviction, even too much history, in proportion to a meager ration of argument. Lacoue-Labarthe and Nancy have wanted to go so far as "to question Arendt as to whether or not the polis or the Roman foundation had actually taken place."[14] Kojève, for his part, cannot reach the finish line to secure his thought on authority. Still, incompletion tells its own story, as did Kant's interruption, when he was contemplating the prospects for perpetual peace. The status of the break-off point is something that continues to invite consideration. One wants to read the interruption, give the unfinished a chance.

Owing to the version with which he has left us, Kojève opens a somewhat indeterminate dossier: questions have been raised, motifs launched, a para-historical layer has been laid out. Such a flourish of initiative should probably not be ignored, even if both Kojève and Arendt will have remained indifferent to other studies of authority when imparting their own reflections, freshened by historical anxiety. I have a tendency, perhaps unjustifiable, to put out a demand for renewing habits of thoroughness, for repossessing the dusty type of scholarship associated with Germanic philology or that comes with fairly typical compilations acquired through *Wissenschaft* (though even these once-generic inventories are hard to come by nowadays—even the Germans have stopped really and relentlessly studying, tracking their sources). I have a way of clamoring for scholarly discipline, advocating for a kind of democratic transparency in the delivery of argument. I tell myself this attitude, this way of digging, is old-fashioned, yet I feel duty-bound to continue with these outdated activities. I used to walk the Nietzschean walk and turn at every rhetorical bend against the scholar, the way they are bent over their work, isolated and isolating. At this point, still in a minor Nietzschean key, I also feel politically attached to scholarly probity—but only up to a point. Not everyone has been gripped by archive fever. I guess, however, that one need not hope for a systematic rendition of prior engagements with the problem of authority—I do not want to relinquish a libidinally invested position too quickly, however. I'll stand my ground, maybe this last time, on the issue at hand: What does it mean to ignore a lineage of scholarly or philosophical inquiry, to go on simply as though others had not offered mappings and a vocabulary of anxiety around a specific problem set? In this case the very *authority of the question* of authority is inevitably destabilized

14. Philippe Lacoue-Labarthe and Jean-Luc Nancy, "The 'Retreat' of the Political," in *Retreating the Political*, ed. Simon Sparks (London and New York: Routledge, 1997), 131.

when questions of transmission and inheritance (the latter being a recurrent focal point of the problem of authority from Luther to Hegel, Marx, and the German Reformation) are set aside in a subtle play of discursive domination (another recurrent trope that culminates in Hegel's analysis of domination and servitude).

Whether located in the domains of scholarship or in critical practice, the study of authority appears to get a running start only after a substantial sector of its history has been lopped off, often assuring a forgetting of prior sources and initiatives. It is as if one had to struggle each time anew to establish the authority of the study of authority—as if one had to make a play, in fact, for a kind of original cut in the authority of authorship on the subject that endlessly reflects and undermines itself. For both Arendt and Kojève, there is the matter of pulling away from Kantian shores or diverting their arguments from the harsher grounds of Burke's insistent claims on the problem they face, and of suppressing the authority-making inroads of Luther and Calvin, bumpy and troubling.[15] In all of the side-swept sources, we find echoes or origins of what Arendt and Kojève in some instances repeat, if for differently stated reasons, and without returns to parented texts. In nearly each of these cases, the world, like a dramatic figure threatening suicide, menaces with ending it all if authority's hold were to weaken. But historical acuity transforms the identical utterance, delivering it to a Borgesian understanding of what it means to repeat a text, duplicating its areas of sensitivity. Perhaps the theological-philosophical kinship network had to be broken in order to bring some order into the question concerning authority, even if some of the results incessantly echoed one another.

The way they were: the scholar as political signatory. So,

returning to our sources, let us get a closer look at the way the problem was relaunched by our principals. In the unfinished work we are considering, *La notion de l'autorité*, Kojève states that the future as such holds no authority: "l'Avenir pur et simple n'a aucune Autorité" (26). Everything can look to a future ahead, but this in no way secures its prestige. The future exerts authority only to the extent that it is "manifested" in the form of a *project* (conceived in the present in view of the future on the basis of knowledge from the past)

15. The evasion of Burke is especially unfortunate to the extent that his work provides the vocabulary and contextual pull that brings some of Arendt and Kojève's reflections into sharper focus. I leave the tie-in of Burke's theories for a future deliberation on authority and the political.

initiated by a *chef*, that is, the vanguard, the executive, boss or leader. The future "manifests" itself in an authoritarian form as the authority of the one in charge ("Autorité de Chef") who procures a metaphysical basis, the "virtual" presence of which is a Present (a human present, that is, a historical present), which is to say, a *temporal* reality. The thought of authority, which Kojève has divided into phenomenological, metaphysical, and ontological domains, is rooted in temporality and, despite an unmistakable tendency to slight or shakedown humanism, the argument retains the figure of man in order to address its points and adhere to historicist narratives.

. . . .

Before pursuing a commentary that may be blind to itself, I stop in my tracks, if only to offer an indication of internal struggle and the predicament of one who approaches the breakdown of authority.

I interrupt myself to question the choices I have made. This happens all the time, every day in so many ways, practically by the minute: the sense that everything could fall apart at any moment, no doubt a side effect of authority's reputed demise. Writing under the erasure of authority doubles the stakes, increases the worry that others, more assured of their footing, would know how to suppress. My "object," even if accompanied and framed by outstanding theorists and their considerable legacies, cannot stand independently of what it purports to show: the demise of authority cannot help but encroach on the project of writing on the edge of its fissures. Tracking the weakening firmness of premise, the work is itself endangered. Less sure, less under the assignment of a recognizable sign or signature than ever before, it becomes all the more brittle. Or not. The work can also choose to take another turn and assume the stance of resolute disavowal, go it alone, without validation or a legitimating guarantee. Even though I feel somewhat at risk exposing this hole in the commentary I was offering, I thought I owed it to the very subject at hand to break off from an assumed pose of serenity, a plausible mood of legitimacy. I'll restart. (Pardon this stumble; it is not self-indulgent but prescribed as part of the task of staying the course with deposed authority.)

Why was I compelled by Kojève for this project, at this time, now? I could have hung in there with Burke or gone for the raw, for Hegel, I mean. Revisiting Burke could have further consolidated my position, I tell myself. Working with Hegel always pays off. I mean, really, why Kojève *au juste*? This is a question that has been harassing my sleep, making me anxious and feverish in the morning, when I wake up. Lacan stokes my sense of distress. Indicating Kojève's starting point in Hegel's *Phenomenology of Spirit*, he matter-of-factly states that Kojève "has always evaded what was there prior to their coming to be," referring to the positions of master and slave and the

54

implications concerning the master's discourse.[16] Figuring out the priors was perhaps not Kojève's area of expertise, nor his assignment. Perhaps he was running toward an end goal without hoisting a genealogical burden; or perhaps instead we are asked to read what he was running from, how his evasion builds meaning without a locatable start or origin, in defiance of an authoritative beginning. Unlike Arendt, unlike Freud, unlike God, he shows impatience with start-up narratives or with a sense of the way we were, even if these are intended to serve, as in Freud's anthropologies, only as propelling fictions and nothing more.

Kojève builds his argument from a kind of genealogical disorder, indifferent to a primal past that his argument nevertheless figures as a defunct father. Maybe Kojève's faltering remains instructive for us, because he thought he could move on without checking with psychoanalysis or pumping precedents for more information about the fate of the paternal metaphor. Maybe the authority of forgotten origins has come to get him, installing obstacles in his important path. Let us suspend the question of Kojève's possibly false starts as we engage his effort seriously. For, whether this effort has succeeded or failed is trifling in our discipline—not to say incalculable, not to say unknowable—given the chances that incompletion still has to play out its game, if only to discover that its exhaustion is interminable. Let me return to my articulation of doubt, pointing to the way I provisionally resolve it, at least enough to go on with the interrupted probe that repeats Kojève's own method of presentation.

I could say that, despite all possible disclaimers, I have considered it important to bring Kojève to the table where political theories for and of the future are being dealt in. I would like to see him put in play with the strong hands of Walter Benjamin and the disturbingly popular Carl Schmitt, placing him very close to Hannah Arendt, whose work on authority has awaited serious integration. Still, the choice of Kojève is and remains overdetermined. I am now thinking that I should cough up an account of the more personal factors that have prompted this study, at least imparting some of their contours. I waver, going back and forth, sunk in the syntax of authority's demise, its implications for writing—something that makes me hesitate over what we're allowed to do nowadays, precisely on those meridians where one enters without a pass, unauthorized. Here I go. No. Well, wait. Yes, OK, here goes.

16. Jacques Lacan, "Interview," in *Le séminaire de Jacques Lacan, Livre XVII, l'envers de la psychanalyse, 1969–1970* (Paris: Éditions du Seuil, 1991), 167. Translated by Russell Grigg as *The Other Side of Psychoanalysis: The Seminar of Jacques Lacan Book XVII* (New York and London: W. W. Norton, 2007).

But only if we understand the place of the circumstantial in the history of poetry, which, in part, I am transferring to theoretical work. I am thinking here of the *Gelegenheitsgedicht*, the poem prompted by occasion, by some sort of circumstance or particular that, compelled or even commanded, cannot be generalized. Here is a brief account of the circumstances under which Kojève's struggle with authority became a serious matter for me. I was first reading his work on authority at a very difficult time for me, sitting next to Derrida in the severe and last stages of his illness. I'd look up and see him stirring, so in order to "distract him" as Marguerite Derrida urged me to do, I made it a habit to summon his teaching self. I would say something about my reading, setting up questions, something in this case on the order of: "Kojève offers four pure types of authority—the father, the judge, the Maître, the leader, but I see no medical authority here, no doctors, not even in the sixty-four hybridized types of authority!" Derrida listens, appears to concur, showing a spark of interest; even Plato secures a firm place for the physician.

Now, for him, for Derrida, in his state of desperate decline, few beings of the human order carry as much authority as does his physician. We get into a brief discussion of the constitution and authoritarian sway of "doctor's orders" before he takes his pills, and then we turn briefly, in the painkiller haze with which I identify, to other prescriptive edges of language usage. This memory seems very personal, but it does not stand entirely outside of philosophy's general tendency to medicalize thought as it shares rounds with the physicians of being and body who probe and diagnose symptoms that may or may not be readable. Perhaps it is not surprising that we found ourselves in areas of philosophy that place rhetoric in a medical perspective. We were reminded that philosophy was a thinking of health that engaged the reappropriation of wholeness in terms of a medico-hermeneutics. We talked about serious philosophical topoi and their often weak or hidden pulses.

One afternoon, we visited the doctor in the *Gorgias*, and considered the one example offered of a case requiring the expertise of a specialist: in this case a rhetorician is shown to be *needed*. This call-up occurs when Socrates, having just distinguished between doctors and experts, and see-ing rhetoricians as amateurs—this is the one thing that Socrates cannot finesse or ironize away: what to do when someone refuses to see a doctor. Call the rhetorician. The dilemma takes us back to and inverts the moment in Plato that calibrates the relation of the shepherd to his sheep and doctor to patient in terms of the authority that the one holds over the other. The rhetor, short on authority, may nonetheless command the force to resolve or deblock an impasse, promote a prescriptive pass.—Well, I do not mean to indulge my own sadness. I am just trying to convey a mood, maybe braced

by the authority of Thomas de Quincey or Johann Peter Eckermann, each poised as a witness to the last days, and in the case of Eckermann, to the last years, of a mentor's destinal embrace. Whatever the source or office of legitimacy for this stylistic intrusion—perhaps none—I cannot deny that reporting a conversation that took place between Derrida and me provokes some anguish on my part. I think of Eckermann, I think of the great addict, de Quincey. I hesitate to note my own fragments of experience as if I were reissuing *Dichtung und Wahrheit*, where the compulsion to tell is linked to a world historical exigency. That is not the case, of course, though the need to self-interrupt is assuredly a matter of the historicity of writing, its faltering steps and disturbed authority, no matter how viable in outreach or possible significance the breach may seem.

But why swerve away from the sturdy handle of commentary? I could have been a contender. I suppose that something requires me to keep it personal, like a wound and a stab, especially nowadays, when things have become so departicularized, often split off and evacuated—or conversely, hyperparticularized, crowding out thought and its barely reachable grasp. Sometimes I think that I owe it to someone to tell nearly all, as if I'm on trial. Telling nearly all, I can't say why or to whom: the saying, nearly compulsive, is like a durable liability, just short of the assumption of guilt. I owe it to *say* the conditions and pressures under which I feel compelled to write and to disturb the writing as I-write. This may come off as a blunder, or it may keep something alive between us.

Another reason to seek help from Kojève, to bring him to the table (other than for purposes of tapping his rich Hegelian affiliation or eating him alive, as I have seen done): It has been observed rightly or wrongly, but often enough to weigh in consistently, that the Bush administration under which the United States has strained the Constitution and disgraced any reasonable sensibility for justice derived unmistakable "intellectual" go power from Professor Leo Strauss. How could one not, as a scholar and citizen, return to the works of Strauss in some way, if only to visit with the site of purported academic arbitration of failure? Strauss's work is said to provide the basis for a recent history of national decision making of the early millennium by the group around the American presidency. The damage that has been done under this insignia cannot be said to disappear with the G. W. Bush administration, which will take a long to time to clean up and clock out, if at all, especially as the Obama administration has both continued and even sealed in the greater part of these scandalous misreadings of the law. The toxic residue and disturbance associated with the episode that bears this name will not simply vaporize but is bound to take other, less transparently indecent forms and poses. Nor can the damage that reverts in large measure to the Bush-Cheney-Rove-Rumsfeld names be blamed on the scholar Leo Strauss alone. Nonetheless, something very recent, on the order of corrosive governance, has been signed by this teacher and scholar, if posthumously. The purported influence of Leo Strauss on the usurpations associated with this name remains persistent in referential reach. The damage may be definitive. I cannot now open the dossier on pedagogy, the scholarly signature, and political excess. This would take us far afield, but needs nonetheless to be considered, especially in light of the diminished power of the scholar in the very place that still seeks the authority of a *Staatsphilosophie.* How did the scholar Leo Strauss become the posthumous philosopher of state, and why was his signature needed?

To get some purchase on the problem, one might consider by way of cinematic interpretation the plight of Jimmy Stewart in *Rope,* Hitchcock's allegory of pedagogical hate crimes, where, weakened and shaking, whiskey in hand, the teacher discovers that his signature was used to seal a crime. In the case proposed by Hitchcock, a Nietzsche course was translated into murderous consequence by Stewart's literalizing, Nazi-identified students. The expropriated text of philosophy provides the impetus for opening a political abyss and ethical disaster. Something in Nietzsche was left wide open to allow for such a hijacking of philosophical meaning, turning a work into a manifesto or manual for rogue takeovers and raw implementation. Or, offscreen, one might revert to the still-stinging history of the philosophical faculty that, to a great majority in Germany, supported the Third Reich. There is no doubt that Heidegger's desire for and enactment of historical praxis, which was promoted in terms of *Geschick*—destiny's mark—remains unprecedented among philosophers. Not even Plato signed up with or for the actualized State. What happens when philosophers or their outsourced affiliates, so-called intellectuals, leave the reserve or relax the gadfly function of which they once were relentless practitioners? These instatements and signups invite further discussion and a carefully delivered idiom by which to gauge the zealously consensual parasitism of philosophy and state.

To return to the homeland's investment in scholarship and teacher's political directives, whether mandated or largely dreamed up by slouch readers, let us take a closer look at the report cards of recent leaders: I don't know for sure what kind of student Karl Rove was, or the GPA that Paul Wolfowitz managed, but we do know that Richard Cheney was an ever-failing pupil in the eyes of the university and that George Bush was satisfied with his C minuses. Still, as a group, they are said to be followers and actualizers of the teachings of Strauss. Again, the question arises of what requirements

are met when a polity attaches to a strong scholarly or philosophical name. Are crossovers into policy making structurally bound to disastrous misapprehension à la Hitchcock or Heidegger?

Kojève, for his part, did not shy away from moving in and out of stated textual limits, mixing them up and reconstituting at every turn the boundaries of the scholarly signature when shifting into modalities of political praxis. He played a significant role in promoting the construction of Europe after his 1942 writings, acting on the peripheries of administrative hierarchies. His commitment to civic forms of governance and to the induction of the "ineradicable idea of justice" in matters of administration are articulated with special clarity in his famous controversy with Leo Strauss, whose *On Tyranny* was published in 1954 in France as *Hiéron ou de la tyrannie*. The French translation is followed by Kojève's substantial critical study, *Tyrannie et sagesse (Tyranny and Wisdom)*. The text not only takes on Leo Strauss and the early stirrings of the movement now designated as neoconservatism and fueling some aspects of the tea party launch; it also gives a view of Kojève's thoughts on history seen as a chain of political actions guided by philosophers "who are themselves assisted by 'intellectual mediators.'"[17] All in all, it would be far-fetched to see Strauss seriously backing his rogue disciples, even though they have in common a disdain for the common, a suspicion cast on the *demos*. Strauss did not believe that truth telling was meant for everyone. Only the rare few are seen to possess the fortitude to approach the truth, the content of which may well be that there is no truth—a state of voided affairs therefore that cannot be handled by just anyone. More recently, the Platonic disdain for the *demos* has been addressed by Jacques Rancière, who points out the default position out of which democracy must repeatedly climb. Strauss's rebuffs take a different turn, of course, and the Bush team was certainly not under the sway of Althusserian reflections on politics. Nonetheless, an original stain of the democratic drive somehow got circuited to them via the corpus of Leo Strauss, landing the group in the vicinity of a Platonic undermining of democracy's prospects for which they sought, and partially obtained, legitimate footing. They did not wait for Plato, or Strauss's broadcast system to actualize their contempt or destructive roadmap, but they did seek licensure, an academic seal to close the deal on disrupting constitutional law and democratic probity. Despite this group's abomination of law and strains of poor scholarship, despite their

17. Victor Gourevitch and Michael S. Roth, eds., introduction, *On Tyranny* by Leo Strauss, ed. rev. and exp. edition, including the Strauss-Kojève correspondence (New York: Free Press, 1991), xvii. Subsequent references are cited parenthetically in the text.

smirky destructions, we cannot simply oppose philosophical reflection to corrupt political practice: something in Plato, something in Strauss invited these historical perversions and appropriations.

In the correspondence with Kojève—the published version of which begins on December 6, 1932, with the salutation, "Dear Mr. Kochevnikoff" and progresses in later years to "Dear friend," often ending "With best regards, also in my wife's name," and by 1948 to "Dear Kojève"—Leo Strauss underscores an aspect of their dissention in terms of philosophical separatism, which is to say that unlike his interlocutor, Strauss sees philosophy as needing to keep to itself. He goes only as far as to concede a need, on the part of philosophy, to negotiate tolerance with a state that is, if not outright hostile, then at least wary of philosophical troubleshooting. Victor Gourevitch and Michael S. Roth show how Strauss in sum rejects Kojève's "reconciliation of philosophy and society root and branch. It is not necessary, it is not desirable, it is not even possible. . . . In his judgment that review [of the *Hiero*] only confirms that the effort to reconcile philosophy and society is bound to be destructive of both. It thus once again confirms the need to sort out—to 'de-construct'—their entanglement, and to restore their classical separation" (xviii). I will not yield to the temptation of the "de-constructor" to read the quotation marks that neutralize or immunize the type of work that the authors call for, but will limit myself only to a few remarks regarding the failure and limitations of political theories that have tried to capture the fissuring qualities of the tyrannical takeover.

Strauss's point of departure is rooted in the failure of "our political science" to face tyranny, "a kind of tyranny that surpassed the boldest imagination of the most powerful thinkers of the past" (xi). The excess that our political science cannot handle has crept up on it in many ways. Tyranny has taken its practice shots on philosophy according to Strauss in the sense that "society will always try to tyrannize thought." Both Strauss and Kojève, however, concur that there is a history of conflict between philosophy and society (some Straussians appear to have introjected Hegel's separation of "state" and "society" yet revert for the most part to using the popular high school word, "society," justified only in some contexts). Strauss and Kojève moreover "agree that philosophy or wisdom ranks highest in the order of ends, that it is the architectonic end or principle." They meet on uneven playing fields, where philosophy takes the glory but is pummeled consistently by the weakening effects of social forces. Thought finds itself subject to incessant bullying. But who started it, and how can a peace treaty be brokered?

The two political theorists disagree about whether this conflict can and should be resolved. In fact, Strauss prizes the conflictual impasse, shun-

ning any such resolution, which only could prove false. It seems that philosophy acts as major disruptor to the extent that it attacks social trust and inescapably pokes holes in authority's claims. Kojève and Strauss organize a few matches around the disputed values and the possible relaxation of the tense stand-off. This is not the place to go further into their *différend* or to watch them duke it out over aims and the problem of "recognition," which largely pits Strauss's Plato against Kojève's Hegel (although Strauss's Plato takes a sudden swerve and morphs into Nietzsche, but that is neither here nor there right now). Kojève infiltrates institutions, linking philosophy and revolution to what would be the culmination of world history. He was a principal in calling the end of history, calculating the takedowns and losses that our predicament implied. "The expressions 'the end of history' and 'the end of philosophy' have become fashionable and hence virtually empty slogans. In our time Kojève was the first seriously to think what such expressions might mean" (xiv). Throughout the drama of their respectful but irreconcilable difference, Strauss and Kojève maintain a silence over a shared mentor who is everywhere present as a veiled enigma, a theoretical scar, and persistent danger signal. The abyss over which they correspond bears the name of Martin Heidegger, a teacher who also mentored Hannah Arendt and Herbert Marcuse, disciples who equally became preoccupied with the tyranny of thought and the locus of authority.

Our modernity: a brief discursive map of who said what and why about Authority. At the time Kojève took on Strauss, the question of authority was not in open circulation among contending philosophers. The character and genesis of authority were not entirely unflagged either, as I have indicated, "mais l'essence même de ce phénomène a rarement attiré l'attention."[18] Kojève pulls authority out of its hiding place. It is impossible, contends Kojève, to consider state power and the structure of the state itself without knowing what authority is. He considered that a study of authority had to precede any reflection on the problem of the State. To be sure, earlier studies of authority had been linked to reflections on power, which Kojève wants to see dissociated in terms of essential state and legal relations. There are two strong sets of affiliations that stand out among those who have investigated the relations of authority to power without necessarily effecting the specific separations to which Kojève is committed; one branching from Alexis de Tocqueville to Marx, and the other extending from Émile Durkheim

18. Terré, in Kojève, *Notion de l'autorité*, 18.

to George Simmel.[19] Friedrich Engels and Max Weber offer their theories on authority in the context of industrial formation and bureaucracy. Their arguments have had a long run and establish the vocabulary by which the question of authority has been broached. Rich and suggestive, these works, from where Kojève stands, appear to have encountered a strict limit. Relations of domination and obedience, power and submission, have organized their discourses on authority; however, from a Kojèvian perspective, such stated relations serve only to enumerate what evades authority—what, in Arendt's terms, it is *not*. Nonetheless, the lines that they form around authority inform and strengthen any serious consideration of contemporary political distress.

Distress, as the modality of anguish particular to modernity, discloses an acute relation to the world of politics as the place where something can be moved or done, where reparations can be expected. This pivot of relatedness holds even where "world" and "place" have been dislodged, where such addresses have been obsolesced or discredited. Transposing Heideggerian *Sorge* to the concerns of the political, the unremitting *anguish of the political* is regularly fueled by differing calibrations and settings of authority according to new constellations, including the ever-evolving elements of bureaucratic freighting and domination. Industrial and technological sutures of authority build and burn bridges in a fissured world—where world, according to Heidegger and his erstwhile disciples, no longer obtains. Some of the arguments stored by the texts under consideration have become familiar and continue to circulate freely, frequently traveling among friendly as well as hostile discursive territories. To a large degree they are processed by literary expanses that define the Kafka-coded terrain, preparing new edges of the authoritarian takeover.

One study of note that should be signaled comes along and settles to the left of some of its contemporaries (if such determinations still make sufficient sense among this politically parented group, though it must be said that this author has been blocked out of view in part because of suspected [communist] affiliations, and also because of his engagement with psychoanalysis). A significant contribution to the question and scope of our subject, the 1936 work by Herbert Marcuse to which I allude is titled *Studien über Autorität und Familie*, translated into English only in 1972 and relaunched in 2008 under the title *A Study on Authority* as part of Verso's "Radical Thinkers" collection. Without recuperating his lost honor or dialectizing a special place for him, I would like to give a sense here of Marcuse's trajectories

---

19. See Terré in Kojève, *Notion de l'autorité*, for a complete account. Subsequent quotations are cited parenthetically in the text.

and perspectives, for his work will no doubt instruct and inflect future reflections on the velocities and petrifications of authoritarian mappings and the way they converse with Kojève and Arendt. Marcuse weighs in with analyses of the critically pertinent strains and motifs that concern us here. Not satisfied to consider authority a monolithic or containable notion, he marks the split in authority, the way it turns against itself and those who would claim to wield authority. The appeal to and of authority has given way to Luther's invention of everyday self-torture, opening channels in Calvin's doctrine of "the right to resist." Explorations of where authority comes from, who signs and which type of authority has the upper hand when and where, guide Marcuse's thinking on the inner breaches of the historical subject. The inward turn of Christian self-interrogation has taken authority to a place of perpetual dispute, internally mulled over, where dissent is groomed and prepared to face external masks of authority. Worldly assumptions of authority's signification henceforth must meet the challenge of the calamity of "Christian freedom"—something that Luther tactically holds up to the peasants only to let the banner of freedom function as a confirmation of their slavery. Turning his sights on the conservative tropes of family constitution, Marcuse investigates the extent to which the "authoritarian family becomes one of the key bulwarks against revolution," which involves an exposition of Friedrich Julius Stahl's theory of the authoritarian-theocratic state—the first truly authoritarian German philosophy of the State (Marcuse 76).

Marcuse's argument demonstrates the extent to which philosophy has lined up persistently with the authority-hungry state. In the *Rechtsphiloso-phie*, Stahl appeals to philosophy to come quickly to the aid of threatened authorities in state and society after the revolt of the Silesian weavers, three years before the March Revolution in Germany; his appeal is a "convincing document on the justificatory and conservative function of philosophy in Germany. . . . Philosophy should take over the great task of 'nurturing respect for all orders and governments which God has set over men, and for all conditions and laws, which have come into being in an orderly way under His directions'" (Marcuse 77). The authoritarian and constitutionalist theories "unite on the common ground of the protection of the family and of the order of property" (82). In the end, Marcuse's theories of counterrevolution allow him to tie authority to the concerns of property among French, German, and English political writers, and to arrive at the materialist-psychological conclusion that "authority is to a considerable degree the authority of property" (75). This conclusion may seem like a letdown, in hindsight somewhat predictable and overly programmatic. Yet the work that Marcuse puts into building his case yields an exceptionally insightful argument and offers mobility to an otherwise recalcitrant "notion," as Kojève says. It also opens a lane to psychoanalysis, though Marcuse at this point does not himself take it. Maneuvering Burke, de Maistre, and others into the weave of contemporary authoritarian strictures, Marcuse observes the state's dependency on family transmission systems:

> The idea of the inheritance of property is one of the most effective factors through which the family is tied to the order of state and society which protects it, and the individual is tied to the family; however, this is not the only reason why the family becomes a matter of life and death to the state. Authoritarian traditionalism knows very well that it is precisely in the family that the "dogmas and prejudices" which it proposes as the basis of society are originally handed down: "we know the morality that we have received from our fathers as an ensemble of dogmas and useful prejudices adopted by the national reason."[20]

A decidedly grim view of something like human nature underlies the property values associated with family, held together with the glue of authoritarian traditionalism. Marcuse identifies a consistent reversion in the works on his reading list to the natural wickedness of man. This natural supplement, wickedness, opens the door for the authoritarian intrusion. The "sad nature" of man proves that "man in general, if he is left to himself, is too wicked to be free." The natural wickedness of man serves to deprive the constellation bearing the name of man of any innate "right" to freedom. This is why the theory of counter-revolution sanctions "the total dependence of men on a few 'sovereigns' by engaging in a total defamation of human reason."[21] There is still a ray of Enlightenment shining through Marcuse's argument, which would see the protection of human reason as a way to stave off authority's depleting incursions. Such hopefulness is short-lived, however.

Offering a perspective that still needs to be reviewed—and not merely discarded—in light of what has been wrought historically by the figure of man, de Maistre sees human reason as "nothing but a beast, and all its strength is reduced to the power of destruction. . . . Human reason. . . only involves itself in [great institutions] in order to pervert and destroy them" (71). Marcuse links the resurgent tendency of the devaluation of reason historically to Luther, who wields a similar view as part of his justification

20. Marcuse, *Studien über Autorität und Familie*, 76, and Joseph de Maistre, *Considérations sur la France*, in *Oeuvres complètes* (Lyon: Vitte et Perrussel, 1884–86), 1:400.
21. Marcuse, *Studien über Autorität und Familie*, 70.

of worldly authorities.[22] Both Luther and de Maistre are seen to count on the destructive streak that defines "human nature" when developing their strategic maps and tactical takeovers. "Men never respect what they have done," de Maistre has declared, which invites anything put together by human effort to become the target zone for a destructive urge: "what I have made, I can also destroy." Man's capacity for destruction grows out of the disdain he shows for anything manmade. This point of departure does not attain to the scope of reflections offered subsequently by Blanchot on the indestructible, nor do we have a theory of *why* man is driven to shatter his objects and world, such as they are, placed by volition and care. These pre-Freudian insinuations about what happens beyond the pleasure principle, or even as cohort to any possible pleasure, whether or not principled, reach for hard-and-fast political solutions, a tendency that has not been snuffed out. Only state-pitched authoritarian force can put a restraining order on such incontrovertible destructive instincts.

The counterrevolutionaries put a primary spin on values that have since gone underground but spring up in displaced sites of political practice. Like Burke who stood up for the uses and usefulness of prejudice, de Maistre asserts that for man "there is nothing so important. . . as prejudices;" they are "the real elements of his happiness, and the watchdogs of empire;" without them, there is "neither religion, nor morality, nor government" (72).[23] Prejudice is another way of deploying fictions and workable restraints on the world of the naturally wicked. But what is prejudice? Both the Enlightenment and Nietzsche tried to fight it down and offer a breakaway plan, a necessary detachment from the bad fiction and grueling aftereffects of prejudice. De Maistre lists patriotism as one of the prime "useful" prejudices. Kant devoted himself to pushing back on prejudicial encroachment. A carefully sifted history of prejudice as concept, whether lauded or phased out, would have to be set alongside the question of judgment and what precedes or upends it in the annals of the authoritarian disposition. Marcuse, for his part, was

22. One can no longer advocate with simple neutrality or innocence for the place of reason. A perspective that examines the dark side of reason would have to unroll from the standpoint of Foucault and Cartesian acts of institution building.

23. Burke primes prejudice not only as virtue and duty but as an essential ally to justice: "Prejudice is of ready application in the hour of emergency. . . . It previously engages the mind in a steady course of wisdom and virtue. . . . Prejudice tenders a man's virtue his habit. . . . Through just prejudice, his duty becomes part of his nature." Edmund Burke, *Reflections on the Revolution in France*, ed. Henry P. Adams (London: W. B. Clive, 1927), 90.

the first to remind and show us how the modern conviction about authority's enduring necessity results from a specific event. Throughout this chapter, we have been trying to read this event. "Authority must exist, for otherwise the worldly order would collapse," hails with unequivocal intent from Martin Luther. Based on hysterical speculation—something close to the end of the world is announced, which Christianity proclaims as its good news—the installation of authority is meant to assure the future of worldly order as an edict issuing from beyond. Luther made his entire world dependent on authority. In countless ways, one is still under the sway of Luther's hold and beholden to the impressive permutations of his signature.

Chapter 3
Archeophilia, Panic, & Authority

Arendt & Kojève, MVPs. A tactically sidelined delegate
from the Lutheran assembly or party line, she comes in from a slightly different texture of concerns and reading habits. Hannah Arendt shows up late
in 1958. Prepared to set a refurbished agenda, she publishes the searching
essay "What Is Authority?" Taking up the relay, she expresses anguish over
the noticeable disappearance of authority. Her investment in the runaway
itinerary of authority takes on different tonalities and sets another type of
intention than that of her predecessors. Nonetheless, Hannah Arendt, too,
tries her intelligent hand at resuscitating authority. Having browsed the
history of theoretical engagements with authority, let us now renew our approach to Arendt's vital work, which in some ways preceded her concerns with
violence. Propelled by the sense that nearly all traditional forms of authority
are collapsing, Arendt traces the destruction of authority to the prepolitical
zones of education and child-rearing, where authority in its most general
sense has appeared to be a natural prerequisite. The breakdown in authority carries consequences not only for politics and constituted civilization,
but also for those whom we diaper and need still to welcome. She revs up
her engines with concern for the youngest among us, the most vulnerable,
reworking the thought of natality. The little strangers, babies, need to be
able *to count on the authority* of those who tend to them. No child could find
stability without the application of authority.{(((This intrusion may appear
premature; I cannot help myself. She gave me the access code when she
folded in the personal with the political. Listen to me, Hannah, are you sure
about this?—Maybe she didn't realize what kind of license she was issuing or
how I could exploit the cleared passageway rhetorically. Hannah? I will be
brief, will not get into the minutiae of lament in full force, but, I mean, as a

Baby Step,
this unceasing
destruction . . .

Before Kafka came on the scene with his hair-raising input, the permanent disruption that childhood routinely works up was profiled in different ways. I am going to skip down to the nineteenth and eighteenth centuries, to a time frame when, for all sorts of overdetermined reasons and theoretical needs, childhood was invented. Philosophy's recruitment of the child in order to pinpoint some of its emerging theorems on memory and human understanding is something I have explored when trying to monitor the empiricist's need to rally the "ideot and childe."* The complicity between figures of idiocy and childhood, in unexpected ways rich and telling, was created basically to prompt the adult capacity for reflective memory. Childhood was from the start a stand-in for live feed—for story anterior to memory that showed, together with the lockdown of idiocy, an uninhabitable space where memories could not be retrieved. The constitutive blur of childhood had to be separated from the expanding discursive empires of history and autobiography, for developmental theories of selfhood and its analogs in historical becoming. By the time Hegel's reflections on childhood rolled in, bringing around concern for a more generally pitched ethical and familial structure, the child in philosophy began serving another function, meant to settle finitude's score: childhood, henceforth, was summoned to put a nail in the kindred coffin.

Hegel puts up a day care center in the *Phenomenology* for the purpose of setting the mortality timer: the married couple maneuver around loss by means of the consciousness implanted in the child. The child exhausts the parents but also is born as savior. This is an old story, but it doesn't explain

---

* See in particular Avital Ronell, "Wordsworth Satellite," in *Stupidity* (Urbana: University of Illinois Press, 2002).

toddler, I would have preferred *mere skill,* some consideration, the occasional hug, and none of the poses of parental authority, always completely off the mark, entirely unhelpful, and, for all intents and purposes, one big joke. The so-called authority of those who tended to me served only to interrupt my already-stressful negotiations with the too-quickly-defeated pleasure principle and the persecutory envois of the reality reps, but let's leave this objection aside, especially at the start of a chapter, for goodness sake, and reinstall the authority that I purportedly needed in a bad way from day one, when a little calm in the household and some skill among those who presumed to raise me would have done the job sufficiently to prop up the good-enough wardens, but, according to my polls, this is off point for some of you who could relax into trust under the very parental authority that Arendt appears to take for granted and affirm. I will get back on track, going toward that place of cultural infancy emblazoned by the Greeks and Romans. Forgive me, Hannah, I am reading with you, I swear. Let me prove myself to you. Ahem.)))}

Relayed by Christianity, our Greco-Roman heritage has depended on three key factors: tradition, religion, authority. In the last centuries, tradition and religion have been undermined—especially, one might add, in this time of the religious death rattle, when the fundamentalisms can be seen to signal the last spasms of an as-good-as-dead history. Now, at the time of Arendt's writing, authority itself appears to be promised to oblivion, even though it has proven more stable than tradition and religion, whatever their returns indicate—regardless of a continued death grip that can be mistaken for vitality. The disappearance of authority in the West pertains, says Arendt, only to a specific form of authority that has been eroding for centuries. At this point and for this reason we are no longer in a position to know what authority really *is*: We have lost our grasp of authority both in practical and theoretical domains. Whatever the case, she continues, we can no longer seek an answer to this question in some definition of the nature or essence of "authority in general."[1] Arendt rolls back to Rome where, at the basis of house and home, one discovers the word and concept of authority. Geographically constellated, authority now has a homeland, a history, and a start-up plan. Convoking other testimonies, let us add on to the cartography that Arendt initiates. In the following and final pursuit of authority's legacy, the crises to which it testifies and the lacerations that it bears, I will travel between Prague and Paris, though maybe also for shorter durations we will continue to shuttle between Washington, D.C., and Vienna.

1. Hannah Arendt, "What Is Authority?" in *The Portable Hannah Arendt* (New York: Penguin 2000), 21. Subsequent quotations are cited parenthetically in the text.

what the couple go through, what parents go through with ego, kicking and screaming at the very stem of the production of children, a death trap. Settled in the speculative dialectics of marriage, the parental couple produce their own death through the child. It is not the case that the child carries or seals the death of its genitors, though some of that is admittedly at work in Baby's symbolic placement system. Rather, as Derrida is careful to point out, "la mort des parents *forme* donc la conscience de l'enfant."* The child's consciousness is formed and informed by this death that the child also unstoppably flags. Marking the law of succession and heralding the disappearance of the parents, the child at the same time permits the parental instance to appropriate its own death. This appropriation of one's own death that the child offers is not all bad, but prompts a kind of victory lap—it amounts to something of a sublation, an *Aufhebung* that supports idealization and preservation: in death the parents, internalized and commemorated, extend their term, deepen the authoritative hold and hang on to consciousness for life. Such an idealizing movement holds for the father in particular, whom Hegel enters as being, more times than not, the first to go. According to this logic of succession and demise, the death of the father in fact demotes the mother who becomes a mere appendage to the process of paternal idealization. (Hegel does not futz around with varying or alternative configurations like, What happens if Mother goes first, or if Sister desires Brother, or if all kinds of incestuous matches are made under the family table of contents.)

Whether by inversion or by means of an explicit tracking device, the Hegelian itinerary fascinated Kafka, who revisits the traumatic implications of succession time and again, but with particular clarity of emphasis in the "Letter to Father." In Kafka there is no dialectical turnover to hand the family its trophy child in one piece. The surviving paternal seeps into the bureaucratic apparatus, goes to court, pulls the switch, breaks the amorous embrace, leaks into relationships—in short, the sprawling paternal stomps on the ego-menacing child in an eternal freeze frame. There is no marriage in Kafka to celebrate ethicity or to fuel state power; but neither was there marriage in the final analysis for Antigone, bereft of the gods.

The child brought forth in Hegel cannot be dissociated from loss, arriving as it does on a losing streak that threatens both the progenitors and the tiny inheritor. As if meant to defer the calamitous Hamlet-like ending or Antigone-like fallout, the loss is from the start recalculated and submitted to transvaluation, however. Loss, to say this quickly, wins out in the end, gets picked up by an unexpected option: "Die Eltern schauen in seinem Werden ihr Aufgehobenwerden an."

* Derrida, *Glas* (Paris: Éditions Galilée: 1974), 150.

The plan calls for a side trip to Weimar, the Negev desert, and Gaza, but this itinerary still needs to be submitted to a higher authority for approval. For now, let us repair to Rome in order to examine the place where Arendt meets up with Kojève.

The sacred founding of the city, the Roman sense of home, are connected to the concept of authority with its diverse juridical aspects. In the areas of private spaces and domestic jurisdiction the father or tutor exercises *auctoritas*, which comes from *augere*, to augment. "Whether it authorizes or ratifies, [*auctoritas*] presupposes an external or foreign activity that it validates."[2] Authority stands moreover as "an attribute attached to a person, originally to a physical person (. . .) as the privilege, the right belonging to a Roman, under the requisite conditions, to serve as the foundation of a juridical situation created by others."[3] Eventually, as François Terré argues, authority, obeying its etymology, *augmented* the very basis of religion and the city in conformity with a mystical and sacred foundation (23). Different from law, authority entails, according to Theodor Mommsen, "less than an order and more than counsel," exceeding an advisory capacity and falling just short of injunction (24).[4] Unlike rules or regulations—and closer in this sense to Kafka's casting of law—authority does not require constraint in order to be established or obeyed. On the contrary, authority, in André Magdelain's words, consists of "a power that accords legitimacy" (quoted in Terré, 86). The heritage of the Roman notion of authority extends to Max Weber's description of charismatic power, which he links to the concept of *auctoritas* and to the power base of leadership constituting the *Führertum* (24).

For Kojève, the largely uninterrogated concept of authority (he says "notion," so it does not properly throne on conceptuality) is a way of getting to something other than power, different than force, but that holds sway over others—sidelining and even, when necessary, sideswiping the law. One might consider here the authority of Antigone as she goes up against state power and the rule of law. Whereas Arendt counts the losses, Kojève, equally disconcerted by the disappearing qualities if not the mismanagement of authority's legacy, wants to get at its structural and phenomenological makeup.

2. André Magdelain, *Jus imperium auctoritas: Études de droit romain* (Rome: École Française de Rome, 1990), 685.

3. François Terré, in Alexandre Kojève, *La notion de l'autorité* (Paris: Gallimard, 2004), 23; subsequent references are cited parenthetically in the text. See also Pierre Noailles, "Fas et jus," *Études de droit romain* (Paris: Les Belles Lettres, 1948), 274.

4. See also Theodor Mommsen, *Le droit public romain* (Paris: De Coccard, 1985), 3:1034.

71

Parental supervision means that the engendering twosome gets to watch the drama of becoming, the becoming-other of the child and of the couple that bore it. The parents get to *see* the swerve that fate takes as they are headed for the disaster of sheer loss—which is a good thing, for otherwise Baby would have to be strapped in like Oedipus, stashed out of sight, kept from Laius and the horde of killer fathers. Something blocks the parental view of Baby's parricidal path, V-chipping the bad news of Baby's survival pattern. *Aufhebung* works on the side of the parents as the economical law of the absolute reappropriation of absolute loss. Derrida calls the absolute reappropriation of absolute loss "un concept familial."* For Hegel, the parents sublate their simple and tightened ("gedrungenes") being-for-themselves. They have had to turn around a losing economy. They are tied to a kind of hydraulic system of giving and drainage: What they give the offspring, they lose; they die in the child to the extent that what they give over is their own consciousness—Baby's first credit card.

It is perhaps important to signal that in the *Phenomenology*, the family arrives only after the Master/Slave or Lord/Bondsman fight for recognition. Children offer another scene of the fight unto death that finds a way to negate death and preserve the being of the one vanquished. The figure or production of the child will have allowed for a passage that keeps the dead alive. Consciousness cannot relate to itself or gather up into a totality and become for-itself—it does not become consciousness—unless it is lodged in family.† This is where singularities and totalities butt up against each other and establish their relations to death and the state along hierarchical stretches of consciousness. Hegel explores the lesions ("Verletzungen"), outrages, and concentrated levels of violation ("Beleidigung") that constitute the child's institution of family, as well as the indwelling collision ("Kollision") that culminates only in death.‡ But let us slow this movement down and suspend a death scene, even if it takes place at the beginning, arriving with Baby—an issue and offspring at once initiating and knocking down family. Bearing these thought incubators in mind—they serve to explain part of the rage and resistance provoked by the intrusion of the child, the fatal markers of progeny about which Mary Shelley had so much to say—let us repair to a different ground, a different aspect of emergence where the speculative playground gets put together. Hegel's warning system can flash in the background. Let me go elsewhere momentarily (as if such an ungrounding elsewhere could be located), remembering that for the German

* Ibid., 152.
† See Derrida's precise explication of this movement in ibid., 154ff.
‡ Derrida, *Glas*, 156.

Authority, downscaled to "notion," cannot boast a surefire enforcement of itself. Yet it stands more forcefully on its own—more stripped down to sheer being than the entire local police force that threatens to bring one under control. Kojève's example is potentially fraught and hanging there without much context. When nailing authority in action, and as a mode of address, Kojève doesn't give much instruction about the individual or circumstance that one addresses and repels at the same time (are you addressing a lover, an intruder, a friend, a fly, or vermin?). He wants to show how authority works, and chooses this example to do so: "If in order to make someone leave my room I have to use force, then I must *change* my own behavior in order to realize the act in question, thus demonstrating that I have no authority whatsoever" (25). If I have to call security or start stomping around, raising my voice, I am lacking in authority. I should be able simply to cast a look, send out a glare, for the unwelcome intruder to slither away. Maybe flashing a glare signals too strong an action. In fact, the less said, the more authority, Kojève indicates a number of times.

The example of "my room" stays emptily private, but Kojève soon enters a more public and politically pitched forum: The ranter or demagogue is chronically low on authority, forcing the other to guzzle up language and locate a loophole. In the *Esquisse*, authority is seen as a capacity to act upon others without provoking a reaction. The one in authority prompts no re-activity, effects no dent that would rattle the one bearing authority—even though others may be eminently capable of responding with force, resistance, or defiance: "By acting with Authority the agent can change the human given without being subject to retaliation or *contrecoup*, which is to say, without having to change himself in function of this action" (25). Authority, formalized into an instigating "agent" but also qualified as human, is immune from reaction, protected from retaliatory damage. Necessarily "recognized" by those subjecting themselves to its considerable pull, any emanation of human Authority must nonetheless have a reason, a cause, or a justified basis for its existence. Kojève dwells on this point, asking why recognition is proffered consciously and voluntarily, allowing others to submit to Authority without reacting. ("Authority": I have struggled throughout these chapters with the matter of capitalization for figuring authority and father; I was tempted to add a chapter on what gets capitalized, according to what constraints or imputations. I even thought of capitalizing all nouns and collating English with German, english with german, until I scrapped the idea in the sense of *Aufhebung*, saving it up for a similar round of grammatical-semantic contention, possibly the next one. Alright.)

thinker Jean Paul, sand was the favored toy, responsible for so many castles and imaginary byways, for so little solidity.*

The eighteenth century was largely responsible for carving out an initiating place for childhood in modernity, for investing the child with interiority and a capacity for historical development—for historicizing the early adult and separating off a distinct status for its peculiar growth spurts, articulations, tendential urges. Childhood, henceforth the new normal of time span—though often cast as hopelessly diluted, semantically smeared, and unreadable—was to be outfitted with narrative supplementation, given its own accounting system and regulative grids. It was not until Freud, however, that childhood received another installment in its conception and became equipped with off-the-charts sexuality, at which point all sorts of later strictures and topological modalities were seen to emerge in the controversial assumption of infantile sexuality, one of the most scandalous discoveries of psychoanalysis—worse even than sleeping with your mother, yuk! Infantile sexuality was another password for the welding of childhood to mortality, putting the youth culture in the seat of the death drive.†

As autobiography tries to inch toward historical reference, it aims for the origin, locating infancy at the site of a discontinuity, at the entry point of language. This is why many world-class autobiographical accounts begin with a stammer, staggering into a place where the so-called speaking subject can register only discomfort, a sear of incomprehension. The stuttering beginnings of the autobiographical trek are often smoothed over by secondary revision or held together with the help of a mythological constellation that opens a particularized history, as in the case of Goethe's self-tracing account of his life. Limiting our remarks to two major starting points in German letters—though *Tristram Shandy* could

---

* Paul Fleming, "The Promise of Childhood: Autobiography in Goethe and Jean Paul," *Goethe Yearbook* 14 (2007): "In Levana, the best toy is therefore one that grants a child's fantasy a maximum amount of free play. . . . In fact, sand is Jean Paul's preferred play instrument, the purest of toys, precisely because of all the possibilities it embodies," 37.

† Christopher Fynsk approaches the topos of mortal exposure from another perspective in *Infant Figures: The Death of the 'Infans' and Other Figures of Origin* (Stanford, Calif.: Stanford University Press: 2000). See also Giorgio Agamben, who defines infancy in *Infancy and History: On the Destruction of Experience* as the transcendental origin of language and the (non)ground of its historicity in general, the (non)ground of human history—a deduction that Fynsk sees as "remain(ing) in philosophy" (New York: Verso, 2007), 94.

His phenomenological procedure tries to respond to the question of sub-mission without ever really establishing a proof or offering a demonstration. Nor does he question the double-barreled positing power of authority and its groundedness in reason, cause, or justification. If authority can stare you down in mute offense, does it necessarily have rational backup? Do its invasive capacities not depend, rather, as Benjamin offers, on more of a mystical endorsement and form of control?

Kojève stays closer to the ground of reason, following closely upon a so-cially pitched phenomenology. To make things manageable, he distinguishes four types of authority that are "simple, pure, or elementary" (26), each of which names a theoretical source and a form of hierarchical relatedness: the authority of the Father in relation to the child, that of the Master in relation to Slave, the Leader in relation to Horde, and the Judge in relation to the Judged. The Authority of the Master reverts to Hegel's elaborations, offering up a general theory of authority that makes no mention of the other, Kojève-induced, types of authority such as those wielded by Father or *Chef*. The latter becomes crucial when reconsidering the trajectories proposed by Aristotle on authority, whereas Plato leads in still another direction, that of the Judge, since all forms of authority are based on Justice or Equity. Kojève lays greatest emphasis on Plato's breakdown of authority, on which he builds contemporary reflections for an independent judiciary. The figure of the Judge offers a way to introduce the most reliable form of authority, and provides the basis for a just polity. The precarious balance struck by justice and authority hinges on this figure. The Judge makes claims for impartiality, objectivity, and disinterestedness, thus commanding at all times authority. In this sense authority attaches to all those who possess these qualities; namely, those who are just or honest command authority even if they do not sit on the bench.

The Authority of the Father, similar to the other designated types, is of divine essence and derives from hereditary transmission as well as from tradi-tion and the past. Authority borne by Father, having in crucial ways declined, now subsists in ways that remain repressed or concealed, and is therefore in need of further investigation—particularly concerning the rebounding structures of parafamilial orders. The expression of paternal power, which was never a manifestation of power as such, has gone underground and dis-turbs the way the world is ordered. Kojève goes after the displaced effects of wayward authority and follows the substitutive chain to mark the ways effective majorities rule minorities, trickling down pressures: bosses lord it over their employees, men dominate women, figures of ideological strongholds maintain their oppressive manner. It is as if we were irremediably bound to archaic have provided a wonderful, if intentionally impossible starting point—we find that both Goethe and Jean Paul, when trying to put together their autobiographies, rifled through other sources in order to get their stories straight. Aiming to retrieve a book of childhood memories, they called upon friends, disciples, various functionaries of recall, and related branches of the self's memory banks, to attach to their largely empty accounts, "to provide them with information, memories, descriptions, and insights into their lives and surroundings."*

Needing to cover for the memory blanks that characterized the greater part of his childhood, Goethe famously called his autobiographical work *Dichtung und Wahrheit,* allowing for the fiction and discursive warping that self-retrievals imply. His relation to his "own" childhood was to be pumped up by fiction, whether or not he had access to memory flashes and images of his younger years. To get this right, this business of starting things from scratch, of unearthing what no memory could be expected to retrieve naturally, a child would have to be invented, not merely falsified, but probabalistically constituted—a near paradox that sets up the autobiographical project. For Goethe, the autonomy of the *autos* was always put into question, from his earliest puppet theater collectivities to his essential conversations with Schiller and other contemporaries, including Hegel, and his later collaborations with Eckermann, who finished and partially dictated the terms of the concluding chapters, writing out his life for the master. Besides its principal meaning as poesy or fiction, *Dichtung* also comes from *dictation,* signaling in this case that childhood memories hail from elsewhere, are dictated to the adult poet, to the accomplished statesman and scientist, as he endeavors to reconstruct or indeed photoshop and stretch a lost history. If *Dichtung* comes first in the title, trailing *Wahrheit* behind, it is not because he means to establish a hierarchy of values—allowing for an organization of signifiers that would have gratified Nietzsche to the extent that fiction takes first honors and precedes truth—but because the poet in him found the repetitive d's of the original title unbearable: "Wahrheit un*d D*ichtung." The poetic reformatting took first place in the end—in itself a telling event, showing that the poetic ear trumped the imperious claims of truth-value—just as childhood was moved up and back to a posited origin, the veracity of which was largely fabricated and multiply mediated. If childhood needed to be propped up through a network of mediations and memory prompts, this was in part because, for Goethe and others engaged in the autobiographical quest, it was dead in the water. Its purported fullness—the golden age for which childhood remained a cipher—entailed a symbolic lesion that required fiction to dress it up and get it going into history.

* Fleming, "Promise of Childhood," 1.

sovereignties that continue to rise up from the four dominant types of Authority and their sixty hybrid forms. Kojève also shows interest in the operation of Authority and its means of transmission: election, nomination, heredity, decree. The very possibility of *transmission* indicates that Authority exists in the absence of a particular or singularized person but communicates and settles according to a specific logic of appointment and transfer. There is also the necessity of setting off temporal from eternal Authority, which involves the negation of time and depends on metaphysical subsets of instauration. Sometimes one of the types of Authority, though prey to contamination and overlap, finds itself isolated, such as when the Judge must go it alone to assume a superior vantage point. Yet each type of Authority marks a stage of consciousness or behavior that elicits corresponding responses or responsibilities. A great deal could be said about the status of the speech acts or propositions, the linguistic and extralinguistic fields that this typology presupposes, including the modalities of *obedience* or the rungs of passivity and orders of oppression that get marked by Authority's exposition. For Authority, according to Kojève, cannot operate in a relational void but implies (unlike force and power) some degree of reciprocal adherence and specific levels of sustaining responsiveness. There is the matter of those who bow to Authority, respect its principle and range, surrender without manifest struggle to its requirements, and let us not entirely forget some among us who need the coveted whip. Even those who rail against Authority confirm its hold.

So. How am I doing? Have we seen authority brought to its stance of urgency? Can a different kind of approach better serve the needs of thinking through authority? Is this the time for greater or lesser degrees of sobriety in terms of exposition and analysis, in terms of prediction and the articulation of *Sorge*? Let me continue to explain some of the choices I have made.

I admit having avoided quite a number of staple discursivities—the phrasal regimens of shared political infrastructures and anxieties that hold sway over the way we treat matters of common concern. I could have done a better job of subduing the extravagant distress that is usually narrowed down by acknowledged forms of political discussion. For starters, I could have mobilized recognizable themes or identifiable arguments that bind our disciplines, that run us safely to the types of suppositions that we return to everyday, that underlie the way we talk to one another. A more grounded procedure would have been tempting—backed, God forbid, by a "methodology," and then there would have been no struggle for legitimacy, internally surveilled or more externally controlled. Finally, I could have disclosed a list of works that have been eliminated for these and those stated reasons and enlisted a cluster of powerful advisors to supplant them. I can say this

Goethe does not make poetry the restorative cover for the hidden truth of childhood. Still, his entitling act accounts for the necessity of the poetic intervention both as a response to the default of memory and as a kind of filler for devastated sites of childhood promises. In rhetorically fitted terms, childhood, for Goethe, is seen as offering a stage of promise that gets broken off. Everything in the construction of childhood depends on smoothing over the fissuring elements of the promise, its continual breakdown. The child promises (and is promised) more than it can keep. The figured plenitude of childhood rests on the structure of the promise. It offers itself as fulfilled by inherent necessity, opening out to all sorts of *possibilities* that it will neither see nor remember: in fact, as Goethe sees things, nature has played a "dirty little trick" to the extent that children promise so much but in the end deliver so little.*

Children, in terms of their development, are thoroughly discouraging, Goethe argues—they let us down as they grow up. Their original genius, artistic inventiveness, and scientific curiosity are snuffed out, punctually recalled. Growth should not be confused with mere development, Goethe warns in *Dichtung und Wahrheit*; the various energies and flows that constitute the growing human being eventually split off—they follow upon, repress, and tear at one another, they switch over to other functions, so that early capabilities leave little or no trace in the adult. One can break down the movement that collapses the child into a place of extinguished hope. There are stages that mark the clear-cut decline into adulthood after initial vaults. For Goethe, the child, taken in and of itself, at first "surpasses all expectations: it is so smart, so comfortable, so cheerful."† Yet, systemic flaws and organic sabotage put an end to the start-up childhood promise. Goethe offers clear analogies between his thoughts on human and plant development, wedging in the principal distinction that the plant's entelechy is disrupted by outside forces—weather, soil, plant nutrition—whereas the human being and frame is susceptible to internal disruption.‡ Paul Fleming argues that the entelechy of plant life, entirely contingent, matches up differently against human life, where the full measure of growth (should one ever be able rigorously to evaluate this) is both contingent and intrinsic. The human being needs to be pulled out of these vulnerabilities by means of education.

Nonetheless, in Goethe's descriptions I see some noteworthy contaminations occurring, as when education nearly resembles the cultivation of a bonsai—with

* Fleming discusses the Goethean dirty trick scandal of childhood in greater detail in ibid., 4.
† Fleming, "Promise of Childhood," 30.
‡ See Fleming's discussion of the distinction drawn by Goethe between *Wachstum* and *Entwicklung* (growth and development), "Promise of Childhood," 30ff.

much for myself, however. Unlike those who make claims for striking out on their own or those who adhere to group formations that exclude stray shots, alien premises, or intrusive contention, I have read extensively the very works that I choose not to mirror, and whose powerful legitimacies I relinquish. This in part is why there has been no pretension to bringing off a political theory here or to restoring a political science.

The cobelonging of the philosophical and the political.

Instead, I have kept the focus mostly on the cobelonging of the philosophical and the political. Maintaining their reciprocal involvement, I account for the political as a philosophical determination, which is not to say that the philosophical simply precedes and trumps the political. It is understood that, for any serious investigation of authority, philosophy owns a time-share in the neighborhood of psychoanalysis, whether this address is given out or kept unlisted. If you are thinking "philosophy, psychoanalysis: no thanks, not necessary," then you are lapsing into the habits of the total dominion of politics that crowds out any critique and inevitably assumes totalitarian qualities.

> This "recall" to the philosophical of the question of the political—which, con-
> trary to what one might think, supposes no assurances as regards philosophy—is
> not a simply critical and "negative" gesture. Vigilance is assuredly necessary,
> today more than ever, as regards those discourses which feign independence
> from the philosophical and which claim, correspondingly, to treat the politi-
> cal as a distinct and autonomous domain (or, and this does not make much
> difference, one tied up with or subordinated to another empirical or regional
> domain). . . . The project of a theory or a science of the political, with all its
> socio-anthropological baggage (and, consequently, its philosophical presup-
> positions), now more than ever necessitates its own critique and the critique
> of its political functions.[5]

At and for this time, Nancy and Lacoue-Labarthe want to encourage a type of vigilance that cannot be satisfied with the apparatus and practice of critique. An intervention that may have lost the power to disqualify or move

5. Jean-Luc Nancy and Philippe Lacoue-Labarthe, delivered in Paris as the inaugural address to the Centre for Philosophical Research on the Political, 8 December 1980. Now published as "The Centre: Opening Address," in *Retreating the Political*, ed. Simon Sparks (London and New York: Routledge, 1997), 109. Subsequent references to *Retreating the Political* are cited parenthetically in the text.

lots of pruning, restricting, and miniaturization pressed upon the living being as it "grows down," to quote Kafka on the matter of his own "downbringing." (Kafka and his delicate peers were not brought up, but brought down, he observes.) The plant gets strapped and slapped down much as the child, trimmed and fit for its nearly ethical appearance, pulling together systematically. Subject to cultivation and culture, the child and plant bear the traces of a largely unavoidable sadistic application—something like Freud's unbeatable reality principle, every time coming round the bend when pleasure is offered. Are plants susceptible to the pleasure principle? Is our botanical population not moved by the joys of dosed-out solarity and the replenishment of water? All this remains to be seen, especially where nature bows to the law of cultivation and is made to submit to very specific training programs. Educated and pruned down, the restricted entity is prepared for the battle of being. Thus the overarching motto for the section of *Dichtung und Wahrheit* dedicated to childhood, part 1, reads: "The one who is not mistreated will not be educated."*

In the early life of that being designated as child, following the first stages of implanted plenitude, the torture officially commences—or: agony takes an official turn, an institutional cast. The death drive receives an overhaul in the form of school, the famous institution of *Bildung* that takes over where genius left off in Kant as well as in Hegel and Goethe. The wings of Imagination are clipped for and by schooling. Some of the highly educated/mistreated, such as Goethe himself and Mozart, did not have to enroll in schools but graduated from home study programs curated by their fathers. The median child, in any case, soon starts losing ground as well as promise, sheds the initial baby fat of genius: the child thins out, is suddenly spent. The promise, as Goethe emphasizes, is without exception broken. (I suppose that mathematical or musical genius allows for a different invoice and report card here.) What the defeated expectation means, among other things, is that the child is already over and out, too old when schooling begins. By the time homeroom and early school assignments commence, the child shows up as the leftover of a once-inexhaustible fund. The sparkle has been extinguished, and barely a trace remains of what had been momentarily made available and instantaneously squandered. That's how Nature set it, according to Goethe. It's over before it begins to weigh in or mean something—the losing streak sets in at the earliest stages, but not without summoning up a glimpse of what was never meant to be. (Freud for his part will roll the clock back even further, not to speak of Melanie Klein, who was a true early bird of human disaster and self-pollution bulletins.)

* For an interpretation of Menander's tough-love credo that heads up Goethe's auto-biographical project see Fleming, "Promise of Childhood," 31.

things, critique in any case would "probably be too quick and ineffective faced with the almost undivided domination of anthropology" (109). These considerations lead them to turn to the philosophical, which they are not trying to manipulate into a position of prestige or declare as winner of any long-range discursive skirmishes. They aim to bring into focus the essential (and not accidental or merely historical) cobelonging of the philosophical and the political. This "recall" should not count as strengthening the dominion of the philosophical, but opens the space of a more original cobelonging, a conversation largely muted by the persistent clamoring of warring discursivities.

Without a doubt, philosophy, stripped of power and more often than not dispossessed of authority, can and must, as Kant once admonished, fire its blank shots at the political behemoth and its brutalizing tendencies. One must stay on guard against those discursive and academic practices that make claims for autonomy or subsist on disavowal when it is a matter of granting significance to a repressed philosophical ground. Nowhere is this more evident than in statements made on behalf of the fantasy of an independently sanctioned political domain. Let us not be intimidated.

In their opening address to the Center for Philosophical Research on the Political, Nancy and Lacoue-Labarthe consider the philosophical essence of the political. They observe that when it comes to the political, the philosophical unavoidably finds that it has been divested of authority. Something about this encounter manifestly weakens the philosophical hold on things, its ability to tell us about the world or to invent a future. In many contemporary forms of political saying and theoretical exploration, it is no longer practicable to yoke politics and philosophy. Nevertheless, as a twosome they have counted on each other, if only behind the scenes; among the Ancients the philosophical and the political of course form an unbreakable pair, requiring each other's attendance and support for family gatherings and foreign outings. At this point, they represent a severed couple, a fissured entity whose history of breakup continues in itself to be of consequence. Putting aside all the differences and distances that separate them, there remains an ineradicable figure, something that cannot be removed from the premises of splintered discursive tendencies.

The political fiction of the paternal.

Let us note the nearly immutable *paternal input* that still intrudes into places where the political gets marked or activated. This is the neuralgic point I'm trying to get at. Even where change is programmed by a discernible social political drive, there remains a relation to Father's worldly energy and familial endurance. This

The situation is the same but a little different for Jean Paul, who measures childhood as origin and goal, seeing it as the pinnacle of human development.* A fall or crash follows upon childhood, which contains the kernel of the *Ideal-mensch*. Education consists in freeing up this ideal by letting the child "unfold," sponsoring "die entfaltende Erziehung" (an unfolding bringing-up).† Still, as with Goethe, Jean Paul resolutely sticks to an angle of youth culture, asserting that "humanity reaches its summit in youth,"‡ defined by potentiality, before external encroachments stamp out desire and anticipatory fulfillment. Jean Paul describes this crumbling motion as a daily destruction, as a countdown of crushing and overwhelming proportion for the subject as it nears the domains of need—the little ones yield to an increasing domination by impoverished being, subjecting them to pressing human claims or aggressions. At the end of the day Jean Paul takes a bleaker view of childhood than does Goethe, who sees a saving possibility for one of the lost sparks of childhood promise.

For Jean Paul, any hope embodied in the child is soon wiped out, taking down futurity with it. Despite a cluster of statements to the contrary, Goethe opens up a secret channel, allowing for the possibility that some inspired or winning aspect of adulthood might pay back walkaway sums to an ever-lost childhood. The future of the child might in the end justify or carry and hand over or return childhood to itself, shining a light on the past from the place of maturity and by means of some fictioning. If childhood has a meaning, it begins in adulthood, metaleptically propped and conditionally remembered. On these counts Jean Paul is the more severe theorist of a loser child-base, holding to his sense that one can roll back only to the could-have-beenness of childhood, its field of possibilities never having meant to be truly supported or realized. Childhood, with its enfolded ideal, offers only a "vorgespiegelte Unendlichkeit," a "pre-flected, simulated, or even feigned infinity": "What is of lasting significance in childhood and what we remember is not what was, but what could have been, what was pre-flected and projected into an infinite future but never brought to fruition."§

For Jean Paul, the internal temporal splintering of childhood, ever breaking off from the ideal, does not bear witness to a lived experience or to an epoch of evolving selfhood that could claim stability or presence: childhood's predica-

---

* "Daher kommt eigentlich der Mensch nicht zum Hoechsten hinauf, sondern von da herab und erst dann zurueck empor," cited in Fleming, "Promise of Childhood," 16.

† Jean Paul, *Saemtliche Werke. Historisch-Kritische Ausgabe*, ed. Eduard Berend et al. (Weimar: H. Boehlaus Nachfolger, 1927 ff.), 5:504.

‡ Fleming, "Promise of Childhood," 6.

§ Ibid., 9; Paul, *Saemtliche Werke,* 4:202; Fleming, "Promise of Childhood," 9.

commitment stands fast precisely when we are dealing with a necessarily failing or fictional outlay of the paternal. A powerful philosophical energizer and political fiction since at least Plato, the assertion of paternity has served many crucial functions that, despite its ubiquity and conceptual banality, still requires interrogation in the manner developed by Derrida in "Plato's Pharmacy," which links the Logoi to the origins of paternal interdiction as well as to particular rushes and writings.

Using another watchword, let us return for a moment to Kojève's casting-off and retention of the paternal function—he manages to do both, remove and preserve the father, disqualify and hang on to the effects of this authority. Lacan has noted the way Kojève skips over the father's very springboard into being—or let us downshift and say merely that Kojève refrains from engaging the onto-legitimacy of the paternal. For some reason, Kojève won't go there, can't look back. One cannot simply enter codes to open up endless new accounts that may explain Kojève's recalcitrance to explore this area and its precedence, neglecting the very premise of his thought. Still, it may be useful to pause and consider the snag to which Lacan's criticism points and wonder what route the philosopher might have taken were he to interest himself in what came prior to the fundamental and master position that Lacan saw as derivative. In terms of a more restricted line of questioning, one might further wonder what the stakes are for Lacan in bringing up this missing link and how it serves the unfolding of his own argument. Lacan may be trying to keep control of the field of the subject, which remained a fixture as he himself navigated through Heidegger, Luther, and Descartes. Despite all the warning signs and breakthroughs along the route, Lacan never gives up on the subject, even when traversing the Heideggerrian oeuvre. The steadfast engagement with the subject on the part of Lacan clues us in to his investment in Kojève's location of the paternal—that which establishes and exceeds the subject. A quality of Kojève's refused "regression" to what precedes the figuration advanced by Hegel comes to light in Freud's own insistence on what is prior to the father and what anticipates something like the subject on which so many of these reflections rely.

Freud underscores the ruptures and breaks that lead up to the paternal positing. What this means can be understood most clearly (I am not joking) in terms rendered by Lacoue-Labarthe and Nancy in "La panique politique," which reminds us of the phrase in *Moses and Monotheism*, "we must recall that the father too was once a child."[6] Freud has always emphasized that the

---

6. Sigmund Freud, *Moses and Monotheism: Three Essays*, Standard Edition of the Complete Psychological Works of Sigmund Freud (London: Hogarth Press,

ment is always to have the little subject jump ahead of itself, lean forward rather than stay in place. Childhood, in fact, was all along lurching forward toward phantasms of its own possible infinity, an inclining stance or pose of readiness that all on its own offered pleasure, anticipatory glee: "What one remembers is the affective intensity of felt anticipation that failed to enter into reality—the unrealized possibilities that still shoot through the present."* It is as if childhood pleasure rested on this failure of becoming. This ungrounded rooting of pleasure may be linked to what Lacan sees as desire's sprouting in deprivation—it is the experience of *not* making it that keeps us going forward. Ask anyone who is not utterly broken about the powerful motors of not-having and the relentless impetus of doing-without. In any case, pleasure in Jean Paul's ruminations on childhood clings to that which never came about outside its space of projection, securing a scene of temporal arousal that never truly got off the ground. Whether or not anything after childhood ever resolves into a more securable lock on the present is another matter.

What concerns me here can be stated through Lyotard's perspective. Childhood is never merely located in the past, at an ostensible first stage on some developmental or growth chart. Never prone to establish its zone as groundable or self-present, childhood also doesn't simply disappear. It suddenly shows up at moments when the possibility of representation or voice collapses, when one loses one's bearings or forfeits one's nearly juridical defense systems—when one is truly at a loss, caught in a disturbing condition of unfairness that the word "dependency" is too weak to cover. The regression to childhood stands always ready to return, prepared to silence the more adult and sturdy parts, should they have taken root. Moreover, what we call childhood cannot burrow into discursive solidity. Whether or not the figure of childhood can be freeze-framed as something that will have taken place in a present, it continually presents problems and eludes the narrative grasp. Yet recourse to childhood fronts as the basis for the biographical and historical impulse.

Besides the rich theoretical implications of Jean Paul's stance, his relation to an unlived childhood—timed and primed for an evasive future—placed him at the mercy of an undeniably rough terrain when it came to writing his autobiography. How are you to undertake such a project when phase one has been definitively canceled except for fragments of an unpolished history of affect and the futile glint of resurrected memory? It is not only the case that the predictions for losing ground provide a slippery thematic brace for any study of historical becoming, but that childhood itself is, for the most part, derailed from the start, based on a relation to irretrievable loss. To get itself going, the faux solidity

* Fleming, "Promise of Childhood," 9.

emergence of the subject traces back "neither from other subjects nor from a subject-discourse (whether it be of the other or of the same, of the father or of the brother), but from the non-subject or non-subjects" (6). To the extent that the non-subject can be designated or named, the priority falls to "the without-authority" or "the without-father." The without-superego—and thus without-ego—is "anterior to every topic as well as to every institution, of an anteriority with which no regression can properly catch up," and has a "broader" base than any founding agency. The non-subject forms "the joint limit of psychoanalysis and of the political" (6).

The unsupportable subject.

The unsupportable subject. Lacoue-Labarthe and Nancy explore the limit that psychoanalysis and the subject share when challenged by power, and the way that power traces the contours of the political. Psychoanalysis, they argue here, "instantly takes us to the common limit of a double question which is as old as metaphysics" (6). Freud searches his own limit "obscurely, obstinately, and repetitively" and proceeds by an "impressive series of admissions of defeat or incompletion" (what they also call when considering his quasi-system "the [false/true] modesty and the hyperbolic circumspection" of his work, 7). Two fundamental questions recur in Freud, asking how the subject supports itself. The problem this raises is especially decisive when one considers that the subject, the substance, is supposed to *be the support* and now is found wanting support in order to be. Importantly, one of these questions runs on the course of authority, involving paternal, political, psychoanalytical dimensions of authority, thus bringing us back to a basic disturbance in any thought on authority, namely, "how does authority authorize itself?" (6). By the time Freud reaches *Civilization*, his thought effectively "bears the mark of the renunciation of the idea of a decisive amelioration of society (by psychoanalysis in particular) such as one found it in previous texts (*Jokes and Their Relation to the Unconscious* especially)." The end of *Civilization* faintly gestures to future researches and hopes that some day the cure of society will be taken up. But the practical obstacle to "surmount in this undertaking will be that of the authority necessary to impose such a therapy upon the group (*Masse*)" (7). The focal points for Lacoue-Labarthe and Nancy converge in the question, "How could psychoanalysis endow itself with this authority? How could this authority be

---

1975), 23:110; quoted in *Retreating the Political*, 6. Philippe Lacoue-Labarthe and Jean-Luc Nancy, "La panique politique," in *Retreating the Political*; subsequent references are cited parenthetically in the text.

of childhood depends on all sorts of fairly familiar rhetorical maneuvers and familial tropologies—family trees without natural soil. In some cases, such as Hegel's reading of *Antigone*, the brother-sister relation can serve to break the very concept of family, to expose its essential emptiness. Family, as Derrida has argued, comes about as something anhuman to the extent that it depends upon an onto-theological home base for every one of its formulations. There is no "family" in nature, no brothers, no sisters. So the drama of the human, with its extensive outlay of convention and contract, is largely our own doing—the bed we have made, so to speak, to lie in. Childhood is not merely lost to us mortals: it is something that we have to lose time and again. Often enough, writing helps the loss to move along, if only as part of the *fort/da* gambit, bringing back something we get to pretend-command.

I'd like to round out these preliminary reflections with a close-up of what Christopher Fynsk writes in *Infant Figures* so that the stakes of my own study on collapsed authority and its loser returns can be stated clearly. Childhood puts a unique stall on the unconscious, and in this regard the question arises of its ever-ventured overcoming. The brunt of overcoming still rests on metaphysical staunchness, so one must proceed cautiously here when shifting from description to exhortation. The overcoming of childhood—the very thing or splice or recollection that could not be stabilized—is what still needs to be thought through according to the red flags raised in the concurring works of Goethe, Jean Paul, Kafka, Blanchot, and quite a few others. The predicament of an impossible recall of childhood proves to be fateful. Fynsk momentarily places the focus on Serge Leclaire's *On tue un enfant* (*A Child Is Being Killed*), where Blanchot finds "another figure of a menacing past that one has never known or lived."[*] The discussion commences with a primary narcissistic representation that is formed, in Blanchot's words, of the "dreams and desires of those who made us and saw us born (parents, all society)."[†] Fynsk sees the *child* as a figure or stand-in for representation—what "Freud, and Lacan after him called *Vorstellungsrepräsentanz*. Its hold on the psyche must be dislodged if desire is to come to speech—a terrible task inasmuch as this representation is unconscious. The child must be destroyed, Blanchot says."[‡] Blanchot underscores the fact

---

[*] Christopher Fynsk, *Infant Figures: The Death of the Infans and Other Scenes of Origin* (Stanford, Calif.: Stanford University Press, 2000), 53.

[†] Maurice Blanchot, *The Writing of the Disaster*, trans. Ann Smock (Lincoln: University of Nebraska Press, 1986), 110. Originally published as *L'ecriture du désastre* (Paris: Gallimard, 1996).

[‡] Fynsk, *Infant Figures*, 53.

analyzed?" The political is seen to encounter its limit here, where authority gathers up the limit-question of power and legitimacy over the meeting grounds of psychoanalysis and politics.

Another way of labeling the designated meeting grounds involves two words: collective neurosis. The symptomatology that fuels the very terms by which we encounter the political emerges with Freud's social theoretical investigations, identifying the breaks and fissures in the psychic ordering of things and naming the difficulty of gathering up sufficient authority for a determined type of social healing. Lacoue-Labarthe and Nancy wrap up a discussion of the contrast (*Gegensatz*) between social and narcissistic mental acts—"the contrast of the social and individual falls within the limits of psychoanalysis" (9)—with a situating statement that underlies their argument:

> The Freudian science is by rights a science of culture, and consequently a political science. Even and precisely if it turns out that this right gives rise to the greatest difficulties, indeed to the greatest disorder, and to the threat . . . of a political panic. (9)

Freud settles into spaces routinely leased out to political science, even where he receives eviction notices or is escorted off the premises of the more recognized forms of social science. His encroachment prompts upheaval, inducing different tonalities of panic. Does Kojève repel Freud at the very place where they share vocabularies and jurisdiction? It is not clear that Kojève lays claim to or wants to be associated with the discursivity identified as political science when he sketches his thought on Authority. Nor is it clear that canonical formations around the discipline feel summoned precisely by the portentous difficulties that an encounter with psychoanalysis implies. Avoiding psychoanalysis—or even that part of Hegel prone to its infiltration—Kojève desists from pressing the panic button, staying on course without feeling the need to probe even the sociological authority of psychoanalysis where it faces off with political science or philosophy. Kojève renounces any accommodation with the way psychoanalysis might situate the *socius* in the ego or mark narcissism as the limit of social formation and the grid according to which it considers identification the shaky ground of the social. At the same time, Kojève was unable to finish his work on authority. The temptation to imagine an ending, or even to invent one for him and for us, is great and would by no means compromise my own repertoire, my habit of picking up where others have left off. I will leave the work of completing Kojève's thought to others, however, understanding that incompletion offers its own mark of an idea's exhaustion, and direct our work toward another that this operation of destruction is ongoing and never disposes of its task in the present—the operation "could never take place once and for all," for it is "not accomplished at any privileged moment of time" and "operates inoperably," situated in the "very time that destroys (effaces) time, an effacement or destruction, or a gift that has always already avowed itself in the precession of a Saying outside any said." The destruction of the child is "perpetuated without term even in the *interruption* that constitutes its mark."*

Without scraping against the sense of Blanchot's reflections and Fynsk's commentary—though such a collision seems inevitable—I would like to put us in touch with this unceasing destruction, often spun unconsciously, yet linked to the very possibility of getting on in the worlds that crowd and vitally, if provisionally, support or deplore us. One could say, according to a Nietzschean scale, that there are many types of destruction, good and bad destruction, affirmable destruction of the kind that clears the way with a quiver of existential "good riddance!" as when a painfully corrupt president must leave office. Recalling and returning to Heidegger's distinction between destruction and devastation—the latter allows no room for futurity, all is razed and rubbed out—the destruction of the child needs to be looked at from its various repressed or reconfigured angles. This is something that cultures and *Bildungs*-formations such as the sprawling American infomercial resist facing as they cover over the child's destruction with riots of youth culture and Disneyland proliferations that double for what has been expunged. To stay with Nietzsche, if only for a punctual stopover, it is necessary to remember that the affirmation of life is seldom far from what destroys it.

* Blanchot, *Writing of the Disaster*, 116. See also Fynsk, *Infant Figures*, 71.

end. I do so with the understanding that our ends will at some points coincide before they part ways.

Let us return to the model of the political that gave both Kojève and Freud a headache. One of the problems that they face involves the bullheaded identification of politics with the Father that sets off a disturbance or disruption to the political within the political. I cannot go into the torsions and frustrations of Freud's tremendous insight now but will have to remain satisfied with stating, following the argument of Lacoue-Labarthe and Nancy, and the careful elaborations of Lacan as well as a number of others—including Samuel Weber, Judith Butler, and Laurence Rickels—that the model of the Power-Father was untenable already for Freud. Freud started erasing and limiting the power effect of Father on the basis of the uncompleted operation on identification. The big troublemaker or troubled site comes up as Darwin, who pitched an enduring red flag on the archeophiliac passages that had Freud consistently returning to the Father.

Darwin, admired and feared, scrambled the code, dragged Freud (and us) through the mud, dusting off any semblance of unaffected human dignity. If he, Freud, based social reappropriation on the thinking of identification, who could hope to make it stick when the lineage traced back to a gorilla? "The figure of the Father was untenable in the Darwinian derivation of *Totem and Taboo* (which will serve right to the end as a matrix): for a gorilla is not a father, and there can only be a Father after the event in the 'after' of the mortal event" ("Panique," 15). Displacing the origin with a gorilla has generated a massive narcissistic breakdown owing to and in the Freudian narrative—one so serious that, let me hasten to add, it in part accounts for the unprecedented maltreatment of animals, the splice of the disavowed "paternal," today. Henceforth, the myths of primitive horde and Father fail to take off: irretrievably attached to Darwinian search engines, they simply don't work for Lacoue-Labarthe and Nancy. This narcissistic shock may be one reason why, in a sense, mystifications such as those sponsoring "creationism" over evolution are on the table, in order to skip the pages sketched by Darwin that undermine paternal license while rattling divine sanctity. Still, we are locked in the archeophiliac edifice of killing the father, which exercises effects of power over a wide range of offenses to this day, raising auxiliary problems of philosophical responsibility and theological authority. One persistent effect of this construction entails Judaism's assignation as a religion of the father (notably in opposition to Christianity, the religion of the son).[7] On another register altogether, though

---

7. See Lacoue-Labarthe and Nancy, "Panique politique," 24. I would add that the motif of the disavowed paternal links up with known forms of anti-Semitisms

What Is Called Father?
(A Fissure in Familialism)

Freud at one point wonders about the victory of patriarchy—something we still have to contend with, he says. I am contending, but barely. On this point I orient myself toward Kafka's work, its starting point and endpoint on the crevice of paternity. An unfinished project of Kafka's, titled "The Sons," was meant to house the horde of loser sons who could not get up from the incessant destructions suffered at the hands of *unwitting fathers.* A savored innocence, an unconscious motor, seemed to drive the paternal machine. Herein lies a principal quality of tension for Kafka: to a certain extent the fathers he examines, no matter how persecutory, remained impervious to transferential fantasies that saw them as the ruling CEOs of psychic plundering, spoliation, incessant familial and political defrauding. Instead, pushing back tyrannical projections, they managed these fantasies by upgrading themselves to the function of loving and tender sovereign brutes whose practices meant little harm and far less damage than they nonetheless prompted. The Kafkan fathers weren't out to smash their kids or send them to Kingdom come, as may have been the case when the ancient predecessor, Laius, deliberately sought to quell baby Oedipus. Kafkan kids were bound over to another set of lethal circumstances, less calibrated by intention or mere power play, less mandated by the so-called instinct for survival. Still, they could not avoid being crushed under the weight of powerful language assaults and the expanding girth of the paternal body, no matter how figurally situated.

In the Kafka family, sexual difference decided whether or not you would be voided. Some girls got away, were somehow stronger, more bridged by Kafka, the disavowed paternal hosts the pernicious spread of bureaucracy and its special brand of cruelty, its rule-binding propensities that circuit into paternal tropologies still requiring discrete systems of detection for their analyses.

The Power-Father, according to Nancy and Lacoue-Labarthe, not only dispatches "the Freudian Political," but comes about in all its forms as the "pervasive consequence of an uncompleted operation carried out on identification" (15). To the extent that the analysis of identification remains incomplete in Freud, suspended, it also however constitutes a blind spot that continues to drive the understanding of the political. Freud recognizes the knot that ties up psychoanalysis's reading of the political and puts in place evasive strategies to protect, as it were, his blindness: "So powerful an *archeophilia* that it is blind to the contradiction which it never ceases to reproduce." Freud's situating the beginning in "'common affectionate tie with a person outside the group' is to presuppose the crowd and the person, it is to explain nothing. The history of the horde at least in this form, explains nothing, nothing but the self-explanation of the political." But here as elsewhere Freud "persists in fomenting and in perpetrating, on his part, a coup which is the political par excellence: *le coup de chef*, the coup of the leader." Lacoue-Labarthe and Nancy make the point that, for Freud, there must in the first place be a head, a leader. Freud, despite any reservations he may have on this point, *wants a beginning*, a head, "an *archeophiliac* drive or passion which forms the very essence of metaphysical (and) political desire." If Freud's trajectory is so evasive, "so difficult to follow, . . . and never completed," this is also, they state, because the archeophilia "does not only proceed from the exterior, from an ideological (metaphysical) remainder in Freud. The politics of the Father is introduced as an external limit because it encounters an internal limit of psychoanalysis: that of identification." With identification something has happened to psychoanalysis, a sort of "accident, the incision of a limit" (16). And it happens to it on "its political limit, which turns out to be both the cause and effect of the psychoanalytical limit" (16).

In terms of the focus I have tried to keep in this work, I can go only as far as to indicate the violent disorder of identities that ensues from the breakage in this description, none of which is Identity, and each of which "nonetheless posits itself only through the exclusion of the others" (21), each of which thereby finds itself deposed. At neither the origin or at the

---

without being entirely identical to that which ensues from the shock of guerrilla parentage. These repressed relations come close on the Richter scale, however.

rebellious, or more compatibly dependent on family rule. The boys were either killed off from the start—Kafka refers to two dead brothers who bailed on him, leaving the young Franz to fight off paternal brutishness on a solitary spin—or they were chronically prone to power failure, as if switched off, suddenly depleted and emptied of being. Their fate, though responsive to Father's sprawling shadow, was by no means planned or designed by the largely hapless creature who came equipped with special effects and liquidating features that were, Kafka contends, for the most part absolved of guilt or any wrongdoing. Paternal power surges in the Kafkan world were by some measures inadvertent, offering the only sign of innocence in the material-familial environs. The sons in the world he pulled together thus suffered, among other things, from an exquisite Nietzschean injunction, disallowing any enactment of *ressentiment*. It might have been easier to hate and resent the Persecutor, to push back and mark succession, calling upon finitude's vindictive edges. But Kafka plays it otherwise. He scores essential points on the outer limits of Freudian ambivalence, subduing the urge to strike back at the ever-encroaching debilitator. These tactics or abolition of tactics serves to keep Father alive and kicking.

Unlike the antipatriarchal heroes of Expressionism, Kafka's sons refuse to take up arms against their fathers, but instead find themselves strapped into paternal machines that slowly buzz-saw death sentences on their bodies. Among the works that Kafka intended to include in "The Sons" was the famous "Letter to Father." This work breaks with the habits of referential discretion to which Kafka committed his writing and in fact resists being assimilated into any stable notion of work. The projected book of Sons could not contain or deliver the "Letter." Difficult to situate in terms of traditional genre theory, slaloming between imaginary and symbolic poles of address, it undermines the epistolary conventions to which it attaches—unless the distress of this letter signals the fate of all epistolary outbreaks. It may be that every letter, no matter how radically rerouted or thematically smudged, asks in its own way, "Father, why have you abandoned me?" and participates in the mystagogy that turns the paternal into a tyrant, an affiliate of the great Depriver. Every love letter, no matter how purportedly remote from paternal precincts, may involve a similar petition of original privation, whether or not it appears to be dissociated from father's address.

I will try to press on with questions raised by this particular nonstarter, Kafka's "Letter to Father," in order to surveil the way it underscores the impossible address, rendering the very notion of "father" summit, nor at the base, "in each narcissus there is no Pan, no *Arche*, no initial Power . . . no *archie*, whether 'anarchic' or 'monarchic.' There is not even the *archie* of a Discourse, Logos or Speech which would already govern the crowd of narcissi" (21). What we are left with, more or less, is the unrelenting tale of an immemorial patricide, for which Freud offers only an insufficient explanation. Somehow Freud's rendering manages to persist in different fields and structures of engagement in his world as well as in subcurrents of our shared worlds. Nailing the ineluctable detachment and the impossibility of the absolute Narcissus—"the Father as absolute Narcissus (as *Massenpsychologie* describes him), is quite simply impossible" (21)—Nancy and Lacoue-Labarthe, by means of a subtle and intricate logic both in "La panique politique" and their opening address, move toward Freud's unceasing allocation of the paternal prerogative.

The father gets set up on the withdrawal of the Other, impelling Freud to circumscribe paternal right, "provided we henceforth understand that Father can only be the unnameable, unpresentable truth of the Mother" (29). Always withdrawing, as the withdrawal of love and face, the truth of the mother hinges on "a relation without relation (a relation of non-relation)" (29)—perhaps the very fearful thing that the incessant return to Power Father covers over. Faking relation and overtaking the political, Power Father seizes a position of privilege with little recourse to foundation. The question of relation and the maternal swerve remerge in the opening address where the question of passage to community is raised, "but it is equally the question of the passage to the subject" that throws off any thinking of self-sufficiency or autocracy (118). The question of relation (of passing into community, into subject) pervades the Freudian text, "from the problematic of originary sociality to those of bisexuality, identification, or the prehistory of Oedipus." Yet relation is hard to squeeze out of Freud's initial register, one that features the autarky of Narcissus, who "is totalitarian," offering the reflection of an unconscious structured like a State "or like a dictatorship." Nonetheless, Freud allows for "the multiple weakenings and fissurings of this political and subjectival normativity," which forces upon itself a thinking, in principle and on principle, of relation and in the end "excludes the position of a self-sufficiency and an autocracy."

Freud thus raises the question of relation *as a question*, a limit question, in terms of the impossibility "of presupposing the solution of relation, whether this be in a subject or in a community" (118). The "social bond," frazzled and assailable, based on an identification that slips away, is something of a gift for (if not from) psychoanalysis, something that Freud, at any rate, presents as a given, by which Lacoue-Labarthe and Nancy mean "the relation which, in disabling, as something that evades us, holding an impossible position, and, from the point of view of the impossible position alone, makes the father necessarily imagined as Depriver. The fantasy of the father manages to break the son and incite a riot of damages to any book or being that would try to place sons in protective custody. When things get bad, father's role consists in carrying out the work of sublime authority, accomplice to death. Kafka decides to write a letter to his shredder. Undeliverable and conceptually suspended, the petition to an unaddressable father necessarily bounces. Still, the "Letter" has a personality and some psychic currency; it tries to chart a history of its nonarrival. Situated between fear and anxiety, it hesitates at every turn between Mitsein and the logic of the Other—between a world of culpability (where the law is given and fixed), and a world of responsibility (where obligation precedes and exceeds the law).

If I state that Kafka situates the "Letter" between fear and anxiety, this is because I am following Freud's understanding of their distinction: the object is at once known, as in the case of fear, and also points to nothing, as is the case with anxiety. With Mitsein and the logic of the Other the signatory of the letter tries to confront the ordeal of an irrevocable, if peculiar, coprimordiality with the father but, at the same time, is tempted by snares in the logic of the Other that places a theological horizon on the relation, entreating an always nearly transcendental Father. Very little can be taken for granted in a Kafkan world that sets up so many intricate instances of relatedness that are prone to collapse while at the same time they prove intractable. It is not as though one knew what a father is, what constitutes his—or her, if we accept the Lacanian rewrite and Freudian pink slips in terms of the paternal metaphor—essential power, particularly when we recognize that Kafka, an unerring reader of the major downsizers of his era that include Nietzsche, Marx, and Freud, contributed his part to the struggle of relinquishing that which cannot be proven or cognized: namely, the authority of Father.

Keenly aware of shrinking metaphysical frontiers and the distinct pressure zones of ever detranscendentalizing effects of power, Kafka sets up shop precisely in the regions flagged by comrades Benjamin, Kraus, Freud, Marx, and Nietzsche, but without leasing the power tools for establishing something or someone like an Overman; nor does he always have the nerves for the appalling complications of neurotic constraints set out in case studies and their terminal/interminable parameters. (Kafka is possibly more Marxist than Freudian or Nietzschean in the end as he struggles with the metaphysics of work spite of everything, Freud *gave himself,* which, like the whole of philosophy, he *presupposed*—this relation of a subject to subjectivity itself in the figure of the father implies, in the origin or in the guise of an origin, the *birth* (or the *gift,* precisely) of this relation." A similar birth implies "the *retreat* of what is neither subject, nor object, nor figure, and which one can, provisionally and simplistically, call 'the mother'" (118–19). The transcendental of the *polis,* provisionally chalked as the mother, does not lead to the hysteria capable of projecting a primal harmony or communion, "nor that of a distribution of functions and differences" (119). Nor does it devolve merely to anarchy. It is "the an-archy of the *archê* itself (assuming that the demonstrative pronoun 'it' can still apply in the lexicon of the transcendental)." The essence of retreat, linked to Derrida's treatment of the trace in his essay "The Ends of Man" and elsewhere, calls us to reexamine all sorts of disinstallations for which Derrida's work is still responsible, beginning with newly set edges of the question of the political.

It is not clear that relation can ever be spoken of in the singular, so the retreat or the nondialectivity for which the mother stands—and falls away— gives relation as relation, "insofar as the nature of relation (if it ever had a nature) is the reciprocal retreat of its terms" (119). Retreat evokes Kant's ethical prescription of relation and Heidegger's problematic of the work of art, where political retreat becomes a question. The issue of the retreating that retraces what it distances brings Nancy and Lacoue-Labarthe back "to the question of a disjunction or a disruption more essential to the political than the political itself." The retreat of the maternal, where it lays out a cartography or becomes the effect of empire building, is something that I have tried to discuss more fully elsewhere, giving a progress report, as it were, in terms of war and dispute—*polemos* and polemics—on the deposed maternal force that comes rebounding back as a grab for territory and language, as when in recent decades, for instance, the United States met with "the mother of all battles."[8] But for now this issue of maternal rebound has to stop, for it leads us to another field of thought-frayed battle.

The incalculable that escapes political determination. The time has come to close the question concerning authority and hope for its advent or relaunch elsewhere, according to other inflections and means. The

8. See Avital Ronell, "Support our Tropes: Reading Desert Storm" and "Activist Supplement," in *Finitude's Score: Essays Toward the End of the Millennium* (Lincoln and London: University of Nebraska Press, 1994). See also the war-

and the exertions of the producing subject—of the Subject in the age of techno-bureaucracy; still, he offers none of the hypothetical safe if bumpy landings or promising projections that some of his fellow doubters, despite significant pessimistic edges, bring into view. At one point, however, they all more or less gave up on man.)* Kafka sets his sights on the exhausted side of the things, keeping pace with the class of other metaphysical dropouts and detectors of withering institutions. What does the turf that these language bearers share look like?

Coming at the problems they circumscribed from different angles, this collective points to a singular facet of the same discovery, working it each according to specific means and idiom, managing the discursive levers of dispossession. Something has happened to the very substance or potentiality of man that has also led Heidegger to orient his concerns toward Dasein. OK, maybe this is fast-tracking the fate of man without properly accounting for what happened or slowing down to tally up the damages. Let me put it another way and count up the receipts of another bottom line and lineage. Man can no longer exult in scanning theoretical highlights and achieving crowning qualities of being and historicity. Man has been auctioned off to the toughest bidders. No longer the "son of God" or the "purpose of nature" or the "subject of history," man at this point, divided up and shared by at least four major constellators of irreversible insight, is seen as that who (or *which*) no longer is or has meaning—something that no longer can be grasped as the signified of sense. From this point onward "man" is that being exposed, abandoned, delivered over, subjected. These terms belong to the thought of Jean-Luc Nancy, which has concerned itself with forms of exposition and abandonment. Following the perspective offered by Nancy's work, we come to see that, in the manner of his fellow "master discourses," Kafka revs up the engine of a distinctive syntax of attachment without identity. Dealing in a displacement of the concept "man," Kafka constellates figures or surrogates that no longer point to the substantiality of a pregiven identity, but to the being, as Nancy puts it, susceptible to exposure, marked for expulsion. However dispersed and disbanded, these figures put out cables to neighboring surrogates of man. Henceforth, being does not consist apart from the "with"; it exposes itself as the *between* and *with* of singularities. Throughout their curriculum of fiction and

* See Philippe Lacoue-Labarthe, "In the Name of . . . ," in *Retreating the Political.*

insistent reversion to the paternal—even where it has been disqualified, yet continues to run out the clock—still models the essential pull of authority, or Authority. Authority.

We don't know whether we need it or flee from it, if we need it in order to flee, to keep the motor going for the purpose of questioning its empty essence. As a start-off point that doesn't look back or look down, as fantasized lever, the paternal still has a hold on power, the way it's shaped, the way it's justified and used. The paternal goes hand in hand with the fantasy of Identification—something left over, Nancy suggests, from monarchical and other forms of divinely appointed regimes that require identificatory passes. These habits, linked as they are to paternal subsistence, spill into contemporary democratic formations. By contrast, opening the lens on democratic multiformity, let us imagine that democracy had room for a Nietzschean lifeline and could affirm itself as a nonfigural opening for the incalculable that escapes political determination—for unaccountable inlets of joy, poetry, delight, and the wide embrace of creativity. These waves of an unaccountable exorbitance comprise qualities or belong to practices that, for the most part, have fallen to the political wayside by means (or lack of means) of *undervaluation*. They have become undervalued or *nonvalued*—hence Nancy, for his part, revisits the Marxist notion of surplus to retrieve an *undervalue* that ought to be gauged with or without capital's insistence on equivalencies. Let us understand that such a democracy—fired off by Nietzschean velocities and aneconomic surges of poeticity, carried over by the abandon with which music rips into existence, and that calls for the overflow of what remains undervalued—strictly *refuses Identification*, refuses the coercive pull of paternal adhesiveness and patterns of valuation. Undervaluation operates alongside the thought of transvaluation. Its affirmed recedence approaches in Nancy's vocabulary a kind of breakthrough deauthorization of prized qualities and practices, whether transcendental or flatfooted and decidedly empirical.

The disbandment or renunciation of the major spectrum of identification indicated by Nancy, "whether it was borne by the image of a king, a Father, a God, a Nation, a Republic, a People, a Man or a Humanity, even indeed a Democracy—does not at all contradict the demand of identification in the sense of the possibility that each and everyone identify (nowadays we like to say 'subjectivize') with a place, role and value—each inestimable—in the situation of being-together" (50). Never entirely effaceable, identification

---

related essays by Tom Cohen, Gil Anidjar, Thomas Pepper, and Elisabeth Weber in *Reading Ronell*, edited and introduced by Diane Davis (Urbana and Chicago: University of Illinois Press, 2009).

correspondence, Kafka's texts appear to inch toward the predicament of exposed being, undeliverable and abandoned.

Very little can be taken for granted in Kafka's world. The paternal stabilizers, glowering and inescapable, phase themselves out in peculiar ways. Though cast in their omnipotence, we never know for sure what fathers are, nor can we be sure to call down what identifies the son. Kafka makes us start from scratch over and again as he stages the inevitability of sharing what cannot be shared, of discerning between Mitsein on the one hand and the logic of the other from another perspective—fundamental if intrusive structures that make continual claims upon his writing. Bound over to the other or to the strictures of being-with, the creatures or "animots" and figures that populate these works show the contours of copresence in a world devoid of substantial measure. In the "Letter" that has been entrusted to us, the stakes of this "co" are precisely what Franz tries to negotiate with the elder Mr. Kafka. He measures continually the spaces allotted to the "co" that defines his characters, such as they are, and around which language is constructed. The son remains confounded by the *between* and *with* that dominate scenes of unbreakable attachment and reveal the strange co-parenting of reciprocally stifling histories.

Kafka's writings show tremendous restraint and the struggle of *responsibility* that emerges with his depositions. For the most part, Kafka subscribes to that responsibility which thought is—what Nietzsche and Nancy have designated in different ways as the responsibility of the *not*: not to let oneself be taken by a clench of sense, not to identify with it, not to assign or embody it definitively, not to figure or reify it.* In a way that compels me, sometimes despite myself, Kafka makes us start from scratch over and again, back peddling toward a region of troubled origins: Neither father nor son is assured a place in a work that still embeds these functions. The fissuring qualities of the figures and functions on which he must rely is something that Kafka's texts underscore emphatically. Yet, these very figures, ever in default and on the edge of extinction, are shown to codetermine worlds and take us outside.

The abiding complicities of these figural anchors allow the grammars of politics to behave as though we all knew what the meaning of these

---

* I have discussed the Nietzschean "not" (*nicht*) of responsible self-legislation and signoff in *The Test Drive* (Urbana and Chicago: University of Illinois Press, 2005).

still has its run, though without substantial backup or recognizable goalpost. Democracy is not figurable; or rather, it is not in essence figural in the sense that democracy "dispenses with the assumption of a figuration of a destiny, or a common truth" (50). Democracy, however, imposes the need for configuring common space in such a way as to allow for opening an infinite breach to sustain figures of our affirmations, declarations, shouts, desires. In the section titled "Partage de l'incalculable" (The Share—Or Division—of the Incalculable), Nancy calls for an excess or loosening of the oeuvre, a "plus-que-l'oeuvre ou un désoeuvrement" on which existence relies. What does this mean? We have been too greatly fixed on the order of exchangeable goods to the detriment of what escapes exchange value: the inexchangeable, the without-value. If we have been unable to summon the courage to focus on the inexchangeables, this is simply because what is without-value is outside any measurable value: "La part du sans-valeur—parti du partage de l'incalculable, et donc à strictement parler impartageable—excède à la politique" (33). The place where capital and democracy lock in on each other gives rise to an overreliance on measurable determination, presupposing a culture that latches onto every side (or inch, or dimension, or shard) of existence with the demand for overevaluation or the belief that everything must and can be submitted to measure, evaluation, distributable shares.

What about those events or things that evade the calculable or any cognitive grid or system of quantifiable returns? This is where the consistent particulars of psychoanalytic "devaluations" come in handy. When psychoanalysis takes measure, it inescapably downsizes and disrupts the headcounts and evaluations on which democratic politics tends to depend.[9] Henceforth what counts (and miscounts) must be submitted to a more fraying logic posed by qualities of ambivalence, postponement, compulsion, vicissitude, discontent—disorderly axioms, broken categories, the aporias bleeding into the spreadsheet to shake up what may have settled in the columns of the political unconscious and various accepted practices, which leave out for the most part what disturbs or ignores "the political" as it scales itself upward in contemporary theories and behaviors.

My scope is more restless than to stay put with what can still be identified as political. By compulsion or scholarly habit, I need to keep digging, if only to come close to the phasedown and refused calls that appear to block the

9. From Derrida's count-off and deconstruction of majorities to Rancière's notion of democratic miscount, numbers and ratings have entered the contemporary philosophical weigh-in on political existence. The third and the One, differently assessed in Sartre through Levinas, also attempt to resignify how politics counts.

defining words and their referential radius might stipulate—as if the material habits of world could still be mobilized by the implacability of these paleonyms. If anything, precisely by taking recourse to radical disfiguration, Kafka was the one to take down the modern family and the burdened assurances of meaning that familialism has continued to exert on political tropologies. Little can be taken for granted after Kafka, and even the positioning of the son cannot as such be redirected, with a quasi-theological push, to represent a grant or gift that could be said to originate with what is called Father.

❁ ❁ ❁

For his part, Freud started us off on the story of an immemorial *Vatermord,* digging deeply into the unconscious history of parricidal rage. Kafka, heedful of the totems and taboos set down by Freud, contributed to the world irrepressible stories about fathers banishing and destroying their children. Sharing the same insight, both Kafka and Freud start up their search engines to fix on the crime scene of ur-clashes. The effort to determine whose killer impulse started the row is possibly a trivial matter. Is it not sometimes childish to wonder who's at fault? Who's to say which of the posited roles can be charged unhesitatingly with having prompted inversion, projection, displacement, or with hiding the murder weapon? Perhaps we can investigate how the expertise of strategic survival techniques has been trained on its object—or, according to some evidence, rescinded. Something happened in the anahistory of a still-gripping psychic heritage that leads one to engage the residual virulence of the paternal metaphor. The work of disinstalling a lock on the imaginary that holds these figures over the fire of material consequence remains a vivid part of the Kafkan legacy.

very areas that I investigate, often against the grain of sanctioned protocols of reading. Perhaps this is where we might situate some of the questions that rise up around authority—precisely in the reluctance to propose a new protocol or prescription for identification. Nonetheless, all movements or addresses of revolution—including those of reform, rebel causes, mutiny, disobedience, refractoriness, protest, and insurgency—start off by turning against a standing authority in the hope of resignifying its intentional stances and discernible effects. Thus in his analysis of the implications for us today of the more-or-less-aborted rebellion historicized as "'68" (and what it means to name an event or advent with a date), Nancy observes that '68 consisted of an irruption or disruption that introduced no new figure, no new proceedings, and certainly no new authority. What mattered was not so much the bringing to light of an "anti-authoritarian" demand. Rather, one of the critical facets of '68 resided in showing that "authority" (Nancy hangs it up in quotation marks) can be defined by no prior authorization, be it institutional, canonic, normed, but only by the expression of a desire that is recognized in it. He keeps this political desire empty of any psychologistic aspect or subjectivism, making it rather a matter of flexing a genuine possibility of being, and thus retrieving a true power of being ("l'expression d'une vraie possibilité et donc d'une vraie puissance d'être").[10] Locating a powerful, perhaps even empowering potency or the abundance of sheer being (without sliding into power politics or bolstering the self and its filial agencies), Nancy orients his thought to the entwined fates of democracy and authority. If democracy is to have any meaning, it must be linked to exercising and *showing* reservation about what gets authority's imprint.

Democracy's meaning comes about when we show ourselves capable of being reserved about attaching authority to such significations as bear the stamp of an identifiable elsewhere, enlisting any register other than that of a desire, even an anticipation. Democracy involves a thinking in which a genuine possibility of being can be expressed and recognized *for all concerned*, for each and everyone. Maybe the attraction to such an indulgent degree of possibility, exhilaratingly endless and radically apportioned, is what in some cases has fueled the enthusiasm for revolutionary promise. Why is it that enthusiasm is off the table when democracy rises up for discussion? Of course, too much enthusiasm, as Nietzsche, warns, is not a good thing: its perkiness can come close to stupidity or ideological error. Still, why must

10. Nancy reads 1968 against the grain of reflections marking its fortieth anniversary. See *Vérité de la democratie* (Paris: Galilée, 2008), 29.

democracy be treated by so many fine minds as a bummer, too dull to engage critical valor? Perhaps when democracy fails the reality tests to which it is always submitted, it depletes the *demos*, and is no longer recognizable as democracy and its exuberant exposures. One would also have to probe the enthusiasm for democracy where it is not, as revealed by fantasies or promises or uprisings that have stirred in its name. We should remember the difference in tenor, the nearly contradictory fervor that words such as "communism" and "socialism" have carried historically in comparison with the pallid advocacy that "democracy" has summoned to its side. Putting itself in a serious dilemma, democracy has discarded all too quickly, with a facile if not phobic turn, the portion of communicity that it enfolds—in part because it is too caught up in managing, accounting and counting, tallying up its gains, standstills and losses, in a space deprived of desire. Who feels the pump of desire in today's so-called democratic formations? Something of the kind spread around the world with the election of Barack Obama, only then to vanish into the dreary spaces of the undesiring machines of problematic governance. Nancy, in a Deleuzian phase of his cycle, which returns every so often, puts more store in desire than I might be able to defend. I can attach only to Lyotard's critique of affect, asking about the drainage of affect that chronically afflicts democracy. I understand what Nancy may be advocating when he calls up desire, and I sympathize with this turn, provided that it stay complicated, positively hounded by the prompts that take us beyond the pleasure principle, exposing itself to risk and failure at every bend. Where our democracies try to stay risk-free, they run the greatest risks, and in this sense desire might supply the motor for facing the lack that democracy requires and sustains.

Revolutionary promise and democratic practice. For now, can we integrate a lesson from '68 into our reflections on politics and authority? Clearly, as rebellion, what we call '68, whether in France, Japan, or the United States, was halted, aborted before it took down a number of walls—much in the way revolution in Hegel stops short of itself, breaking its stride.[11] In practical terms, '68 pulled the brakes when, instead of recoiling, it could have made a startling pact with its own incursive potential. But at a level of political legibility, '68 stopped itself from bringing in a new

11. See Rebecca Comay's discussion of shorted rebellion in Hegel's reflection on revolution in *Mourning Sickness: Hegel and the French Revolution* (Stanford, Calif.: Stanford University Press, 2010).

team of managers, new and different models for governance, or a different performance of authority. Nonetheless, something did come through from the mangled history of a near revolt: '68 managed to deliver an affirmation that freed itself up from any and all identification. In sum, it gave authority some slack, a bit of a free pass without the noose—without the executioner or partial interest group standing by with the machinery of law enforcement. This gives "authority" a new face, if only in a discrete way. Withdrawing some of the more restrictive qualities that we tend to associate historically with authority, Nancy situates it in terms of a kind of replenishment for our life together in this world. He places authority alongside powerful enhancers of being, as an expression of a desire and commitment that moves existence without letting it regress or reduce to a figure of substantial destiny, a people, a religious attachment or definitive identity.

In more Derrida-on-Nietzsche terms we can ask about the *responsibility* of authority and how it counts for a vitalized sense of existence, how it can be addressed to the everyone to whom democracy owes its explanations and proposed generosity of care. We still need to consider in terms of address who and what gets left out of the politics of all in democratic practice. The emphasis placed on the incalculable yet precise cipher of "any and all," "each and every single one" to whom authority is answerable and from whom and of which it springs, requires a calculating machine rigged differently from the ones that have been counting too many of us out.

Never one to ease up on my colleagues or myself, I must question what it means to propose an action or restart, no matter how restrained, what it could possibly mean nowadays to call for another breakdown of how we go about things, projecting a different way of calculating or "incalculating." Does it make sense—enough or too much sense—to call for essential reworking? Is such a call even feasible in our day and ages? Perhaps, in terms of the algorithms of *feasibility* to which so much has been steadily degraded, one will raise the objection that all this—the reopening of the case of democracy, strengthening its tether to the authority of the each and every one—is not workable. "Workable!" I say. Maybe this is where we part ways, or maybe this is when a friendship can be imagined among us, because I grow suspicious of what has been established as workable. This tendency to settle on the workable is part of the structure of dismissing inventive inroads, whether speculative or pragmatically wrangled, as unworkable. The dependency on the workable—or the fantasy of the workable, I should say—relying on that which gets dragged down to the limiting perspective of what can be calculated, known, understood, exchanged, is, to my way of thinking, what needs to be broken.

103

So. Where does this leave us as we head toward the struggles of Kafka, Lyotard, and others as they prepared to face the very same professions of concern—well, admittedly not every single one of them—that have filled these pages? In the upcoming sections I would like to convince myself of how committed Kafka was to taking on these enigmas and, from another perspective, not incompatible with that of Kafka, I'd like to get Lyotard to show you his cards and play out his acute regard for historical disturbance, due in large part to the pressures of patriarchal overload. The engagement with authority opened the way, I hope, for another type of encounter with the aggravation and distress that has beset our fractured worlds. There are still other routes to take, other ways to explore some of the stinging implications of authority's reach. We have not closed the reflections on the corrosive swell of authority, its indwelling improbity as long as it takes off from the premises of the father, shutting down the incalculable dimensions of its reputedly protective registers. If these reflections have not been closed, this nonclosure tells us something about the persistence of the paternal with which Freud is still contending. How indeed would one distinguish between bracketing the paternal function in order to encourage an alternative thought from the very parricidal gesture that the law of the paternal function dictates?

◎ ◎ ◎

PS—Permit me one more round with the paternal signifier, its complica-tions and call-outs, for, to believe Kafka and Lyotard, one will never finish with the "mainmise"—the hands-on or throttle—of Father or knockoffs of God and leader. There are still other narratives that stage the torment of those who assume the signifier, find themselves ambushed by its claims, beginning (at least) with Abrahamic tradition, and ride out the disturbed endowment of paternity. Levinas, who does not as such debate the warrants of paternity, nonetheless proceeds from the certainty of its traumatic edges and uncanniness. Even where the "relation with the child [. . .] establishes relationship with the absolute future, or infinite time," the certain inex-haustibility contains the trauma of this unhappy father-son lock.[12] There is the angle, moreover, beginning (at least) as soon as Laius is up for his turn, of seeing the designated father's horror of paternity when faced with the monstrosity of his "son." Of a mirror-quality in filiality, Levinas writes, if not quite letting go:

12. Emmanuel Levinas, *Totality and Infinity: An Essay on Exteriority*, trans. Alphonso Lingus (Pittsburgh, Penna.: Duquesne University Press, 1969), 268.

Possession of the child by the father does not exhaust the meaning of the relationship that is accomplished in paternity, where the father discovers himself not only in the gestures of the son, but in his substance and unicity. My child is a stranger (Isaiah 49), but a stranger who is not only mine, for his *is* me. He is a stranger to myself.[13]

Expropriated and dispossessed by the very relation in which everything seems to originate, father, ever a victor—Frankenstein, that is, a Victor Frankenstein—comes to himself only to be estranged in the son. I have by no means meant to simplify things or imply that one knows even where or how to locate the terms of these relations that nonetheless commonly exert oppressive effects and exercise dominion. Whether or not we can seize upon paternity with cognitive levers and recognizable descriptions, we continue to return to this petrified configuring of finite being as if, precisely, it could spring us from the strictures of finitude. Following a number of decapitations, downsizes, and strikeouts of the paternal, Lacan has suggested that the father finally is possibly better than nothing, though one is the worse for it. At the end of the day we are saddled, when we go after ground and figure, either with the *père* or *pire* (the father or even worse). Everything indicates to me that you should go for the *pire*, risk the worst. Choose your weapons.

13. Ibid., 267.

Chapter 4

The Good Loser

Kafka Sends Off a Missive to Father

"Was wissen die Kinder!" ("What do children know!")
—Kafka, "Letter"

"Bittendes Kind" ("Pleading Child")
—Schumann, *Kinderszenen* op. 15

Without fail, writing looped back to the submissiveness stipulated by childhood. The experience of surrender had its unstoppable velocities from day one and carried the day, every day, seeing the leveling effects of childhood into political majority. The thought of "becomings" was dashed from the start. One was stunted—except, possibly, for the sudden assault of an occasional metamorphosis. For Franz, in any case, the writer was hard-pressed to stand up straight, to shake off an iron grip that was pushing down, it seemed, from above—or maybe from within. Like the aphonic call in Heidegger's work, an obligating menace appears to come *from beyond me and within me.* You don't hear it but you know it's there, wherever "there" is, and that it originates both from above and within. I'm already repeating myself, above and within, above and within. A teacherly habit, to repeat oneself, but is it transferable to writing, I wonder. Already repeating myself—in the first paragraph! (Sometimes I proceed too quickly and leave a blur in my trail. I want to be clear with this text, stop the drive-by speed up of writing. It's good to repeat. Often it's necessary, if you want some sense-making to happen after all is said and done.) So, in Heidegger—we're talking *Being and Time*—a call comes at you simultaneously from beyond and within, tracing a double provenance. By the time Kafka was at the desk, the "within" part was no longer locatable, though. He had scuttled interiority and was working under the new management of variant strains of self, for the most part unrecognizably handed down and in many ways mangled. To be fair, Heidegger, too, when his turn came, was not merely shoring up an interiority of self. But I don't see much evidence of a childhood trauma in Heidegger's motif of the call with maybe one exception: the dramatic residue of a lost friend that stays forever on the line. Kafka offers a different delivery and storyline for the call he had to take. Whether or not he was equipped to handle its damages is another story still.

Kafka, for his part, could barely climb out of the traversals of passivity, the determined constraints of childhood. Rigged to last, childhood outfitted the writer's pose: one is bent over, writing at the behest of another, ever prepared to submit. The so-called "Letter to Father" reprises such a history of submission, and, if I am not mistaken, the greater part of Kafka's works meet their limit of intelligibility whenever prodded by thematized adulthood—a defining birthday, a sexual encounter, a job, the time and responsibilities of manning up, attaining legal majority. The only way to have made it over to something like adulthood would have been by contracting to marriage, by starting a family and becoming Father: so goes the critical narrative that crawls under Kafka's texts. The dilemma of becoming the father that one wished to avoid had Kafka doubled over in pain or in stitches, depending on the day or on the momentary stakes. He was under the sway of an injunction—his very own categorical imperative strapped with unbeatable aporias and destructive contradictions. The law of the Father was always closing in on him, taunting, yet proposing, despite it all, the seductions of a takeover. The one way to get out was to go in, to take it on.

Well, this strategic plan was not limited to Franz Kafka or hardly ran off the charts of filial ambivalence; yet, he remaindered it like no other.

⊗ ⊗ ⊗

He gave us the close-up of parasitical existence but only by giving it a paradoxical run: on fast spin cycle, the parasite turns into predator, shedding all substantiality before receding back into parasite hell. Unwelcome and excremental, the parasite in Kafka, bloated on guilt and primed on shame, experiences itself as predatory excess. Nonetheless, parasitical vigor proves ever prepared to pounce, to scratch, and to sink back into the system of traces that we understand as writing. Existentially unavoidable, the parasite marks the spot where writing begins and life is sucked out of any internal field of expectation. Kafka, like Lyotard after him, teaches that every child arrives on the scene as a parasite, prey to the infanticidal phantasms of predator

107

parents. Among other things, the starting line of nearly human existence has meant that, in order to avoid this crushing knowledge, we have had to divinize the child and airlift it up into transcendental zones, making it God and angel-like. Kafka shows up right before the dialectical switch is implemented and keeps the child down on an existential ground level. If you are still hugging representations of a toughened and secure state, however, or are still inclined to side with Mr. Kafka, father of Franz, and other authoritarian figures in crisis, the child (a first immigrant) is powered by the potentiality to arrive, from the get-go, as gruesome predator, invading and parasiting hapless parents. That said, it is still possible that every child arrives to destroy the family, as Hegel already knew.

Franz Kafka wants out of the parasite-predator polarity, if there might be an outside to such a consistently sticky ordeal. He imagines and posits that becoming a father could spring him from the oppressive quagmire of predatory parasite or parasitic predator. To embrace fatherhood would mean, as Kafka several times indicates, to have arrived, to have coincided with and nailed a destination. As father, he could have coincided even with a proper death—to the extent that destination and death always imply each other, as let on in a "final destination." The address of father—as phantasm, rhetorical custom or biogenetic prop—is set as literature's telic anxiety, the homecoming for which poets have stood and rhetors posed, from Odysseus's address to Zeus to Saul Bellow's sit-down in *Seize the Day*, to appeals made in Dennis Cooper's work to Daddy, to Daddy's appeal in Kathy Acker's Oedipalizations, to Hélène Cixous's counterphobic laugh of the Medusa, and so on and so forth. As complicated as locating the father gets in his works, Franz Kafka, for his part, will never have reached the station of father, just as the letter cannot reach its registered destination, but in the end allows the fiction of paternity to collapse on itself. The failure of the letter to arrive, the failure of Franz to make it past a highly invested boundary, involves a number of deflections that are crucial for the fate of literature. Bearing in mind Freud's statement that "Fate" and "Father" (**FAT**h**E**r) share the same structure in the unconscious, we will trace their merging itineraries in Kafka.

Now a free-standing book, the "Letter to Father," which traces a history of traumatic interruptions, is, as Heidegger might but could never have said, a destiny for us. It is a destiny to the extent that it corrupts destinal presumptions and reroutes literature around paternal markers never to be reached or assumed. Fiction shoots out of the wound of unbearable paternity. Among the things that it has going for it are the crucial stalls and breakdowns, the persistent parasitical drainage of which this text remains an unprecedented record. The letter enfolds a destiny that cannot come

to pass, if only because the terms of arrival have been withdrawn from its account, delegitimated. The "Letter" tells us of its impossible itinerary in so many ways and sets itself up as a substitute for a type of writing that it serves to erase. Up close and intimate, the "Letter" refuses to disclose its subject or open a historical account.

For rhetorically rigorous reasons, Kafka is no longer capable of full-blown biography, though the "Letter" unavoidably gathers up and posts biographical material. History and its satellite narratives have been exhausted as Kafka edges toward a limit of the sayable. Memory, in any case, is always thrown into question, as the attempt at history persistently falls prey to false memory, disruption, aberration, secondary revision, and other transmission problems such as unavoidable static (which the French language designates as "parasites" or "phantoms"). Any trace of a history or development has been crushed by the expropriation of experience that Father flags. As in "The Judgment," the patriarch stands up for a hijacked experience of friendship and love when, for instance, he takes away the friend from Russia—a destination crucial to the imaginary mapping and letter writing of Georg Bendemann. When Father shoots down the friend, he cuts off Georg's supply line and escape route; he removes the life-sustaining destination that gave Georg a sense of a possible history, if only in the transmuted form of a geographical remove—the promise of distance. He needed little to get some protection from paternal encroachments and pernicious outreach programs, for remote geographics sufficed to keep him going in a world where tropes of referential overflow, when they were not closing in on him, were in any case defunct. Biography and history, which imply an inner transformation and some type of locomotion, are halted by the father's imperious inflations and by the son's corresponding incapacitation, his inability to separate from paternal annexations: the father takes up space and poaches figures that might mark out a separate existence or an independent motor experience. If anything, the "Letter" tells of the drainage of experience, of life flattened out, impoverished and parasited by the paternal predecessor. (The father is not only predecessor, however; he vampirizes the future—he is the *suckcessor*.) Few things can be translated into experience; it is as if Father were the affective correlative of a mall or time stuck in an elevator, or perhaps he evokes the rising rage of idling in traffic, where one is slowly wasted, in a perpetual slump, pretending to move forward or advance in life.

Stuck with Hermann Kafka for a father, Kafka starts up the *Hermann*eutics that keeps Franz running—or creeping, as he often writes—in place. As with the war-weary soldiers that according to Benjamin return from battle worn down and emptied of experience, unable henceforth to accumulate stories and history, Franz has traded in experience for authority.[1] Authority, though emptied by now of transcendental mooring, props itself up in the space vacated by history, forked over by experience. Deregulated and eerily pervasive, authority cannot be proven or demonstrated or even easily recanted, but is imposed as a force that experience, weakened and run-down, can no longer unhinge. Abandoned by history and bereft of the rumored solidity of experience, the son can offer only testimony, an attestation to his muffled voice and diminished pose in an experience-less space. There is no question of initiating a story, replenishing a world, or starting off on an adventure. Even "adventure" implies an overload of agency in terms of possible experience. At best the son can negotiate a position between reactive rage and responsive marginality. Franz chooses to agitate on the margins of a history occupied and closed off to him by Hermann. His letter starts as a citation, as if picking up a call: "You asked me recently why I maintain that I am afraid of you" (Du hast mich letzthin gefragt warum ich behaupte, ich hätte Furcht von Dir). The text continues: "As usual, I didn't know what to answer, in part due to fear. . . ." (Ich wusste Dir, wie gewöhnlich, nichts zu antworten, zum Teil eben aus der Furcht, die ich vor Dir habe). It is not possible to speak before Father, to answer his call live and within his range of reception. Franz offers instead a written response that also threatens to crumble under the weight of the father's demand, but he can at least give it a go. Granting fear its due, Franz partially rebounds to take up an engagement with the very thing that paralyzes him.

Franz Kafka, the megawriter as parasite, can practice a politics of address only in a dead pose, which is in any case inherent to the logic of deferral dictated by writing. Even efforts to speak to the father end up as a kind of writing, to the extent that it is technologized into a stammer, never gelling into intelligible speech but at most resembling the squeaks and screeches that Kafka's talking animals nervously emit. Kafka, stumped by the question that repeats the violence after which it inquires, picks up the interrupted relay with the characteristic ambivalence of a remembered prod. For his part, the father had not asked, "Why are you afraid of me?"—a question that would imply a specific protocol of possible responses—but, "Why do you maintain," or, "Why do you assert that you are afraid of me?" In other words, the question goes after language as much as after its ostensible object; it

---

1. See Agamben's treatment of Walter Benjamin's "Der Erzähler" in *Enfance et histoire: Dépérissement de l'expériènce et origine de l'histoire*, trans. Yves Hersaut (Paris: Éditions Payot, 1989), 19–25.

delivers an accusation, insinuates a pose, and announces the addressee's rhetorical duplicity: it asks about the legitimacy of the child's fear and his right to maintain it—as if fearfulness ought to and could have been renounced, as if the child should have signed a waiver, given up a certain type of truth claim. "Stop claiming or pretending to be afraid of me, stop using language in such a way as to betray and fight me." The father's question as resuscitated by the "Letter" is more a philosophical indictment than an affective-psychological or even ontological query. Still, it hits home. "Why do we *maintain* that we are fearful," his father wants to know, rather than, more psychoanalytically tilted, "What is the source of fear?" or more simply even: "Why do you fear me?" I will not approach other possible versions that would have him asking, "What do I do to instill fear in you?" Such a redescription, cast as paternal concern, would have him skidding off the parameters of the Kafkan predicament as regards the orientation of this phrase. Nonetheless, this being Kafka, the indication of possible paternal concern is also what trips him up. For nothing guarantees that Father is not stating his weakness and bewilderment, wondering why on earth his son, so resourceful and competent, so capable of outmaneuvering his hapless father, feigns fear.

The record of fear that Franz presents at the "Letter"'s beginning progresses like an anasemic narrative track, for it reveals an alternate semantics that rules over the range of response. The earliest memory of being menaced by the father is recovered fairly quickly in the text. A child starts tallying the episodes that have led him to maintain his fear. He starts checking off punishing memories. The first and primal scene takes place as a splash of water (*Wasser*) and simulation of thirst, recalling an early desire or *demande* put out by baby Franz. A call for water opens up an entire switchboard of aggression. A first provocative language attack, the call gets circuited as something unremittingly addressed, as part of the wearing-down that the child practices upon the father, and for which he is traumatically punished. The scene is set by two initiatory events of some consequence, so let us hold off on going directly to the spout. With or without the water episode, was Hermann survivable?

I claimed to locate the beginning of the letter in its statement of fearful reticence on the part of the writer. In fact, the letter characteristically begins with the salutation and address, with a struggle over how to open the address. The manuscript shows a hesitation here. In the end Kafka settles on, "Liebster Vater" (Dearest Father) over "Lieber Vater" (Dear Father)—dear or dearest? Dearest? Dear Father? While I do not wish to go into an exegetical flurry over the address, I do not see how tuning to its implications can be avoided. The accompanying interpretive difficulties lie at the heart of this address and the multiplicity of ambiguities for which it allows. Among other things, "dearest" prompts the supposition that Kafka has chosen to call upon the dearest of all fathers, one most dear among others less dear, thus splitting up possible fathers toward which the letter orients itself. I do not necessarily want to "overread" this initial moment, wishing only to signal that I could spend many paragraphs on the way the address already calls on its own trouble-making potentialities, splitting and doubling Father in such a way as to take him down, or at least pull him away from his purported unicity. This being Kafka's world, one is authorized to stagger before things properly start, assuming that Kafka at all allows for any kind of running start, and not just a slump before the law of composition. Kafka struggled over the address, making the decision to summon the *most beloved* of his fathers. Will the smart missile find such an address?

Franz claims that he would have been able to survive Hermann Kafka had he been known to him as a friend, a boss, an uncle, a grandfather, "even (though more hesitatingly) as a father-in-law."[2] (The irony of the hypothetical marriage that would render Hermann father-in-law, marked with hesitation by Franz, leads to vertiginous interpretive calculations that we'll leave to the side.) Kafka adds, "Only as a father you have been too strong for me." Too close, too powerful, the father's authority is moreover consolidated by the death of two brothers and by the fact that the Kafka sisters were born long after, leaving Franz in early youth to fend for himself. "Only as a father you have been too strong for me, particularly since my brothers died when they were small and my sisters came along only much later, so that I alone had to bear the brunt of it (*ich also den ersten Stoss ganz allein aushalten musste*)—and for that I was much too weak." Franz had to take the first hit all alone, *ganz allein.* Hélène Cixous has offered a reading in her seminar of the hyperbolic doubling of "all alone." Why, she asks in the context of Proust's "tout seul," does being alone have to be further qualified by the totality of all (*ganz*)? For Kafka the surplus totality indicated by *ganz allein* may work differently than in Proust where "all" inches toward cosmic depletion and doubles the sum of possible aloneness. For Proust, the addition of "all" to qualify "alone" implies a subtraction, an intensification of the experience of being alone. In Kafka, the "all" suggests an add-on. It is as if Kafka, for his part and parties, were arranging a spectral colloquy, an *all*-inclusive gathering of the living and the dead when addressing the father.

2. Franz Kafka, "Letter to Father," trans. Ernst Kaiser and Eithne Wilkins, in *The Sons* (New York: Schocken Books, 1989), 117. Subsequent references are cited parenthetically in the text.

If Franz found himself *all* alone in childhood, this is because they were *all* there, crowded in his aloneness: he was not only alone but in the haunting company of dead siblings. Two little ones preceded him but could not make it, leaving Franz at once stronger—he made it—and weakened, a kind of degeneration or parasitical remnant of the perished brothers. Franz does not say how or why they died, but he lines up their disappearance with his father's persecutory powers. Nietzsche, another loner who invents free spirits for company, furtively mentions a dead brother in *Ecce Homo*, where the father is positioned as an existential passerby, possessing qualities of a fleeting memory. Here the corpses are stacked up against the father, further numbing the son's chances of viability. It's not entirely clear if Franz has incorporated the dead brothers: is he now doing their bidding for them, working pro bono for the dead? In terms of now-classic theories of mourning disorder or pathology, is he putting in claims for restitution? The unmournable brothers create a blockage in the passageways of the "Letter." Franz is enfeebled, vampirically seized by the strictures of unmournability. His experience of weakness is linked directly to their demise. Being *"all* alone"—what about this hyperbolic surplus, why are we *all* alone, isn't it hard enough to be just alone?—this predicament of aggravated aloneness appears to mean that he stands in the buffer zone *with* the phantom brothers, *with* the trace of their extinguished existence. His stance, up against the paternal wall, tethers him to a frayed concept of the *with/without*: he is being-without, arrested at the premature deaths that mark his toppled upbringing, indicating from the start that he was always and ever raised from the dead.

Abandoned and exposed, part of a muffled history of the undead, Franz has to go it alone. He starts out, very young, as a survivor or parasite, paradoxically strong enough—precisely because of his fragility and minimalist life—to crawl past a first marker. The structure of his survival is such that the immemorial fault is distributed equally between his father and himself. Keeping things ambivalent, his sense of who did what to whom remains at times weak. There are no indictments, no witnesses, no subpoenaed evidence, just a structural insinuation: the brothers were killed off/Franz somehow got away. Alive, he's more dead, or at least more vulnerable than the terminated children. At the same time Franz weighs in on the *strength* of his parasitical existence, living off the dead brothers to whom he owes an unpayable debt. The way he settles the narrative account gives a Freudian-Derridian orientation to the matter, as he goes over territory covered by *Totem and Taboo*. Deprived of the fraternal horde, he had no chance of overcoming his father, no primal alliance or secured lineage to support patricidal rites. (To recap: *Totem and Taboo* establishes the law and lay of patricide, the mythic core of any serious reflection on *Vatermord* and is dependent on a notion of vital fraternity, which Derrida follows all the way up to political structures anchored in the orders of *fraternité, liberté, égalité*.) The sisters were late in coming and the brothers had been dealt a fatal blow. Franz Kafka does not examine the impact of the decimated fraternal horde, the dead weight that thematically holds down the halfway launched letters; he goes only far enough to nail his exposed solitude on the missing brothers. Without the living fraternity, patricide is off the table. If anything, they owe *him* interest and taxes for the exertions he has had to make as the solitary successor, with and without his brothers, going it alone, all alone, as the pretender that father evermore took him to be. One of his brothers, Georg, returns in name, harangued by his father to commit suicide at the end of "The Judgment." The other sibling, Heinrich, leaves less recoverable traces.

Whether pretender to the paternal throne or henceforth lined up with the world of pretense—without the siblings covering his back, he'll have to fake it relentlessly—Franz signs up for the school of make-believe. Pitched against the virile claims of truth and phallus, he sees himself becoming girly. Father, we are informed time and again, cannot abide the world of pretense. The values of pretense, artifice, parasitism, and language manipulation quickly load up on Franz's side of the line. Allied with and proxy of truth, Father disavows pretense, what Derrida in his essay on this text translates as *feindre* (to feign or make believe). Kafka's father sees himself as courageous, capable of dispensing with politeness, and other surplus niceties, en famille. Other fathers, the argument pressed by Hermann Kafka is quoted as saying, feign interest, pretend politeness, they lack the courage to judge or act according to the sometime brutal precepts of honesty. This well-known logic conventionally covers for rude oppressions and pseudo-dialogue ("I was just being honest"). Let us get a close-up of this rhetorical standoff and examine its life-threatening edges. Paternal frankness cuts an incision in Franz's stance with the world and lines up with the law. How does the "Letter" drop into the abyss of their relatedness, configuring the paternal as emissary of law?

One of the first disputes that the letter tries to settle involves the father's assertion that he is different from other fathers only insofar as "I can't pretend as other people can" (116). Franz responds in the letter, "You can't pretend, that is true . . ." The response becomes more intricate, indicating in the main that the father seeks a no-fault escape, which Franz cannot grant—though neither party is simply free from blame (or innocent), either. What interests me is the inventive extension of "other fathers" when we know that Franz shows up as artifice, the solicitor of pretense, the prince of make-believe. Colloquially, Hermann's rhetoric serves to set him apart from a whole class of fathers who might indulge their sons, feign praise, stage pride, lather on fictions, or something of the sort. But in this face-off another logic soon emerges, especially since the notion of father is highly contested or a matter of considerable pretense, creativity, and construction.

The other father referred to by Hermann would be Franz—the defending champion of fiction, the fiction-father, the one who puts his father to fiction and carries off the pretense from which Hermann repeatedly dissociates. Hermann and Franz circumscribe different fields of battle for the purpose of motivating their plaints. In order to fight the father, Franz has to prepare a plan for taking down the father's name, or at least for taking it on for another round. Brought up between the dead brothers and not yet manifest sisters, Franz enters a battle of proper names, unlinking the very sign of survival—the name, whose mark is meant to secure surviving beyond the perishability of its bearer. Who truly belongs to the name *Kafka*? Who or what gets to live on in and as this name? On the other hand, who gets cast as a parasitical hitchhiker living off an eminent patronym? The name, apart from any act of subjective volition or eventual agency, is in principle passed on from father to son as untamperable inheritance. But something occurs in the transit. The young Mr. Kafka wears his father's name uncomfortably, as a fake ID of which he can only expect trouble. This is where pretense and fiction—what his father accuses him of perpetrating—begin to serve him, for his is, he claims, only a pretend-name. It thus turns out that Kafka is his improper name, truly the name-of-the-father. "You, on the other hand, a true Kafka in strength, health, appetite, loudness of voice, eloquence, self-satisfaction, worldly dominance, endurance, presence of mind, knowledge of human nature, a certain way of doing things on a grand scale, of course also with all the defects and weaknesses that go with these advantages and into which your temperament and sometimes your hot temper drive you" (117). The signatory does not bear his name fully, to the extent that a truly binding signature is possible. "I, to put it in a very much abbreviated form, a Löwy with a certain Kafka component which, however, is not set in motion by the Kafka will to life, business, and conquest, but by a Löwyish spur that impels more secretly, more diffidently, and in another direction and which often fails to work entirely." Thus the "Letter"'s hand-delivered scandal: Kafka is *not* a Kafka.

What we in the meantime understand as Kafkaesque reverts in reality to the Löwyesque, or to that part of Franz that failed to make the Kafka grade. But it is not simply as though Franz could make claims for an original authenticity of the name that would be borne by his father. The defect already emerges in his father's relation to the name, so that the name of the father gets transmitted with a fault line and compromised lineage, offering for each of the contenders only a strained fit. There's no power-punching, patriarchal passing-on of a name-of-the-father here that wouldn't turn around and bite the paternal bearer. The father himself hasn't fully grown into the name "in so far as I can compare you with Uncle Philipp, Ludwig, and Heinrich. That is odd, and here I don't see quite clear either. After all, they were all more cheerful, fresher, more informal, more easygoing, less severe than you" (117). The essence of "Kafka" comes down to that which escapes the manifest essence of Kafka.

Both father and son owe their outstanding features to what fails to meet the Kafkan prerequisites. Where they deviate from Kafka, the Kafka signature begins. What has by now settled into a registry of sheer Kafkan dispositions—severe father, anxious son, punishing bureaucracies, night sweats, world-emaciation—skids off the history or accumulated substantiality of the name and drops what it has come to mean in terms of iterable and recognizable features. Franz can offer the account of the ill-fitting name only in abbreviated form, he writes. Kafka's readers will identify the irony of the abbreviated relation to the name in terms of the K.'s that wander through Kafka's voluminous novels, compressed and deformed, pointing to a never fully knowable name, moving through the sequence of episodes like dissociated letters, partial initials of larger or lost programs. The strength of the name-of-the-father seems to reside in its lapse, its defective and deflected itinerary. Even though Hermann Kafka cannot fully own or live up to the name Kafka, it is still a name that he carries off without question while Franz remains clandestine, going about as a stowaway in the father's name.[3]

This hidden and illicit transport offers him his one chance and solid diminishment, the kid's survival kit: Kafka as Löwy is more stealth, timid, more failing. In this sense he sneaks past the name of the father who was posed as his fate. The playing fields uneven, he avoids collision and collusion, diverting the inevitability of a fatal runoff because, as it turns out, the name behind which he hides—the name itself of hiding, secrecy, timidity—is that of the mother, a Löwy, a lioness. Switching names and scrambling the codes of paternity, Franz, the unKafka, can no longer be mowed down by the

3. For acute readings of the Hebrew lineage of Kafka's name, *Amschel*, that Kafka links to his maternal grandfather, see Werner Hamacher, *Premises: Essays on Philosophy and Literature from Kant to Celan*, trans. Peter Fenves (Cambridge, Mass.: Harvard University Press, 1996), and Michael G. Levine, "Spectral Gatherings: Derrida, Celan, and the Covenant of the Word," *Derrida and Democracy*, a special issue of *diacritics* (Spring–Summer 2008) 38:64–91.

assumed father, not on these terms and turf, anyway. Despite the skirmishes and perpetual standoff, the so-called father's authority has been rigorously impugned. Franz does not say that he is more like his mother but that *he is a Löwy*: "Ich, um es sehr abgekürzt auszudrücken, ein Löwy" (I, to put it in a very much abbreviated form, a Löwy) (9). In terms of rhetorical delivery Franz interrupts the statement ("I, a Löwy") by cutting himself down ("in a very much abbreviated form"), offering the cut and cutting away from the name-of-the-father while retaining a Kafka component—a speck or specter that allows him to hold off on complete disavowal. Refusing to substantialize the name, Franz at no point says, "I *am* a Löwy." He cuts himself down to size, saying in abbreviated form his name: "I . . . a Löwy." The stealth byway supplied by the not-name-of-the-father grants him his peculiar survival skills and password.

With an added twist of Kafkan irony, the difference with regard to the Kafka name between the father and son in itself proved dangerous. "In any case, we were so different, and in our difference so dangerous to each other that if anyone had tried to calculate in advance how I, the slowly developing child, and you, the full-grown man, would behave toward one another, he could have assumed that you would simply trample me underfoot so that nothing was left of me. Well, that didn't happen. Nothing alive can be calculated. But perhaps something worse happened" (117–18). Incalculably, Franz has survived extinction, but such a fate and this fact have exposed him to something worse than total annihilation, something that makes him permanently prey to the incalculable—the non-death with which he must face the non-name-of-the-father. Kafka explicitly states at this point that their essential dispute does not amount to a matter of culpability—his or father's—but to effects that cannot be controlled. He sees and classifies the cluster of effects his father had on him as unintended. This must remain the presumption that enables any address. Nor can anything that passes between them, including his own claims or imputations, be regarded as malicious, such as his fearful responsiveness to the *effects* of the father.

A timid child, he would have benefited, he now conjectures, from a "kindly word, a quiet taking by the hand, a friendly look" (118), all denied him. Let us take a close-up of this grievance that consists of a withheld hand paired with a severe paternal gaze. The play of hands proves crucial to the unfolding of the plaint and appears here in its speculative positivity, projecting the type of tranquil reaching-out that might have reassured the martyred child. A lot turns on the destiny of hands, and the "Letter" is replete with a variety of hand positions or practices, many of which Derrida explores for other purposes in his work on Heidegger's hands. In Kafka, whether withheld or given—a hand might be given in marriage, or raised and threatening, or meant to calibrate a grip, the *Griff* (18), or set to determine the way the law itself comes down on the child when the father exclaims, "Do whatever you like. So far as I'm concerned you have a free hand. You're of age, I've no advice to give you" (126)—the hand, whether in use or off-limits, waived or waving, slaps meaning and punishment into the child's memoir even when it is lifted, that is, removed and figurally declawed. The scary part that Kafka divulges is, you can't tell which is worse in terms of a rogue pedagogy—hands on, or the other way around: giving you a free hand, letting you off at the unbeatable juncture of your own little hell. The narration continues, "and all this with that frightful, hoarse undertone of anger and utter condemnation that makes me tremble less today than in my childhood only because the child's exclusive sense of guilt has been partly replaced by insight into our helplessness, yours and mine."

In the parable "Before the Law," Kafka shows how the law gives a free hand. Law, as Derrida notes in his reading of this text, isn't in the first place an inhibitor or interdictory bar, but lets you go ahead and make your fateful error. The difference between child and adult in the passage dissolves into the recognition of reciprocal helplessness—the experience of *Hilflosigkeit*, the sheer unprotectedness that becomes so important to Freud and is then picked up in Lyotard and Lacan. Part of the tally of a somewhat stabilizing analysis relies on the understanding that the *Autre* is in trouble, fissured, hence the sign, A̶, barring the Other from access to its own imagined plenitude. The adult signatory behind the "Letter" . . . (I need to interrupt myself here, because, let's face it, every one of these terms is shaky. Kafka will switch off with the father and it cannot be said with certainty who signs, who makes it to adulthood or backslides into childhood, and whether these positions can be stabilized or are consistently prey to corruption: this is Kafka's doing, not mine, I'm just doing my job and keeping close to his logic, following his instructions, taking note of decoys, false indications, baits, and exegetical lures. Let us resume, then, with a firm sense of the fine print and as if this interruption never happened.) The adult signatory behind the "Letter" consistently concedes the paternal scission, honoring the pain of the father who shares his part of weakness with the child. Still, the paternal hand countersigns a childhood memory never as such effaceable: "Your threat, 'Not a word of contradiction!' and the raised hand that accompanied it have been with me ever since" (126). In fact, the specter of the raised hand, as threat and horizon, is responsible for the child's fall (or rally) from the stammer to utter silence. The father's hand is raised above the "Letter" that had begun as a substitute for speech:

> What I got from you—and you are, whenever it is a matter of your own affairs, an excellent talker—was a hesitant, stammering mode of speech and even that was still too much for you, and finally I kept silent . . . I could neither think nor speak in your presence. (126)

The menacing hand, Franz continues, and the accompanying, "Not a word of contradiction!" were responsible for the major power playoffs in the relation between father and son, for "the effect of it was too strong for me, I was too docile, I became completely dumb, cringed away from you, hid from you, and only dared to stir when I was so far away from you that your power could no longer reach me—at least not directly" (127). Hermann Kafka has operated the coinciding clashes of hand and utterance, threat and injunction, in such a way as to render language searingly competent, loading the ability of language, in collaboration with body, to land fateful swipes. Silencing the child ("Not a word"), whose insertion in language necessarily involves contradiction and protest, a rub against authority, father manages to shut down the link between language and presence. The writer backs off from speech at an early age, something that stirs a manoeuvre of subterfuge on the losing side of logos. I will try to make this clear. For now let us retain the way Kafka offers the description of cringing and humiliated silence as he slinks into the space of writing.

From his corner, Franz maintains a relation to language other than Hermann's, another system of feints and *demande*. The convergence of intention and meaning, the sweep of reference, has little to do with the child's first throws of catastrophic language usage. Only one memory remains in the adult's registrar of primal clashes. For this reason alone it is of supreme interest. "There is only one episode in the early years of which I have a direct memory" (119). Kafka brings it on early in the letter. This is the only unparasited, no-secondary-revision total recall to which the adult signatory lays claim; he goes so far as to suppose that the addressee may share the same memory: "You may remember it, too." I need not remind anyone to what extent the very notion of childhood depends on narrated memory. Such narrations often come, as Lyotard states, from an adult source. (Lyotard does not care for the critical tendency to emphasize narrativity, since this line of inquiry proves too straight to offer coverage of linguistic damage, of the blanks and blurs of ostensible childhood. But that's another story—or maybe also part of this story, as the very possibility for narration continually cuts itself off and down at determined junctures of infant retrieval.) So, to resume, here we have the only direct hit, an undoctored docudrama of which the writer evinces no doubt: "Direkt erinnere ich mich nur an einen Vorfall aus den ersten Jahren" (I distinctly remember only one thing from the first years) (11). The memory grows out of a whimper, part of a phrasal regime that barely makes it to the Super Bowl of language games. "One night I kept on whimpering ("Ich winselte einmal in der Nacht") for water, not, I am certain, because I was thirsty, but probably partly to be annoying, partly to amuse myself" ("um mich zu unterhalten").

"Not, I am certain, because I was thirsty": thus the first and only unalloyed childhood memory, says the signatory. It announces the night of a first relation to language, the squeak or peek of the primal call out: putting forth a desire without object or need, banked on ambivalence, the whimper was meant to annoy the other while amusing (or "maintaining") the solitary child. Though formulated as a *demande*—as that which urgently puts upon the Other—the whimper does not arise out of want, nor does it expect reference to emerge, to materialize out of nothing. Asking for water, the child does not want water; the child is neither a thirsty empiricist nor philosophy's primal man but he—or *it*, since the evolving "I" whimpers and does not directly speak, though it is already bilingual, as we learn from the next sentence—he, that is, it, *das Kind,* will nonetheless meet up with Rousseau's hulk, at the origin of language. Squeaking "immerfort" (repeatedly), for water, the child, on automatic whimper, ignores the threats that come to the encounter of his unstoppable *demande*.

This sport of "Fetch!" without reference cues the first war of the Kafka worlds, priming the dispute of language usage that irreconcilably separates son from father. The first direct hit, angering the father and entertaining or maintaining the son—one thinks of Blanchot's infinite maintenance, *L'entretien infini*—volleys language, shoots blanks, and makes use of the senseless as his locutionary site. In fact, the first direct hit is not a direct hit, wanting nothing more than the *jouissance* of false positing (yes, imagine, the child's first target practice exercises the pleasure of scattershooting off the range of meaning and reference, not pointing but propping up the pointless), saying language's noise and nothing, evincing the nearly random word not of *milk, pee pee,* or *mommy* but of *water.* But this may be a child ontologist. "Water" distilled to its anasemic base as *Wasser* in German may be asking after a question of essence: *was er,* what (is) he? The passage emphasizes that the *demande* for water is not in any way motivated by thirst or object. Language perversion (the essence of language) keeps the child going, setting up a scene of illicit delight, to which the father seems privy: if it had been a matter of substance or meaning, the child would have been given his damned water, stopped up, and stilled. The adults could have returned to sleep. But something else is afoot, and parental supervision requires that the inessential spitballs or *jouissance* of nonmeaning be halted. The sleep-

less night of pure feint, of linguistic screeching, needed to be stopped. The father, responding to domestic code orange, counters the child's burbling assaults with threats. The night of the first remembered threat, of the call or order that the child would not heed, dissolves into violence, demonstrating the breakdown in a "diplomatic" idiom that is however backed up by force. This scene, similar to a host of traumatic memories pieced together by Franz, multiplies and escalates the political stakes involved in the languages and names of the father. Every whimper sets off a terror alert, brings home the law and a confrontation with its representatives.

The father moves into action, bursts into the room to deport the child: "After several vigorous threats had failed to have any effect, you took me out of bed, carried me out onto the *pavlatche*. And left me there alone for a while in my nightshirt, outside the shut door" (119). This episode, notarized as the first nonrevisionist history of their relation, indicates, as do many Kafkan parables and descriptions, what Lacan would call an "architecture of pain," a scenography of persecution blueprinted by unjoined domestic spaces. The father removes the child to the outside of an inside that is designated in Czech, doubling the intimate foreignness or foreign habitualness of the uninhabitable signifier. *Pavlatche* is the Czech word for the balcony in the inner courtyard of houses in Prague. The child, according to architectural design, is put out to be locked in, shut up. Removed to an outside, he receives his first eviction notice but still remains too close to home to flee or free himself—a difficult concept for a child, who, nonetheless, often thinks of little else than emancipatory flight. Many things are taking place here, setting into place an irreversible lockdown of the childhood memory.

If language is the house of being, the child has been hurled out of language to remain chained to its peripheral structure, where outside and inside collapse at the same time as a barrier is constructed. The locality to which he is exiled—at once shut out and locked in—switches languages, functions like a swish or a linguistic blur, adhering to the tenuous outside with the fog of foreign subtitles. You sent me to the *pavlatche*, the other side or site of a minor's literature, splash—here comes the water—*ptche, pvltche*. Yet the Czech word also spills into the paternal realm, the paternal Czechpoint, arranging itself around the nearly universal *pa*. As for the nonreferential water the child had obstinately whimpered for, he himself gushes with tears, a victim of his own language teary (there is an aquatic consistency to his plaint, many scenes near or in or productive of water, tidal waves of humiliation, washed over by anxious fret, the moistening forehead, distilled to shivering drops, being exposed, puny and scared at the pool, lots of tears held back or released, raining on his parades). Clearly, if one were trawling for a psychoanalytic redescription of these waterworks, one would look further into suspicious conjunctions such as those that link wetting, gushing, language spilling and spoiling—all leading up to paternal punishment, smack packs that are unforgettable and structuring. As for the signatory of the "Letter," he does not assign blame—"perhaps there was really no other way of getting peace and quiet that night" (119)—but brings up the remembered nighttime drama "as typical of your methods of bringing up a child and their effect on me." The *pavlatche* punishment worked: "I dare say I was quite obedient afterward at that period, but it did me inner harm."

Sent out, the child was struck inwardly, having been brought up or rather down to obedience, reduced to one figure in the biblical history of the name Löwy, the tribe of the servile, the servant's servants, bowed by law to a stance of submissive docility. The concurrence of non-sense and punishment creates an ineffaceable terror base for the child: "What was for me a matter of course, that senseless asking for water [Das für mich Selbstverständliche des sinnlosen Um-Wasser-Bittens] and then the extraordinary terror of being carried outside [des Hinausgetragenwerdens], were two things that I, my nature being what it was, could never properly connect with each other" (119). The German burrows perhaps more deeply than its translation into the essential disjunction that the primal scene of terror narrates. In the first place, the senselessness of asking for nonsubstantial water in what might be called an *irreferential* mood is for the child "selbstverständlich," self-understood (translated as a "matter of course"). The coemerging contours of selfhood and understanding appear to be at stake in the experience of a primary disconnect. The minimalist hermeneutics of the senseless are confronted with the massive Hermanneutics of disposal and punishment. The emphasis and tone of *Hinausgetragenwerdens*, rightly translated as "carried out," strongly implies being carried out like the trash—a recurrent fear and figuring in Kafka's writings, as when Gregor's body is unceremoniously disposed of at the end of his trial. The child has been put out with or as the garbage, a trash body translated into the outside-inside of the paternal empire. What is important to retain, I guess, is that the parental maneuver was carried out in order to silence . . . Franz Kafka. Instead of finishing him off, however, the dislodging act completed another operation: that of starting up a new *litterature*, a new dawn. It had been a long night of lobbing senseless utterance into the bin of writing remains.

The traumatic tremors remained with the inner-outed nuisance-nonsense child poet. But something utterly regressive-affirmative happened in the crowded space of closed parentheses—something burst out from the walls closing in, clamping down under parenthetical supervision. First, Franz

wraps up primal trauma time before he breaks out, generalizing and nearly transcending the prison house of early language exercises. The trauma would not let go: "Even years afterward I suffered from the tormenting fancy that the huge man, my father, the ultimate authority, would come for almost no reason at all and take me out of bed in the night and carry me out onto the *pavlatche*, and that consequently I meant absolutely nothing as far as he was concerned" (119–20).

The timer is set to incite the phantasm and paternal phantom's return, looking for his son, in order to carry him off into the void of his own nothingness, his dead-meat-being, crushable, eviscerable, a detainee, locked up, serving a sentence, outside yet within the jurisdiction, with no rights nor recourse. The phantom raid could occur at any time, any place, for nearly any reason—"fast ohne Grund," practically on no grounds. The ultimate authority has no grounds for the kidnapping—or rather, *almost* none. The irony and double-blindedness of such an assertion should not be lost on us, beyond its chilling contemporary feel. In the end, "for almost no reason" gives the vote to reason—there is still *some* reason for the violence, or the letter writer could have struck the "almost." Instead, the mark of approximation delivers the quiver of the abused, the confession of the exhausted, the caving in of the docile—a concession loaded on the dock of "almost."

At the same time, a chiasmic switch occurs in the rhetoric of the plaint. The whole episode had been generated by the articulation of "fast ohne Grund"—the groundlessness of positing, drawing the water that was funneled through no grounds, irrigating and irritating supervised language usage. The child, by historical and philosophical tradition, deprived of reason, had *almost* no reason to clamor for water. The episode in its entirety, trailing traumatic residue, appears to reside in the terroristic revelation of the arbitrary pump of language associated with unlimited authority—a home-based Republican Party wielding the means by which to deploy constitutive abuses of power. The son's language drips, whimpers, drops with only a pretend pipeline to substance. Father's language, hovering over the kid like an attack helicopter, is packed with the power punch of strategic decision and sudden political action, swooping down on the kid, throwing him into the holding pen of penal servitude, outside the system but firmly held in place, enforcing the architectural grip of what Lyotard will call the *mainmise*—a hands-on relation to filiation and language. There must have been a banister or some sort of gate or support that night, the structure that Kafka's characters crash into when it's all over and they put themselves down—or when they give up, going down, in blindness and fatigue like the man from the country in "Before the Law." The banister figures in Kafka's drawings, holding back the stick figures that look away from you on the cover of many of his published stories.

The narrated episode launches the Kafkan world of language loss and fearful reprisal: "That was only a small beginning," writes the narrator, "but this feeling of being nothing that often dominates me . . . comes largely from your influence" (120). The child could have used "a little encouragement, a little friendliness" in addition to "a little keeping open of my road," instead of which the father blocked it "for me though of course with the good intention of making me take another road." Father wanted Kafka to be a man, like him, or like the imago of regularized virility to which he was partisan. Franz was taught to march up and down the living room in solitary military formation, saluting smartly; he was prodded to eat heartily; he was urged to drink beer with his meals; he was made to prattle father's favorite expressions—all scenes of a futile schooling of incorporation. Downing food, throwing up bits of language, choking on the language of the other that he was consistently forced to swallow, Franz was trained to annex the narcissistic bulk supplies sent across the room or table by his father. The supplies, meant to supplement the dependent's essential deficiency, always came from the paternal warehouse of Hermann's needs. So Franz. The child was encouraged to become the father, to live up to the father; to open and shut his mouth according to paternal pullies. This may seem like a normal upbringing to most of you—the pedagogy of swallowing and identification consolidating and competing with a bully's narcissistic supply line. Usually, at some point, the upbringing business makes it big, and one becomes a more or less efficient import-export branch of the paternal lineage. Maybe it even happened to some degree for Franz Kafka.

OK. I had broken up a citation with ellipses, sneaking something by you (a Löwy maneuver). Let me back up and draw some water from those dots—alpine springwater taken from the regions of the sublime. We left Franz hanging, feeling his nothingness ("Gefühl der Nichtigkeit"). The encrypted primal episode, the "kleiner Anfang" (small beginning) is rather big, irrevocable, leaving the writer hung over with a recurrent Kantian *Gefühl*, or type of feeling at least that Lyotard says philosophy can never really handle. The crumbling feeling comes back periodically; it dominates and oppresses, it takes out the trash that you are, compressing you to the point of your nothingness. OK, normal enough. Nearly every kid comes with the compressor kit. (Though some now claim not to have come equipped with the kit, never needed it, they've had nice childhoods, no Oedipal tracks on their back, very little "baggage," they come from unknown to me regions of childhood-lite. I really don't get it, *Verneinung* maybe, they are in up

to their ears in denial, not even a dead cat to have ruined life's puffed-up hopes, no betraying little aggressor friends or angry looks or lapsing nannies or dismaying colds that make you miss birthday parties, no hunger or yucky food ever to teach you a lesson from finitude's kitchen? As I said, I don't get it—and I sure didn't get it, the mythically happy childhood, which is not the point so let me return to the three points, the ellipses that had me in the cutting room again, splicing the tape, reviewing fragments of a childhood.) There is the matter of a dominant feeling of nothingness. Opening the sentence like an internal canyon, another perspective appears, something that the sentence has swallowed. Here's how it goes unedited. I'll take it from "feeling":

> but this feeling of being nothing that often dominates me (a feeling that is in another respect [in anderer Hinsicht] admittedly, also a noble and fruitful one [allerdings auch edles und fruchtbares Gefühl]) comes largely from your influence. (120)

The parenthetical parachute would be lifeless and merely scandalous if it didn't point elsewhere and instigate some sort of philosophical buoyancy to push it through, if it weren't at least partially identifiable and hence somewhat readable. (Still, unreadability rules in Kafka more intently even than elsewhere, so it can in no case be ruled out.) Terror is shown in this primal passage to yield the sublime, to crush the self-escalating subject under the weight of felt nothingness, which, in Kant (to the considerable horror of his successors) rolls over into a triumphalizing account, recuperating the losses that the sublime had bravely tackled. Like Kant, Kafka decides to back off and beat a retreat when facing a stupefying abyss. He rewrites the scene. There will have been another track: he lays it and lays on it. In sum, he opens up the tunnel of paternal cruelty to meet the expanse of the ethical sublime. By means of a parenthesis, a parent-parenthesis, or parent-antithesis. The feeling—is it überhaupt, in any way, a feeling?—has "another respect," another viewpoint. "Nothingness" gives way to the sentiment of nobility and fruitfulness—"auch edles und fruchtbares Gefühl." Crushed to the point of near extinction—read the *Third Critique*—something bounds back, corrects itself, moving into the field of survival that confers a sense of nobility.

Not only has the trash been recycled and upgraded Nietzsche-style ("I am ugly created the beautiful"—in this case upgraded to the sublime), but it has turned organic. The relentless attack on the psyche has ennobled *and* fertilized this child. In some respects, as said, this is the story of a normal upbringing restating a version of the sublime politics of child pedagogy. Kafka, however, sets his sights elsewhere. In its own way, the text announces

125

that it's rhetorical payback time, turning against everybody and everything it will have called up for inspection. Throughout the elaboration, the whole drama between father and son is said to hinge on and condense to Franz Kafka's ability to seed, his "fruitfulness" (Fruchtbarkeit). His redemption is staked on his *Fruchtbarkeit*, on the reproductive valor that would spring him from father's colonizations. But there is one fertility treatment only, as we now learn, and it is organized around the memorable scene of discipline. The unintelligible punishment has borne fruit, has ennobled and enabled him, in part because of the power supplement of . . . nothingness.

The child has been raised. Razed and raised at once, he is on his way, limping with something like pride of ownership—a small beginning ("ein kleiner Anfang") or the beginning of the little one (German—well, *my* German—allows for this inverted stretch), the beginning of smallness, of all the specks and stains that in Kafka take the house down. If you roll through his texts, you'll notice that Kafka always gets small in order to attack, always marks the spot or jot that unravels the empire of the dominator. The fleck on which Kafka's military maneuvers depends stains the paternal metaphor, polluting literary transcendence and the house of metaphysics. There is always a crumble, a fleck of *dreck*, a piece of newspaper, a fabric stain to unhinge the proper of a highly invested property. Kafka does not inflate his tropes or troops but thins out or waters down the method of attack. Abraham, our primal father ("Erzvater"), is taken down for a piece of dust. His authority in Kafka's parable disintegrates *by means of a mote*. The strategic resilience of the Kafkan defense plan resides in its ability to shrivel the scene of terror, to introduce nano-responses to the encroachment of sublime terror, the incalculable adversary.

The machinery of the offending detail on which the Kafkan world of conflict runs produces a swarm of unauthorized narratives and barely legitimate protests. Still, this was his way of meeting head-on with the master narrative that Hermann—Herr Mann, Mr. Man, the Man, Hermann—embodied, which is to say Franz Kafka rode his nothingness, accepted the existential crumb, traded the flex for a fleck, took the cut in domestic approval ratings, embraced the downsize, and became the first world-class laureate of failure. He taught us how to lose, how to count, to count on the losses as a matter of course, without looking for hidden recompense or transcendental loopholes or last-minute turnarounds. The meek in Kafka do not inherit the earth but are of earth: they rule the dirt. Let me get this right. They rule nothing. At most, on especially good days, they roll in the dirt. They receive little, no pay dirt, no genealogical entry ticket. Inheritance itself is too grand a narrative, untransmissible. He wrote the book on losing the inheritance.

126

For all the guilt he accumulates, the entries in his registers provide room only for no-fault economies of disadvantage and loss. At the same time, he lists a miniscule supplement of profit when accounting for the losses.

When Kafka parenthesizes the gains of terror, he not only repeats a Kantian gesture of pulling in recuperative cuts but manages to offer thanks, somehow, and to embrace his "castration." The *feeling* of the symbolic destruction is also, parenthetically, a noble and fruitful feeling, opening up the restricted narcissism of the martyr, the categorical affirmation of one's own diminished capacities in the face of the Other. Still, at any point the feeling of nobility can exceed itself, can turn into the steaming exaltation of revenge. In Kafka, nobility puts a limit on the *feeling* it nevertheless announces. Nobility implies, in a more Goethean strain, renunciation—a feeling that does without feeling's intent potentialities. In Goethe's language, renunciation is called *Entsagung*, a kind of de-saying, if that's possible to imagine, that corresponds in the "Letter" to Kafka's inaugural phrase of nonsaying. The letter had begun in renunciation—I cannot speak, I can barely write, I cannot win. It seeks only the truth of a possible suspension, a truce; it goes after another logic of the enemy combatant raised on renunciation, pummeled by fate from start to finish, yet able to take a cut from improbable winnings. It provides another version of Kleist's famous text, *Die Hermmansschlacht*—Hermann's massacre or "The Hermann Battle."

The "Letter," a peace offering collated with a declaration of war, takes off from the premises of losing ground. It does not seek to establish or institute anything but a tenuous peace, a withdrawal of forces that could at best hope for a perpetual standoff, what Kafka calls *Versöhnung*, or some sort of nonaggression pact, an attempted reconciliation (elsewhere, other German scholars and I have pointed out the *Sohn* [son] in the word *Versöhnung*).

There is another thing going on. If the father's night strike proved not only catastrophic but in some way fruitful, as well as ennobling, then Kafka's description unavoidably enters a scene of insemination when he says and writes that he bears the fruits of the encounter. This is why, on this other level, he must become in the letter a Löwy, and to the letter, namely, he must become the "wife" of the father. But, as said, all this is fairly normal. If he has become his father's demeaned mate, put out like the trash or a dog, his aim is not to cheat his destiny but, in a distinctly Goethean way, to ennoble it. (Leave it to me to consider the pornological cast of this nocturnal screen memory and to drag Goethe into the script [I can say at least this for myself: he was one of Kafka's beloved superstar writers, along with Kleist].) The traumatic episode says, "You did something to me that revealed to me my nothingness." The disclosure of his nothingness proceeds from a narrated confluence of water, gushing, spurting, harming, issuing from what appears to flood the scene of a spermatic logic. The father's body is all over the place; Kafka has him pressing against the corpus, spreading his flesh over a larger measure of world. Other episodes show the child to be proud of the father's naked body—for instance, at the pool—and at the same time he is scared, shy about revealing his own body, its puny contours and breakability. The double-takes prompted by the appeal of the paternal body and its suffocating menace, hunger and satiation, desire and horror, run subtly through the text. I am not particularly happy with the turn this interpretation of the passage has taken, but I am mostly blameless. I could stay with the restrictive thematic line that deals solely with the maltreatment and hounding to which Franz was prey. I can even handle the ambivalence and vacillation that abuse routinely engenders. Yet, the way Kafka aligns disruptive allegations within the frame of description makes one slow down and crawl under newly oppressive spaces. I would not be forced to crouch and strain in this way if our letter writer had not included-excluded the parenthetical bit about the noble feeling and fruitfulness, perverting an otherwise perfectly tranquil-seeming semantic field, shaking it up so as to expose uneven valences and intrusive tropes of encounter.

The fantasy of the son figured as the wife of the father comes from the culture that has brought us Dr. Schreber and the Rat Man. In itself—and given a larger contextual milieu in which it situates the stakes of desire's disturbances—this setup suggests nothing abnormal. The motherly back-up that Franz often seeks comes in weakly, even when going strong. In some instances, Kafka's mother gets taken up by the paternal supercluster, and the maternal goes missing or is structurally upgraded, if continually sidelined. Franz becomes her surrogate or fills her place. The logic of displacement—she moves around much as he moves in and out of maternal and sororal locations—is something that Franz allows for, and under some narrative lighting techniques he has Mother assume the posture of hidden law when Father is seen as a mere police dog.

But for the most part, Mother only intensifies the power of the father by hiding out in protective precincts—she functions as a decoy that draws the children toward her so that Father can close in on them. She's the trap and trip-up for the child, capable only of installing new and improved registers of ambivalence. The child assumes it has found sanctuary, but then Mother turns out to be another mask, quite simply, of Father. She is harmful to the extent that she appears to hold down a discreet district in the fantasy of household harmlessness, the nudge of comfort. "Mother unconsciously

played the part of a beater during a hunt" (132). Mother, on the home front, set up the autoimmune lab by voiding defense codes that the child might otherwise have been capable of developing. The child might have been able to map a defense, toughen up with a vigilant sense of clarity and enemy reconnaissance had Mother not operated an interruptive machine that served to confuse and weaken her ward:

> Even if your method of upbringing might in some unlikely case have set me on my own feet by means of producing defiance, dislike, or even hate in me, Mother canceled that out again by kindness, by talking sensibly (in the confusion of my childhood she was the very prototype of good sense and reasonableness), by pleading for me; and I was again driven back into your orbit, which I might perhaps otherwise have broken out of, to your advantage and to my own. (132)

Mother, advancing as protectress and assuming the pose of reason, diminishes the child's chances of stocking up on healthy reactivity. She knocks down the transmitters and crucial detection system that ought to have kept the child on alert. Hers is a position sometimes rendered in blunt warfare, resembling the disposition and complicity of counterespionage and whatever blows out bridges or telecommunication centers. But Mother is more stealthy than all that noisemaking, being a Löwy. She fills all the roles of *pharmakon* insofar as she poses as remedy but dispenses the poison and also turns into the family scapegoat in the battle of wills:

> You were always affectionate and considerate toward her, but in this respect you spared her just as little as we spared her. We all hammered ruthlessly away at her, you from your side, we from ours. It was a diversion, nobody meant any harm, thinking of the *battle* that you were waging with us and that we were waging with you, and it was Mother who got the brunt of all our wild feelings. (139)

The child, our narrator surmises, had been right in being wary of Mother even when she manifested kindness and held out the promise of a secure safety zone:

> She loved you too much and was too devoted and loyal to you to have been for long an independent spiritual force in the child's struggle. This was, incidentally, a correct instinct of the child, for with the passing of the years Mother became ever more closely allied to you; while where she herself was concerned, she always kept her independence, within the narrowest limits,

delicately and beautifully, and without ever essentially hurting you, still, with the passing of the years she more and more completely, emotionally rather than intellectually, blindly adopted your judgments and your condemnations with regard to the children, particularly in the case—certainly a grave one—of Ottla. (138–39)

Annexed to the paternal mover, whether exceeding or consolidating his powers, Mother, increasingly fused, is allied to the enemy camp. Where was Franz to turn?

Chapter 5
The Battle of Wills
On Being Cheap

The brothers, as we said, were nonstarters, though their ghostly extinction prevails over much of the domestic front. They mark a kind of nonorigin, phantom predecessors that allow Franz to slip into the Löwy name. Only sister Elli manages a success story among the siblings. Ottla, the other sister, kept the fight going where Franz capitulated quickly. Elli, she breaks away. However success is hemmed in by the Kafkan "almost": "Elli is the only example of the almost complete success of a breaking away from your orbit."[1] A little firecracker backed only by a loser beginning, she suddenly pushed ahead and pulled out. She was the only one, save the eventual grandchildren, to break the circuit, find an off-ramp on the paternal systems of tyrannical enclosure: "When she was a child she was the last person I should have expected it of. For she was such a clumsy, tired, timid, bad-tempered, guilt-ridden, overmeek, malicious, lazy, greedy, miserly child . . ." (140). Elli is the one with whom Franz most closely identifies and who leaves him, gawking, in the dust. Her way out: marriage, a springboard to a history of generosity, cheer, hopefulness. A question arises. Why is marriage, a confining institution, understood to be a refuge from the encroachment of the patriarch? How does Elli become the exalted party in this text? So desperate is he for a way out, that Kafka evinces a surprisingly rigorous ambivalence to marriage. For some reason, when it comes to Elli, he is unable to shake off fully the mythic stabilizers of marriage. Still, when Franz Kafka finds a match, seeing himself in his sister, he

1. Franz Kafka, "Letter to Father," trans. Ernst Kaiser and Eithne Wilkins, in *The Sons* (New York: Schocken Books, 1989). Subsequent references are cited parenthetically in the text.

is at the same time repulsed, averts his gaze, loses the faculty of speech: "For she was such a clumsy, tired, timid, bad-tempered, guilt-ridden, overmeek, malicious, lazy, greedy, miserly child, I could hardly bring myself to look at her, certainly not to speak to her, so much did she remind me of myself, in so very much the same way was she under the same spell of our upbringing." Locked into identification and ever on a regressive traveling plan with the abhorrent other—he can't stand his identical sister—Franz falls away, rolls into a silent corner, refusing the gaze or address.

Elli, the inner Franz, feminized and externalized, engages in a game of deadly dispossession with her sibling. They are both shadowed by *miserliness*, a quality that defines them and underpins their struggle over an elusive object, fronted by metonymy and stand-in. Pooling their resources, Kafka offers the groundwork for a thought on what it means to be cheap—a greatly underrated modern phenomenon. What does it mean to hoard for oneself when one starts and stays on zero, inhabits the near nothingness of a withholding existence? Let us bear in mind that Elli is both miserly and greedy. Kafka doubles the taker's position with which he identifies (if this were a seminar, I would probe the doubling and difference, if there is one, between the two forms of avidity.)

Elli and Franz, bereft from the start, play out a domestic politics of cupidity, taking from each other what neither has nor can give. They spin their mutual lives on the sullen rigidity of nongiving. Franz, for his part, starts out by giving neither language nor look. The letter writer is treading on thin ice when he levers the withdrawal of speech on the syntagm led by Elli: he identifies the unwillingness to speak—the impoverished space under which faltering, diffident speech occurs—with greedy withholding, the compulsion driving miserliness. Though Franz purportedly addresses his father and not his sister in the "Letter," his plaint is henceforth accompanied by the mania of greed, even if this round of calculations should be played on the sidelines. According to the logic introduced via Elli, the "Letter" does not so much deliver a sign of something he wishes to give or offer, but packs tightfisted ungenerosity, a way of scrimping and pinching and withholding— the bargain basement of tracings only paradoxically "offered" to Father. He learned from his sibling's pleasure to appreciate the returns of withholding tactics: Elli, as a child, *enjoyed* "taking away from me" (140). For the young Franz, the predator twin deprives him of any comfort possibly taken in life's at-handedness:

> Her miserliness was especially abhorrent to me, since I had it to an, if possible, even greater extent. Miserliness is, after all, one of the most reliable signs of

profound unhappiness; I was so unsure of everything that, in fact, I possessed only what I actually had in my hands or in my mouth or what was at least on the way there, and this was precisely what she, being in a similar situation, most enjoyed taking away from me. (140)

The two miserly children—Franz exceeding Elli in this hunger-bitten match—feed off each other in a way that serves only to increase the daily dosage of deprivation. Still, deprivation fuels and supports desire, according to Lacanian scripting and the Kafkan text: it is—or is *not*—what keeps things going, wanting. Kafka of course stayed the line of deprivation, having produced the mock-mastery of destitute being in the figure of the Hunger Artist, who comes by his means dirt cheap—as the one who refuses sustenance, feinting at aneconomy, the aneconomy of anorexia.

Kafka passed the mic to those who reject nurturance as part of a system of wanting too much. Miserliness, however, is about wanting at another, ground level. It piles up on the want, grinding and recycling, hoarding the bits and pieces of provisional ownership. It swells up on near nothingness. Interestingly, when his sister swells up in pregnancy, miserliness bucks the infantile trend and rolls over into generosity, unselfishness, and hope. Elli's submission to the allegories of breeding buys her time and a one-way ticket. According to his calculations, she makes the grade and breaks away from both Franz and Father. The repellent adhesion to her brother disintegrates, identification collapses, and Elli, for her part, draws a home-free card. Marriage and childbearing—the "Letter"'s principal stakes—effect the leap from aneconomic stinginess to extraeconomic generosity. In the process, we have to assume, Elli will have lost the Kafka name: "Elli no longer lives with us."

To the extent that Elli mirrors Franz, giving us an inroad to the scope of textual disturbance, self-defamation and transcendental crashes, we need to follow her closely—especially when she splits off from him, having left him once again "all alone." She has headed in another direction, according to the "Letter"'s recap, and has found the only available off-ramp to the lifelong Hermannic harangue. In Elli's life, something gives when she marries and starts a family. Franz by contrast shuttles between the minimalist byways of giving in and giving up. He proves generous only by exceeding Elli in miserliness, by refining the art of bringing things down to a bare minimum, by withholding and making himself small: these gifts give Franz, who was fated to remain hostage to the unrelenting paternal machine, his edge—an inverted blunted edge, no doubt, but that's the plan he came equipped with.

Kafka stays attentive to the sororal track, sticking close and defending against the sisters for whom he doubles, often taking the part of the "weak sister." Ottla Kafka outbids Franz in a different way and magnifies a stain of negativity. In fact, his sister Ottla presents a problem for the "Letter" as well as the letter writer to the extent that she, vilified by the father, can only induce paternal furor. The mere mention of her name can tear up the "Letter," violating the implicit contract that Kafka tries to establish. If he can scarcely speak to his father but finds himself capable only of writing, Franz can barely even write *of* Ottla. She disturbs the letter's destination and puts a hole in its destiny, in principle undermining the entire range of its possible effects: "I scarcely dare write of Ottla; I know that by doing so I jeopardize the whole effect I hope for from this letter" (140). Nonetheless, she's in there, ready to destroy the letter, a virus that he lets in. Why is she so dangerous for the fate of this epistolary experiment and its inbuilt program of locating and stabilizing its addressee?

Their father hates Ottla, feels persecuted by her, seeing her as "in other words, a sort of fiend" (141). Outrivaling the disjointure between Kafka and his father, she remains the cipher for the greatest estrangement, "greater still than that between you and me." So remote is she from the father that a specter is put in Ottla's place "where you suppose her to be." Ottla, resembling something "like a kind of Löwy equipped with the best Kafka weapons," paradoxically in the end has posed little mimetic problem for Franz: unlike his feisty counterpart who goes one-on-one with Father, he quickly caves, practically turning his diapers into a white flag of surrender. "Between us there was no real struggle; I was soon finished off; what remained was flight, embitterment, melancholy, and inner struggle. But you two were always in a fighting position, always fresh, always energetic. A sight as magnificent as it was desperate." That was then. "All this, however, is today only a dream" (142). Ottla no longer trains her enemy eyes on her father and "has to seek her way alone, like me, and the degree of confidence, self-confidence, health, and ruthlessness by which she surpasses me makes her in your eyes more wicked and treacherous than I seem to you. I understand that." Again, Franz inches past his sibling on the strength of weakness.

Ottla—sad, suffering but "not desperate (despair is my business)" (142)— may have given her father hints that she is accomplice to Franz. They band together often enough to whisper and laugh, "and now and again you hear us mentioning you" (142). The impression the downbeat siblings tend to put out, despite their declared intentions, is that of "impudent conspirators, strange conspirators." Father is the locus of their discussions, Franz avers, but not as an object of derision or as a designated target of some conspiratorial scheme. They pool their resources only in order to review "this terrible trial [Prozess] that is pending between us and you, to examine it in all its details, from all sides, on all occasions, from far and near—a trial in which you keep on claiming to be the judge, at least in the main." The narrating couple so often caught in the act by Father-Judge prepares to go to *Trial*, to present their case, to write the book on authority in crisis. The explanation takes a crucial swerve, beginning with the neat concession, "at least in the main" (wenigstens zum grössten Teil).

The rhetoric of the plaintive pitch deserves a closer look here, for it clues us in to the reading protocols of the other works to which the "Letter," while all alone in its kind, remains parented. "At least" shrivels, ironically inflating to "the most, the greatest or largest part": at least for the most (greatest, largest) part, giving us *least and most* at once, as signals of withdrawal, pinpointing a semantic fluctuation characteristic of paternal designations that range from tiny flecklike disturbances to inflated monstrosities. If Father were only huge and not also capable of compressing into horrifying miniaturizations, some sort of sibling strategy might have been concocted to countenance the paternal overdrive. The thought phrase ends, then, "at least for the most part (here I leave a margin for all the mistakes I may naturally make) you are party too, just as weak and deluded as we are" (142). End of paragraph. The next paragraph has its own life, beginning with: "An example of the effects of your methods of upbringing." (Note how careful the letter writer's articulation remains—the focus rigorously stays on *effects* and makes no pretense of nailing a cause or assigning substantial blame. Kafka shares the censure, divides the imputation of wrongdoing and, as a modern insurance lawyer, he refrains from apportioning liability.)

So, what has happened here, and why am I inclined to fuss over it? Franz, preparing to go before the judge and ultimate stay-at-home take-no-prisoners authority recognizes the fissures and blanks that constitute paternal authority. Henceforth, he can only orient his language, his appeal and plaint, to a troubled site of incapacitation. He can rally little more ("wenigstens zum grössten Teil") than the certainty of nonresponse. Lapse and the panic of delusion are carried over to the Other, just as the hopeless Kafkan bureaucracies are mere (but still killer, death-penalty sponsored) compromise-formations, stupidly mechanistic and faltering—. Of great effect, the minor shift in enemy targeting is in fact huge, at least for the most and largest part, and serves to splinter once again the addressee of the missive/missile and its phantasmatic stronghold.

Faced with a pending "terrible trial," Franz remains a dependent, a loser without means and without a truly targetable opponent. He wears or is worn by battle fatigues, there is no doubt about it, equipped only with the suspicion that he cannot take down the adversary, that his life will be a perpetual piece of warfare, one unending blood-and-guts skirmish over hopeless boundaries controlled by a looming indictment. Kafka's uncanny night vision of catastrophic clashes penetrates the obscured logic that configures every interminable war scene. Franz Kafka has already been to Vietnam and Afghanistan. The trial, the home entertainment version of the last judgment, is pending, hanging in the air, awaiting the child who understands that the Other, too, comes at us blind and deluded. How much more leverage he would have enjoyed if he could project shrewd, shifty yet determined hypercompetence, the bigness of cognized efficiency, onto the Other. Having the father's weakness in his sights, he cannot shoot or conclude; he cannot finish off the imaginary declination of enmity. He can only offer, that is, *surrender* this peace treaty, handing over a position statement that appeals to the unstoppably injuring yet ever injured other. The weakening effects of Hermann's intrusive fragility proves more destructive than any embodied traits of sustainable aggression could ever be.

Enmity in the household will have taken many forms—it is stored up in secret accounts, explodes frontally, or suddenly comes to a halt, due to some clandestine act or negotiation such as occurs when Hermann Kafka hovers at the doorway, anxiously watching over the ailing child. He just stands there, not daring to step inside Franz's room for fear of disturbing his vulnerable charge. This ineffaceable image—father anxiously looking in, fearful, embarrassed, utterly humbled by his powerlessness to help or heal—makes the grownup writer cry as he writes.[2] But the memory of paternal anguish does not mean that the state of exception has been lifted. The condition of house enmity prevails. The restored battlefield also absorbs what appears to belong outside the home, in historical avenues and on political sites. Emergency

2. I have often wondered about this exceptional moment in the "Letter," when Father is posed at a threshold in anguished paralysis. The doorway has long puzzled me, as if it provided a dimension in the work to which I could not find access. I went through my literary Rolodex and discovered Cixous's Dora, who "foutée(d) Freud à la porte." I recognized *Faust*'s Mephistopheles, who had an obsessional neurotic thing about doorways and required that everything be put in writing. His lingering at the doorway is cited in Freud's case of the Rat Man. I see that for Laurence Rickels in *The Devil Notebooks* (Minneapolis: University of Minnesota Press, 2008), the pre-Oedipal father—meaning also prepunitive with tender concern for his children—soon swings over into satanic projections of rage. The switchover from benevolent father to his hellish counterpart in malevolent figuration may well provide the hinge of this scene of a psychically revolving door. For the moment Hermann is frozen in a pre-Oedipal pose, the "memory" of which has Franz weeping.

measures need to be taken. We know that Kafka took anti-Semitism seriously. He read the *Prager Abendblatt*, preparing to respond to the outrages of the actively anti-Semitic writer Hans Blüher. "Kafka was familiar with Blüher's earlier work and took him more seriously than he did other anti-Semites."[3] But the Jewish problem began at home.

From early on, the implications of the "Letter" begin their ethico-political work of establishing a social palimpsest. Thinking that political strife takes root beyond domestic boundaries proves to be deluded. Franz has to battle homegrown anti-Semitism, must put up little insurrections in the name of class struggle—his father demeans his workers, Franz's inner social policy forces him to cough up restitution and workers' comp—and he constantly rebuilds the antiballistic shield to protect himself from father's rage ("wüten"), the furious rant. The ranting of a tyrant or boss, of the one buffed up on power, a political director, stays with Franz as the key grievance of one of his internalized claimants. The way one speaks to one's "inferiors"—to those who cannot in any case talk back, bereft of voice and vote—is one of the recurrent concerns of the "Letter"'s argument. The father's unleashing, even when emanating from a place of powerlessness, is remembered consistently as the trauma of *Schimpfen*—the ceaseless volleys of words of abuse. The little one that Kafka was (and continues to harbor as a kind of political refugee) ducks for linguistic cover, hitting the deck of a daily familial bustle.

Sometimes Franz, for his part, was prepared to put up a white flag of surrender, as when he gave his father—the only such text mentioned in the "Letter"—Benjamin Franklin's memoirs of his youth. Franz Kafka gives Hermann Kafka a gift, a book. I need to slow this down, not the least because we've suddenly crossed oceans of meaning and literary checkpoints. The passage is extraordinary, without parallel, and tells of a literary-historical impasse that requires further reflection, particularly since it revs up a political engine and connects us to what will become Franz's engagement with *Amerika*. Let us take a close look at what occurs when Kafka's "Letter to Father" swallows up *The Autobiography of Benjamin Franklin*. I'd like to consider the consequences of this singular incorporation of another, strangely pertinent volume.

When Franz deals in Franklin, something happens to the letter that tries to contain the new addition/edition that henceforth rides piggyback on the "Letter" itself. To overlook this determining intrusion—that of America, of a brother-text, a fellow vegetarian, a political visionary—would be to mismanage the interpretive sails that push this text to other shores and unexpected

3. Nicholas Murray, *Kafka* (Croyden, Surrey: Abacus, 2005), 342.

exegetical borders. "I really did purposely give you this book to read, though not, as you ironically commented, because of a little passage on vegetarianism" (149). The volume of Franklin's memoirs cues up the passages in the "Letter" on Judaism and the father's "disgust" ("Ekel") for Franz's writing; it belongs to a sequence of highly invested battle scenes and represents a gift, a book, another text and pretext that Franz has offered and addressed to Hermann. As such it also organizes a strategic dimension of the present text (never as such present, a present not offered in or as presence, as is by now well understood), reaching out of its discreet positioning in the "Letter" to install codes and ensure modalities of reading, in some ways meant to remain covert but, according to other signals, capable of opening up a significant transmission channel. The Franklin memoirs, as embedded text, inhabit the "Letter" and shift the valences of what is said here by inevitably signifying, contaminating, corrupting its course, reorienting all possible exegetical claims on the "Letter" itself, as if it stood all alone. In a sense the "Letter" breaches itself, reaches out to pull in another's memoirs, creating an enigmatic fold, and—given the strident thematics of Benjamin Franklin's filiations and political breakout points—it succeeds in repositioning father and son. Why did he do it? Why did Franz tap his father with the American autobiography, or say he did?

Vegetarianism is a bone of contention between son and father, but this is not necessarily why he feeds Franklin's book to Father, though the themes of carnologocentrism and problems of incorporation cannot simply be ruled out as motivation. Franklin's vegetarianism (if the practice is assimilable to an "ism"), moreover, puts murder on the table: "Hitherto I had stuck to my resolution of not eating animal food . . . I considered the taking of every fish as a kind of unprovoked murder, since none of them had, or ever could do us any injury that might justify the slaughter."[4] Let us look more closely at what could have compelled Franz Kafka to take up Benjamin Franklin to the point of relaying this work to his father and making it part of the "Letter," or the letter within his letter, a place where he could read himself or provisionally write his way out of a system of constraints. Partnering up with Franklin, Kafka is able to get closer in the letter to his aims of presenting himself and making his case. In many ways, Franklin mirrors his own attachments and language habits. Franklin in fact names himself in the very terms that Kafka uses to code his ur-experience with language. We thus learn, following an aqua-logic that takes a few laps around the textual margins—and linking

4. Benjamin Franklin, *The Autobiography of Benjamin Franklin* (New York: Dover, 1996), 27. Subsequent references are cited parenthetically in the text.

the French language with reading and swimming (Wygate "spoke French and lov'd reading. I taught him and a friend of his to swim by twice going into the river, and they soon became good swimmers," 37)—that one of the names by which Franklin was called matches Kafka's primal experience with acts of naming: "the *Water-American*, as they called me," and "I drank only water" (34), creating a textual womb that holds them both by means of an explicit signifying chain. Franklin's *Autobiography* underscores both his "thirst for knowledge" and a lifelong though troubled relation to books ("I have since often regretted . . . that more proper books had not fallen in my way," 9). By the age of twelve he was book-bound and indentured to an older brother who was a printer, which gave him access to books but also initiated the Kafkan drama of being forcibly severed from letters—in this case, from poetry—by paternal edict or dictation: "I now took a fancy to poetry. . . . but my father discouraged me by ridiculing my performances, and telling me verse-makers were generally beggars. So I escaped being a poet, most probably a very bad one; but as prose writing has been of great use to me in the course of my life, and was a principal means of my advance-ment, I shall tell you how, in such a situation, I acquired what little ability I have in that way" (10). Franklin became a writer by the crush of paternal default—Father had pulled him away from poetry. Yet, this being Benjamin Franklin, he finds his advantage in the smothered passion and starts up the mythologies of Yankee ingenuity. Kafka's American journey would be notably different, if still maintaining a detectable relationship to Franklin's trials. Let us consider why Kafka assimilates Benjamin Franklin to the work before us. In what ways does Franklin's text call out to the Kafkan dilemma?

Addressed to his offspring, the *Autobiography* describes to his own son the fate of the writer, or rather, the fate of poetry sublimated into prose writing. Franklin considers and calls himself "bookish," the attribute with which he saddles up in life. His bookish being undergirds his existence, carrying over in some measure to the Kafkan *Schriftstellersein*—the writer-being by which Kafka identified himself in his diaries and correspondence. Franklin roots everything he does in his relation to writing. Even his refusal to eat meat comes from the dictates of a book that young Franklin devoured at the age of sixteen. Clearly, Franklin broke out and broke through the material parameters of sheer bookish being in its restricted sense; he drove into scientific fields, added diplomatic tracks and the pragmatic-speculative ventures leading up to *Poor Richard's Almanac*. These purported breakouts remain inseparable from a bookish Dasein and confirm time and again Franklin's original relation to writing—something that he never lets go of. Franklin is known mostly for other activities, and no one would have dreamt of seeing him take a seat close to Kafka in any lineup or write-up or chronicle documenting the fate of letters. Franklin famously flies a kite. Apart from their shared bookishness, they appear to have little in common. Kafka, for his part, enjoys little mobility and no particular form of public sanction; above all, he cannot address the letter to a son. But it is hard henceforth, looking backward and forward, for anyone to get out Kafka-free. Kafka will have put his mark on all writerly beings and has his copyright on every text, whether ancient or not yet on the scrolls. Benjamin Franklin was officially adopted by Kafka, so in many ways he is in the machine and must be read, if not written, by Kafka. The scrambles and unauthorized entries that we associate with the Kafkan legacy now accrue to Franklin. Returning to the work of Benjamin Franklin, we can now see that the itinerary of address gets complicated and it's no longer sure who does what to whom, or from what station. Some actions or beatings that have become classics of Kafka's world now return in a displaced form to Franklin's work. The violence associated with the Kafkan father in Franklin's recollections reverts to a tyrannical older brother who beats him regularly, inscribing on his battered body an enduring passion for justice. The Franklin father, on the other hand, inverts Hermann's aversion to reading his son, picking up Benjamin's writing, often in order to engage it . When Benjamin put in writing his side of an argument—one topic involves the propriety of educating the female sex in learning (young Franklin was on our side)—something happened that, on good days, Franz only dreamed of:

> Three or four letters of a side had passed, when my father happened to find my papers and read them. Without entering into the discussion, he took occasion to talk to me about the manner of my writing. (11)

So, once again: Why did Kafka present his father with this work? "Because of the relationship between the author and his father, as it is there described, and of the relationship between the author and his son, as it is spontaneously revealed in these memoirs written for that son. I do not wish to dwell here on matters of detail" (149).

That's funny. The "matter of detail" that young Kafka skips, uncharacteristically sprinting ahead, necessarily gives pause; the suppressed matter of detail would halt the machinery of ostensible reconciliation or jam up the textual claims department. What does Kafka's gift do or say? Does it model these relationships in a particular way? The sudden clip, the blind aversion to speck and detail, appear to be contagious. Even Kafka commentators who take note of the book, perhaps primed by Franklin's historical stature, see in it a picture of harmonious family relations. In other words, they have not read the autobiography nor do they appear to have considered the famous clashes that defined these relations and that collapse family. Franklin and his son were acknowledged enemies; their relationship was fraught with issues of legitimacy, governed by notorious disputes and a history of piqued nerves. This is the poison pill that Kafka would have fed his father, though he himself appears to have thought he was administering a vitamin—something to energize, steel, and strengthen their own perpetually flagging relationship. Uh-huh.

What Kafka does mention, skipping the details, is that the memoirs are addressed to the son, "written for that son." Franklin will have written the inverse, on first screening, of Kafka's letter-memoir or antimemoir, anamemoir (so much is forgotten, he writes, halting sometimes in the midst of a sharp accusation). Addressing his own son, Franklin wants, per usual, to teach a lesson. The first impulse, though, goes to pleasing the son, to the extent that "it may be equally agreeable to you to know the circumstances of my life, many of which you are yet unacquainted with" (1). The pleasure of recounting equalizes them, Franklin the father imagines. More impossibly significant for the gift-giver Kafka, the paternal Benjamin Franklin writes of his memoirs, "I sit down to write them for you."

The particulars of address, a strong motif throughout the "Letter," become especially important for reading the end of Kafka's letter, supposing it ever ends—or, given all the complications of *envoi* and delivery, supposing that the letter takes off. Let me simplify the task of tracking its itinerary by becoming a straightforward materialist-deconstructive examiner assigned to its route of transfer. The letter allows Kafka to break through some transference stations and meet his obstacles head-on. He trades off attributes with the purported other, introjecting and perhaps converting the paternal object—living with it so that he can die with it. By the end of the document, Franz assumes his father's voice, becoming the father or parasiting his position, reversing and transcoding their putative roles. Embedded in the text, Benjamin Franklin's *Autobiography* diverts Kafka's "Letter" and neutralizes the identifications it appears to support. As peace treaty or pedagogical model the *Autobiography* opens different registers of Kafka's plaint. It could be that the strategic placement of Franklin's text indicates some sort of wish-fulfillment or inscrutable reproach, a beseeching plea: "Daddy write me a letter. Write me the 'Letter to—I mean *from*, Father.'" Or, given the ventrilocating acts and parasitism that define the "Letter"'s end, perhaps we are being fed a clue whose purpose discloses a truth about the letter's origin and aims—namely, that Daddy *did* write, dictate, submit this letter, going so far as to shove it down my delicate throat . . . But woe to him who makes himself Franklin's addressee, the unwitting "dear" in the headlights of "Dear Son."

The *Autobiography* turns up the volume on the textual directives set up in the "Letter." Franklin's *Autobiography* belongs to a sequence of allegorical writing desks that Kafka arranges carefully, if only to block the passage to the mere correlation of circumstance or semantic transparency that he also asserts. What could he have wanted to get across when giving his father a copy of this book, which moreover appears to have been available not in German but in Czech, matching the *pavlatche* trauma? A gift, the book also involves the disclosure of massive betrayal and the theme of a father's inability to forgive his son's trespasses. Benjamin Franklin has let it be known that his son William was a devastating disappointment for him, particularly when he chose to remain loyal to the King during the American Revolution. "Nothing," he said, "has ever hurt me so much . . . as to find myself deserted in my old age by my only son."[5] Ben Franklin himself was the most reluctant of revolutionaries, but he made the necessary push away from the mother country (as did 80 percent of the white American population). Benjamin could never get over the filial breach and "never forgave William for his 'disloyalty'"—to America, to the father, henceforth synonymous and guarded by quotation marks.[6] He had pushed away from William's mother and raised his illegitimate son as part of the new family. Their estrangement, by the time it came to choose or lose America, was unbridgeable. The son was virtually cut off from the will and sailed from his native country in exile to England in 1782, solitary and broken. So this about wraps it up for the exemplary father-son relationship that Franz-Franklin has determined to share with Father—a story of disinheritance, political enmity, desertion, irredeemable strife, illegitimacy, abandonment, exile. One remaining irony is that William enacted betrayal by being a loyalist, by choosing King over Father, or possibly mother country over *patria*, the paternal, if femininized, revolutionary version of nation.

Nothing ever really trumped Father for the signatory of our letter, none of the emissaries or metonymies of paternal sovereignty matched the drive or power of Father—no King or Kaiser or throne or scepter, themselves subject to paternal faultlines and pretensions—could overtake the invested territories staked out by the paternal, which ensured only an inescapably crushing

5. Quoted in Sheila L. Skemp, *Benjamin and William Franklin: Father and Son, Patriot and Loyalist* (New York: Bedford/St. Martin's, 1994).

6. Ibid.

defeat. The Kafkan emphasis on the father's authority was something that, on first reading, would have bolstered the father in Franklin, though it calls for a rewrite of Franklin's own assertion of authority and the concept of paternity. To the son addressed in Franklin's work, Kafka appends and in some measure opposes in the "Letter" a story of himself as disinherited son. Even where Kafka has wanted to show his father the fantasy relation between Franklin and his son, he runs into an alias of his own father, however, and encounters a disinheriting force—something he can recognize and that subsequently dissolves. Franz runs into dead-end mirrorings, delivering only identificatory breakage, finding or denying a destiny that is somehow enscrolled in the gift he gave his father. The gift is loaded with contradictory directives and self-canceling perspectives. How do we read the double-decker letter from this point onward?

As readers trained by Kakfa, we are enjoined to offer several interpretations of the nearly unreadable present, none of which crowds out with certainty the others. Kafka's descriptions make clear that both father and son prove unable to read Franz's intention when offering the book. Let us at least keep this dossier open and fill it with questions on the margins of its deposition. We may as well start with the most extreme hypothesis. Does Franz want a father like Franklin—one who actually *banishes* his son? This would cut him some slack, apportion a space of exteriority, if only in the mode of pain. Still, it's a way out and corresponds to the traumatic memory of being set outside in the earliest clash of frustrated desire. Some traumas, as we have said, are structuring. Franklin's intervention in the letter points to other facets of *demande* as well, in some ways more structurally inflected. Inserting the model text, Kafka evokes another scene of writing, one in which a father writes to his son. Franklin's *Autobiography* could have borne the title "Letter to Son," offering the countermodel to a "Letter to Father." Embedding Franklin's letter, he reorients his own text to another origin, pressing the "Letter" to become that of his father, addressed to him. In a sense, he gets his wish, he gives himself the switch as the letter progressively becomes that of his father—addressing, precisely, his son, pushing the son from the signer's position, making him progressively disown the fantasy of autonomy with which the letter appears to have begun its mission. Kafka, after all, will have given up claims in the letter to the Kafka name.

Handing over the speaker's place to the paternal locus and function in the work, the writer has made way for Father's domination of the scene, clearing him to accomplish a hostile takeover, even that of the "Letter." In order to make room for the encroachment of the paternal, Kafka's works move out from tiny claustrophobic bedroom spaces to the wide expanses marked by the bloating signifiers of Russia and America. Palestine and China flag still other outposts of the Kafkan imaginary scope where inner and outer domains of unsettled being are rendered and exchanged. Some of these countries plot shaky correlates to their more referential counterparts. For there exists in Kafka a quietly mythic Russia, as "The Judgment" manifests, providing a textual radius that measures and supplies distance, that proves to be as important as the Russia that might be mapped beyond psychic determinations—though the idea of a vast nation or series of nations, huge or small, that would exist without psychic appropriation is never a sure thing. What America means to Kafka, and why he migrates in the "Letter" to America in order to score a futile point, requires a study of its own. Nations and territories, too, model their breakups on filial tropologies and colonized grammars of intention, ordering the vision of pioneered selfhood. These considerations of land maps and their rhetorical markers form a small part of endless Kafkan runways. There are many reasons for jockeying the meaning of Franklin's residential status in the "Letter." Kafka will have reached out for America on several occasions and made this journey part of a failed trajectory of self-reappropriation to which he returned time and again. Kafka's oeuvre lands in America to expose a degree of failure in the histories of second chances. In terms of the development of his own work, Kafka will have pointed us in the direction of Benjamin Franklin to complete a phantom cycle in his unfinished *Amerika* novel. It is very likely that he lets Amerika and its attendant phantasms finish or sign off on the "Letter to Father." One should not forget that, for Kafka, the trope of going to America was part and parcel of a punishing send-off, a very particular inflection of loss and exile. "Amerika," moreover, vast as it is, offers another abbreviation of the name Kafka. It/she shelters and supports an adventure of the incomplete name, a signature on the prowl, a slant in naming to which our writer was demonstrably sensitive: Amerikafka would be the nicked name for America. Or the other way around.

○ ○ ○

So much has been staked here in order to give some buoyancy to the understanding and predicament of the idea of a "good loser"—one who occupies the default position without eliminating the ambiguities and blind spots, the impossible binds implicit in the write-up of a complex contract of submissive abandon. Beginning with the posture of surrender, the syntax of a bow to the other, we have traveled through regions of submission reminiscent of Levinas's description of the very bestowal of the poetic word—a bow to the other, the bow that Paul Celan traces as inclination—a bow that may

take place in the giving of a handshake. Or one practices the "après vous" of ethical obeisance. Benjamin Franklin writes a letter to the banished son, leaving an offering, perhaps a mandate, in the form of an autobiographical text. He offers his life up to his son, who, disinherited, can enter succession only as recipient of the father's story and life, a son henceforth infused with the paternal letter. Kafka incorporates this letter in his own undeliverable letter. The address is vulnerable to destruction at every turn of the letter's destination, pointing to its incineration and scarce survivability. I've turned the page to Derrida, to the place that seals the concordance between a destination and a destiny, or the adestination signaled by the *Carte postale*, where, from the very beginning, on the cover, the relations are inverted and the legendary speaker becomes the secretary to the other: Socrates is shown taking dictation from Plato, behind his back, reversing the gears of our shared metaphysical heritage. The nonwriter poses as the writer, supports and supposes but also menaces the writer, and in this sense presupposes the writer, to the extent that the progenitor gives himself over to his son who lingers on the edge of doing himself in. At some point we discover that there is no such thing as a nonwriter, that the address to the nonwriter is in itself a fiction. The map of broken destinations provides us with a complicated scenario or wish.

What was Kafka thinking when he posed *The Autobiography* as the gift/book that would bind and newly relate him to his father? Was this the beginning of an incorporation of a foreign object or crypt-formation signaled by the deposit of Benjamin Franklin's address? I have indicated this before, but let me restate it in the prose of researched inquiry. The *Autobiography* was not available in German at the time Kafka made a gift of it to his father in 1919, and was handed to Hermann in the Czech edition of 1916. The commerce between father and son remains bilingual, binational, distributed between two experiences of the foreign, bridging two family members infinitely foreign to each other. The book enters the "Letter" within a kind of *pavlatche* structure traveling outside the inside of the language barriers that may constitute a minor literature or a split mother tongue. The internalized foreign body, Franklin's work, is pushed toward one edge of Kafka's plaint, permitting a double signature of near homonymic dimension, binding "Franz" to his translation in "Franklin," both of whom enter the scene of language by means of a *water*-signifier. The inclusion of Franklin as a sign of unreadable exchange between the Kafka father and son also establishes the blueprint for what will form the end of the "Letter," when Kafka ventrilocates a final exchange with Father on the subject of the "Letter," writing through the one who speaks in his stead, expunging his voice. Wedged between father and son, Franklin attains a place as unreadable remainder, as what the Kafkas still have to give each other and read together without however being able to do so. The identifications and failure to forge identifications with the characters put forth by Franklin create a vertiginous series—the Franklin son, addressee of the *Autobiography* qua letter (it begins "Dear Son"), cut himself off from his father and fatherland by declaring himself a monarchist and returning to the mother country. The futility of address staged by Franklin gives pause, for the lost son was not to be reeled back in by means of a letter. These considerations, and so many others, the detail of which I must now skip, put red flags on the possibility of writing up family return trips or wishing to reach and stabilize the fugitive relation.

Taken in by Kafka, the Franklin text begins to grow some Kafkan features. As odd as it seems, Franklin cooperates with his own alterations by posting some frankly Kafkan motifs in his autobiographical letter, quoting for instance a critical appraisal of his writing that binds them together, nearly matching Kafka's first page of his letter. He describes the stuttering start of a shared writing machine: "'In his common conversation he seems to have no choice of words; he hesitates and blunders; and yet, good God! How he writes!'"[7] Like Kafka—though this may be a staple feature that many writerly beings remember—Franklin takes recourse to writing in order to address a storm of violence that he could not stave off or take apart by speaking out. He recounts the "blows," the constant pummeling, to which he was subjected as a young man, placing him near a writing machine—the printing press, not unlike the one, slightly metamorphosed, in "The Penal Colony." Both writers had writing beaten into them, even as it provided refuge. Franz locates the cruelty of his up-and-downbringing in the father's *preparations* to beat him—when his father starts the engine of rage, puts the strap on the chair, rolls up his sleeves, shooting hard and deliberate looks at the shivering child. The last-minute reprieves served only, writes Franz, to install a guilty conscience, as if the child had gotten away with something grave. As if the adjourned beating were in itself an injustice that the child had perpetrated and for which he stood condemned. Had Hermann not each time aborted Project "A Child Is Being Beaten," Franz might have been able psychically to pay him off, he offers, and to emerge mostly unscathed in comparison to the one who could only witness the damages being collected by an indelible creditor. The meter is still ticking.

Franklin broke through the confines of a paternal penal colony by taking the beating, by receiving the blows. There's another thing that gave Franklin

7. Franklin, *Autobiography*, 29.

the advantage, a displacement of the paternal that lifted the American out of his prison yard. I will get to that momentarily. I must not lose sight of the fact that Benjamin Franklin is brought into the fold of the letter as a father. Franz Kafka may not have delivered the "Letter to Father"; but he brought home this "letter from Father" and pushed it across the table, to Hermann's side of things. Giving the father the gift of this life story, fathering his father by offering the letter from Father, Kafka may have gotten as close as he could to the fiction of becoming-father. It was a historical fiction that slipped into the house under the authority of Benjamin Franklin, one who domesticated the electric flash. Franz makes it clear that Franklin's text is meant to domesticate a raging disturbance in the household of Kafka. It may invite Franz to stow away in a vessel that turns the address of letter, reassigning a beginning so that the signatory of any letter henceforth attains the status of origin and paternal locus: "Dear Son." You are my lost son, whom I have disinherited, but toward whom I write. Or, I must disinherit you, as son, in order to write. Henceforth every missive, at once calling out and disinheriting, will have included this structure of broken address postmarked by Father.

But let us back up on the genealogical track of paternal fictions. Before leaving this text, incorporated into the body of the "Letter," a question must occupy us concerning the hookup with Benjamin Franklin, whom Kafka triangulates with Hermann, or of which he creates a supplementary fold, citing the American father-son example. Beyond the possible projection of a father writing to his son, or an American father writing to his father, Hermann Kafka—since he reinstates the field of the remote destination of the letter—has Kafka not irremediably disturbed the example he wished to provide by reintegrating the story of abusive relations? Has he managed once again to find, if by inadvertence, an abusive father—one who could only recycle, or precycle, themes of repudiation, exile, irreversible separation?

The dossier is complicated, and we have only begun to investigate the migration of Franklin's autobiography into Kafka's text and its effects upon his fissured world. If Kafka could not give his father grandchildren, he gave him Benjamin Franklin. This writer inserts a remark by means of an * to a passage that describes a scene of judgment linked to fraternal punishment. Let us install this passage and its supplement now. Writing of his brother, Franklin describes their "differences":

> Though a brother, he considered himself as my master, and me as his ap-
> prentice, and, accordingly, expected the same services from me as he would
> from another, while I thought he demean'd me too much in some he requir'd

of me, who from a brother expected more indulgence. Our disputes were often brought before our father, and I fancy I was either generally in the right, or else a better pleader, because the judgment was generally in my favor. But my brother was passionate, and had often beaten me, which I took extreamly amiss, and, thinking my apprenticeship very tedious, I was continually wishing for some opportunity of shortening it, which at length offered in a manner unexpected.* (15)

Well, this version of Franz/Franklin had a few things going for it. Franklin was able to manage pain by displacing familial hierarchy and indicating a pattern of workable governance. Paternal cruelty reverted to the brother as master, which, at least in this limited case, proved benevolent to the extent that the father assumes the position of judge in a space that no longer allows for a death penalty. Not uncharacteristically, Benjamin Franklin turns torture into a good lesson, putting it early to bed and early to rise, a penny saved in the nick of time. Applied cruelty was part of his democratic training grounds. Perhaps the political transvaluation of affliction can happen when your first name, Benjamin, bears a promise and means that you are the favorite son—the son of the right hand from whom a whole tribe is said to descend. The reading of names and their fateful inscriptions is Franz Kafka's doing, not mine. His "Letter" continually recalls to us the extent to which the fate of the son is tied to the name with which he is saddled or crowned, or out of which he must try to climb.

As for Kafka, he eventually turned against his "Letter," disinheriting it, at least for the most part, evaluating the effort as the "schlechten, unnötigen" (bad, unnecessary) piece of writing through which he may have worked something out with himself—or not.[8] In terms of what comes close to intention, it had started out as part of a pact to secure a better life for his father and, where possible, for himself as well. It was meant to offer them the expectation of relief as an untenable couple, bound for life, inexorable. By the time he plowed through the pileup of textual-existential requirements that awaited clearance of some sort Kafka, however, had to change the last sentences to include a death sentence. The ending was freighted with

---

* I fancy his harsh and tyrannical treatment of me might be a means of impressing me with that aversion to arbitrary power that has stuck to me though my whole life. (15)

8. Franz Kafka, *Briefe an Milena* [Jesenská], ed. Jürgen Born and Michael Müller (Frankfurt a.M.: Fischer, 1983), 196.

another need. The asserted wish for a better way of dying was appended to the letter, because, ailing and significantly weakened, Franz was also signing off on life. I am writing, he states, with the intention of reassuring both of us and "mak(ing) our living *and dying* easier" ("daß es uns beide ein wenig beruhigen und Leben *und Sterben* leichter machen kann. Franz," italics, like "and dying," added).

Yet the letter hits a snag as it signs off on itself because on some level it has tightened up on its intention, offering a kind of evidentiary overkill and, all in all, by means of a Kafkan paradox, too snug a fit. Graphically honed, it finds itself *too close to truth* if it aims to cover the reality of the puzzled and irrecuperable relationship of father and son: "Naturally things cannot in reality fit together the way the evidence does in my letter; life is more than a Chinese puzzle. But by the correction made by this rejoinder—a correction I neither can nor will elaborate in detail—in my opinion something has been achieved which so closely approximates the truth that it might reassure us both a little and make our living and our dying easier. Franz" (125). The extreme coherency of his case causes the "Letter" to falter, prepares it for further trial and scrutiny, subjecting it to the fissuring that any text worthy of the name attracts to its distressed premises. In fact the entire letter, marked as rejoinder ("Einwurf"), now folds back onto itself to cast the text as a battery of exams and tests that Franz had all along—and all alone—administered to himself.

Kafka once again decides to skip details. Yet, he offers one incitement to justify an address to his ever-forsaking Father. Kafka, the unmarried, has thrown in the towel. His recent failure to nail a marriage contract served as the springboard to the text of failures. The "Letter to Father" project emerges from the voiding of a contract, an abandoned vow. Filling in the blanks after the last failed attempt at marriage, Franz writes shortly before wrapping up that he had in fact failed the better part of all other smaller tests and quizzes put to him by life's exigencies. Of these, *Ehe* (marriage) is pronounced as having constituted the greatest test ("Ich prüfte mich ja nicht erst gegenüber der Ehe, sondern gegenüber jeder Kleinigkeit. . . . Jetzt kommt der Zwang zur Bilanz, das heißt der Heiratsversuch," 56–57; "I tested myself not only when faced with marriage, but in the face of every trifle. . . . Now comes the coerced balance sheet, the attempt ["Versuch," test, tryout] at marriage," 119–21, translation modified). He does not relent, turning himself over time and again to the authority of the test. The most horrific fright—the repeated attempts at marriage ("Heiratsversuche")—was prepared by an enduring, decisive and in effect, the most bitter test ("eine dauernde, entscheidende und sogar die erbitterteste Prüfung," 46). These attempts, testing out the possibility for any kind of redemption in this life ("Rettungsversuche"), were all the more grandiose, he writes, for their failure. Franz wonders if, after all is said and done, the failure will have been so great that language cannot capture its magnitude—he can only be thwarted, he surmises, in his attempts to make the experience of failure itself intelligible.

Yet the fate of the entire letter, its singular success—the success wagered on the slim chances for bringing home a description of failure—hangs on making the failure of these tests somehow readable ("Und doch hängt das Gelingen des ganzen Briefes davon ab, denn in diesen Versuchen was einerseits alles versammelt"). Everything depends on reading the pulse of his failure, the "Letter" appears to urge at the core of its self-understanding: its entire success hinges on getting such a failure to expose itself, giving way to the sum of its uncountable losses. But the deficit that has accrued to this loser son's account is so considerable that it cannot properly be rendered without burning a hole into the pages of its improbable telling.

I cannot say for sure whether the texts before us belong to literary telling or point to yet another form of recognizable language usage. Perhaps they suggest an anahistorical account, telling us how to begin the work of testing the limits of authority, the markup of the paternal, the shadow-side of domestic policies and the early exposure to what is constituted as foreign. The encounter with the foreign, Kafka has shown, begins at home. For those who still wonder how poetic ventures might tell us more about stark political realities and the way they slide off or are tethered to reference, I'd say that we might consider the way the Freudian notion of "secondary revision" helps us understand the unavoidable nearness of poeticity to matters of political determination. Literature can and has played a decisive role in the development of national identities, transnational formations, political and social endeavor as part of its exegetical push. Breaking open frontiers and sticking to the impossible rigors of its telling, literature is our teacher, asking that we read nearsightedly, and with great suspicion, what passes for democracy or truth or the solidity of knowing. Literature, for its part and parties, has stayed the course with the feints, improvisations, and revisions on which language relies for its startling disclosures. Let me introduce a somewhat paradoxical formulation: There is a glimmer of hope in knowing that language is from start to finish unreliable, requiring vigilance and endless flexibility, demanding at every turn a real sensitivity to its positing antics, slippages, revisionary tendencies; language ceaselessly tells and repeats the story of

the doomed sense it carries of its failure to tell what is happening to us, or to locate with any certainty the addresses that we imagine befall us. Yet it has on many occasions a tracking number for the addresses that miss us and can account for our many deconstitutions. Traumatically insufficient to itself and world, language makes you responsible, alert, ready to restart even in moments of greatest depletion. There is hope in the fact that language is relentlessly self-tormenting—a glimmer of hope, but perhaps not for us.

What Is Called Father?
The Sequel

One reason to revert to childhood at this point of histori-cal reflection—and to confront the familial delusion—is to get a close-up of ORIGINAL IMPOTENCE. The child's impotence, Lacan reminds us, is a far cry from the omnipotence of which the neu-rotic feels capable and seems culpable. One recalls Freud's declension of the neurotic tot's obsession with the idea of an omnipotence of thought that leads head-on to his father's demise: "he's dead because I wanted him dead, at least in my head, but I didn't mean it and now I'm in for it!" There's a spark of power behind such thinking, a hike in self-importance.

By contrast, ORIGINAL IMPOTENCE—the unshakable sense of being-in-trouble, the rage of start-up incapacitation—opens the dos-sier of the cornered, the perpetually startled, those who feel throttled and can't find a means to break out of the first scaffolding of serially decked confinement. Things snap severely into place without much wiggle room. Frustration, aggression, despair, and extreme forms of dependency have their way with childhood, even if more cheerful nar-ratives overlay the inset of its fundamental constraints. While it is the case that frustration is imaginary, privation is real, if not also situated with respect to the symbolic.

Restauration

"Home cooked meal evokes terror for me," writes Thomas Bernhard in the novel, *A Child.** The perversion of reinstalling the home front where it might have been repealed, at least for the time of a meal, sends shudders down the young spine. The family restaurant hosts aversion for the Bernhardian child, blocking the emancipatory edge that going out to eat offers. Restorative and exteriorized, the restaurant should in principle release the hungry child of modernity or one of its subpersonalities from the shackles of the family table. Eating elsewhere, on furlough from the dinner table, could even function to stimulate the child's appetite, turning the tables on the child's staple sentence, "I'm not hungry." Every little one, at one point of formation or another, is already signed up at the tryouts for the special Hunger Artist Olympics, standing with Kafka's figure for the refusal of sustenance. In literature, the ordeal of the Hunger Artist serves as one reproach to the integral anorexia imposed by the family gathering, its sloppy communion and pile-on of values. Refusing to eat, terrorized by the concept itself of a home-cooked meal, the child is itself invariably served up as the first course and the main course—the curse habitually clocked as mealtime.

Give us this day our daily dread: it is difficult to imagine the Kafka family going out to eat, though that is what it would have taken for the death grip of mealtime to loosen, let go. At home, at the table, little Franz Kafka was eaten alive. By the time of the famous "Letter to Father," he was vaporized. He says so himself: A good deal of the damage done to the young psyche occurred at table. The neighborhood restaurant might have rerouted the oppressive domesticity of home rule—it might have introduced a hiatus or suspensive regime change that would

* Thomas Bernhard, *Ein Kind* (München: DTV, 1999), 31.

allow for hunger's pacing. Part of a spectacle of public generality, the theater of ingestion—possibly also of incorporation—the restaurant causes the hold on the child to slacken, if only because there are witnesses and waiters whose work consists in diminishing the intensities of paternal law and the sacrificial rites that underlie their daily distribution—the daily apportionment of dread.

In Kafka's works the family table locks the child into a site where Father presides; it offers one of the prime occasions for paternity to enthrone itself, conducting prescriptive raids on the child's bearing—invading his plate, entering and altering his body, adjusting his manner of being. The table becomes the metonymy for all law, the place where sovereign exceptionalism asserts itself: Father does not have to obey his own law, he can pick his teeth or clean his ears while the eaters submit to the severity of his rule. The children, in Kafka at least, and in the simulacrum of home in which many others were grown, are consistently downgraded to the status of unshakable refugees, parasites, those who quiver under the thickness of anxiety while laws, like platters, are passed and forced down one's delicate throat.

Chapter 6

On the Unrelenting Creepiness of Childhood

Lyotard, Kid-Tested

Unde wenn die Prüfung
Ist durch die Knie gegangen,
Mag einer spüren das Waldgeschrei.

(And when the trial
Has passed through our knees,
May someone sense the forest's cry.)
—Hölderlin, "The Ister Hymn"

From Socrates' predatory urges to Locke's invention of the "Ideot" or Hegel's racist assignments—for the moment I shall take this no further—philosophy has demonstrated a need to impound those who could not speak for themselves, who had not reached a certain legislated majority. Under the reign of Locke, Hume, and Condillac, empirical philosophy assembled the figure of the idiot in order to put some reality behind established hypothetical assumptions.[1] The idiot pinned down the first folds of language in the essays on human understanding. Made to stand for an epoch, lost to civilization, of originary memory the idiot spanned the chasm between the asserted polarity of nature and culture. The entry on philosophical pages of miscreants helped, moreover, to rehabilitate the "empirical" basis of empiricism. Much can be said about the induction of wild children, savages, idiots, and infants into the realm of philosophical

---

1. I discuss the relation of idiocy and its correlates in philosophy more fully in *Stupidity* (Urbana and Chicago: University of Illinois Press, 2001).

speculation, and it would be important to investigate more fully the peculiar yet crucial status of these minorities as philosophy conducts its adult raids. No doubt Nietzsche may be seen to have turned this state of affairs on its head when he invited the animals to participate in a new tropology.

Now comes Jean-François Lyotard, who talks to children. No matter how polymorphously perverse, punctually pampered or pacified, these are the distressed among us, the fearful and hungry. They squeak and peek and try to get their meaning across. They panic; then smile and burble, then panic. Held in abusive custody by the laws of becoming, they hang on to your finger for dear life. From the get-go, the reality principle sneaks up on them to snap them out of the domain of the pleasure principle (of course this is a complicated relay, as Lacan has shown, for the reality principle is always in defeat; but still, it goes after you). As in Goethe's ballad, the Erlking is out to get them, poised to snatch the child from the arms of momentary reassurance.

In the case presented by Lyotard we are faced with the figure of the minor, often oppressed, for whom language and representation may not be entirely foreclosed, though surrender, the predominance of muteness, and a reper-toire of stammers often govern the thwarted scene of childhood. Still, there are reprieves and the event of memory; language, however jumbled, mimetic, deregulated, occurs and belongs to the existence to which childhood—some-thing that eventually goes into remission but returns in waves throughout the lives of the wounded—is fitted. Interiority does not necessarily take hold at the early stages. Yet even when these children are silenced or a hand is laid on them, they are traversed by what Lyotard understands as sheer feel-ing—maybe a pinch of joy, a sting of melancholic regret, a straitening both pleasurable and painful, a body memory that trembles. With no language of interiority to vouch for feeling, the children are more or less stranded, bared to colonializing projection.

Vaulted and shut, their subjectivity—if there is one—offers little in the way of an account; even so, in most cases they surpass or at least scramble the master codes of philosophical claims made on their behalf and elude the cognitive scanners that try to detect and classify them. The child constitutes a security risk for the house of philosophy. It crawls in, setting off a lot of noise. The figure of the child, which in the end inserts an imaginary lesion in philosophy—a condition that calls out for endless symbolic repair—may be borne by the anguish of the *différend*. That is to say it enters, or is entered into the places where speech falters and language chokes in the throat of a political body, where the question of fair representation is peremance to-rily dismissed or simply not addressed. But it is not as if the child had the means of representation at hand. The child is given over to extreme forms

of defenselessness: "dependency," Lyotard indicates, is too weak a word to describe the condition of such minority-being, the ever-chafing condition of childhood.

How did they stumble into philosophical headquarters? Well, their proto-type, the essential child—the idiot—appeared alongside or at the head of the train of blind, deaf, or mute subjects (whose implications for subjecthood, precisely, provoked crisis), and was most closely leagued with the prestige accorded to the construction of the wild child—the teachable idiot. They were pressed into service, assigned to uphold mythic assurances of the humanly clean slate, presenting such a possibility, in theory, at least, to the extent that they—idiots—donated their bodies to the cause of a science that staked everything on what appeared to constitute observable traits of human origins. Recruited to the cause of philosophy to make a philosophical point, the idiot belongs outside the philosophy whose integrity it promotes. The child, as I said, crawls in at unexpected moments or morphs, as in Kant's critical reflections, into the ambivalent purveyor of genius—the irresponsible, often puerile excess to which we owe the poetic word.

In *The Inhuman*, Lyotard, for his part, writes of the debt to childhood that is never paid off. A matter of the traces of an indetermination, childhood continues to hold us hostage. The obscure savageness of childhood reminds us that all education is inhuman "because it does not happen without constraint and terror."[2] At once savaging and civilizing (there is never one without the other), education straitens the little one, who is cornered by cultural demand. Childhood, in any case, will leave us with inhuman surges of deregulation, with a level of fear and distress that can come up at any point in the trajectory of so-called human development. "Shorn of speech, incapable of standing upright, hesitating over the objects of its interest, not able to calculate its advantages, not sensitive to common reason, the child is eminently the human because its distress heralds and promises things possible" (3–4). Lagging behind itself, the child's "initial delay in humanity," moreover, "which makes it the hostage of the adult community, is also what manifests to this community the lack of humanity it is suffering from, and which calls on it to become more human" (4). Childhood, with its unrelenting creepiness, issues an ethical call—be it made by the day-

2. Jean-François Lyotard, *The Inhuman: Reflections on Time* (Stanford, Calif.: Stanford University Press, 1991), 4. Subsequent references are cited parenthetically in the text.

care crowd or the operators Antigone, Christ, and Isaac, all loyalists to the child's camp, even though their identity as children must remain at once undecidable and settled. (For some reason—or unreason—some figures of ethical calling are tagged essentially as children, even if by other measures they are plainly in midlife crises when they are tried.) Lyotard asks: "What shall we call human in humans, the initial misery of their childhood, or their capacity to acquire a 'second' nature which, thanks to language, makes them fit to share in communal life, adult consciousness and reason?"(3). Childhood enters a breach into the very concept of the human and makes us ask, once again, what it means to be human. Yet the decision to claim the human is split between the early episodes of initial desolation and the later cover-up schemes that language supports and the community payrolls.

More severe words are reserved for the provocation of childhood in another, later text. In "Mainmise" the child is lined up with the slave, with the one whose destiny is put in the hands of another.[3] Like the slave, the child does not belong to itself, having, Lyotard says, no claim to himself (there is no play of "herself," so out of a sense of frustrated probity I will repeat the complete oppression of the girl-child before we encounter the drama of Emma in the next chapter): "He is in the hands of another. Dependency is too weak a word to describe this condition of being seized and held by the hand of the other" (1). By childhood Lyotard means that we are born before being born to ourselves. "We are born from others but also to others, given over defenseless to them. Subject to their *mancipium*, and to an extent that even they do not recognize" (2–3). The offense is such that even the offenders, by necessity repeat offenders, operate on the level of an unconscious siege. You may want to know when exactly the sneak attacks strike: Childhood

3. Jean-François Lyotard and Eberhard Gruber, "Mainmise," in *The Hyphen: Between Judaism and Christianity*, trans. Pascale-Anne Brault and Michael Naas (Amherst, N.Y.: Humanity Books, 1999). References are cited parenthetically in the text. It may be useful to consider the translator's note: "*Mainmise*—from the French *main* and *mettre*: 1. A term from feudal jurisprudence referring to the action of taking hold of or seizing someone because of infidelity or lack of devotion to the feudal lord. 2. The action of laying a hand upon or striking someone. 3. The freeing of slaves by their lords (Emile Littré, *Dictionnaire de la langue française* [Chicago: Encyclopaedia Britannica, Inc., 1978]). The *Pluridictionnaire de Larousse* adds that *mainmise* can also refer to the action of laying a hand on and having an exclusive influence over something or someone—as in a state's *mainmise* over certain businesses (Paris: Librairie Larousse, 1975)" (12).

is an age that is not marked by age—or rather, it does not age but recurs episodically, even historically. Childhood can last a whole lifetime if you find yourself throttled and unable to root out some representation of what is affecting you; this can happen every day. "I am speaking of this condition of being *affected* and not having the means—language, representation—to name, identify, reproduce, and recognize what is affecting us" (2). If I am not mistaken, Lyotard uses childhood to resist the modern Western ideal of emancipation; he manages to deflate the reverie that has you thinking you'll get out from under the grip of the *mancipium.*

The *mainmise,* which travels in many disguises (parental love "may have been a calamity—it may have engendered such a *mainmise* over the child's soul," 3), often remains unknown to the child as an adult. Something is taking her down, even as she meets the world with measurable instances of "success." Under the thumb of an invisible yet persistent *mainmise,* the adult child regresses to minority following an unpredictable rhythm of being that beats the drum of an impossible emancipation—the emancipation promised by humanism, whether Christian or secular, which teaches that "man is something that must be freed." As for the nature of this freeing, "there are many different possibilities, from Augustine up through Marx." These promises say in effect that the *mainmise* can be thrown off, even dealt with definitively, according to some calculable program or redemptive ground plan. If we could get over it—this would suppose that we had some grasp of what is keeping us down.

The *mainmise,* a condition of extreme captivity, can be so powerfully effective that, like the child, the adult has no access to it by means of memory or cognition. To bring the terms of this condition into focus, if only by projective inversion, it is almost as in those stories of *The Twilight Zone,* which end with a shot of a miniature house where normalcy was played out under the gaze of a gigantess, a playing child. The shadow thrown on you was in a sense too big to be perceived, much less fought off. One is left dumb and unknowing about the *mainmise* that nonetheless accompanies your every move and persists in calling the shots. The imprint is so profound that the child, well "it will not even occur to him to rebel, nor will he have received the gift or grace to pray that his *mainmise* be lifted" (3). Because of the untraceable fingerprints of the *mainmise*—I am surmising here, as Lyotard is unclear about how this works—the condition that he describes redounds not only to severe psychopathology ("I am not just talking about severe neuroses or psychoses"). There is no account or narrative that could contain or point reliably to the *mainmise,* no anamnesis, as he likes to say. At the same time, the surrender is so pervasive that it need not be pathologized in order to be conceded. One does not have to be psychotic to understand that you're barely out on bail on good days and back in the hovel of wretched captivity on other days of your so-called autonomous being. The possibility of a given freedom—freedom as unquestionably given, and before all else a given, thrown in with the *da* of our Dasein—in other words the kind of freedom that Jean-Luc Nancy with his Kantian signet posits, seems to be absent from the scene.[4] Childhood, in any case, has never been philosophically or politically posed together with freedom (unless one reverts to the story of the wild or ineducable and unharmed child). The civilized child is always in tow, the emblem of unfreedom, the "too soon" of any emancipatory trek or movement. The child's logical exemption from the discussion of freedom requires, precisely, that one *think the child* for the purpose of political headway and ethical starters.

The hold on the child translates into an irrevocable wounding on which childhood in fact depends. The timing may be slightly off, because in this instance Lyotard hints that pleasure may be felt prior to the wound, while elsewhere he indicated, I thought, that the wounding hold had first dibs on the child. To the extent that the rhythm of unconscious time bombing is included in the depiction of these experiences (which often bypass "experience"), it would be petty no doubt to insist on strict synchronicities. Lyotard offers this wounderful observation: "For the child, everything is a wound, the wound of a pleasure that is going to be forbidden and taken away" (3). The *mainmise* is raised as a sign of what is about to happen, namely, of what has always happened: it is raised to slap the pleasure out of the child. In this round the *mainmise* is, we could say, the hand of time. Time beating pleasure, given over to the stranglehold of the reality principle. "The suffering that results and the search for the object, something analogous, in short, to emancipation, arise out of this wound." The emancipatory urge, prompted by the early experience of essential deprivation, starts with this figure of analogy, weak but soldering. (In Lacan's reading of Freud, the fundamental desire—the incestuous one—is prohibited in one of the starts of life: everything else flows from the initial withholding pattern, including the battering search for the object neither entirely lost nor altogether found.[5]) Alive with the memory trace of early forfeiture, the subject tries to free itself, at least

4. In this regard a careful reading of *L'expérience de la liberté* (Paris: Galilée: 1988) would complicate the trajectories we are pursuing. Freedom is linked to the singular experience of existence, an experience that does not obey a logic of *fact* which would be opposable to the law.

5. This becomes one of the fixed points of the ethics of psychoanalysis. See Jacques Lacan, *Le séminaire: L'éthique de la psychanalyse Livre VII* (Paris: Éditions du Seuil: 1986).

enough to cover the losses. Thus originates the call, a call to emancipation or of exodus—a call, in any case, that initiates the movement of flight. The call positions the constrained child in relation to elsewhere. The children of Israel (why are they children?) are said to have taken the call as they headed for trouble or, rather, for more trouble, and elsewhere.

Lyotard links the temporal wounding to the flight from Egypt. He observes, in reference to the exodus of the Hebrews, that they "escaped the Pharoah's *mancipium* only by placing themselves under the *mancipium* of Yahweh" (2). The fantasy of a promising elsewhere is broken. It is not as though there would be a locatable exteriority to the primal hold. Permit me to introduce an analogy, another hand to play in the negotiations with the *mainmise*, for it is still necessary to elucidate the difficulty of obtaining a truly valid exit visa when it comes to the anticipation of an exodus. As with the plight of addiction elaborated by Thomas de Quincey, one can move only from one addiction to the other, even if the second term is that of a cure; the oppression of dependency, the demand of adherence to the addiction or to that which opposes it, is structurally the same.[6] What joins the disparate events consisting in the *mainmise* of the child, the flight from Egypt, and the call from elsewhere (Lyotard persistently figures the flight from Egypt as a response to a call, a "vocation"), is the unknowing in which they originate and continue effectively to hold sway. One is dumbstruck, somnambulizing, rising to a call that cannot be identified or in any meaningful way secured. Perhaps it comes from the past or resounds in a future dimly awaited. "It comes from beyond me and within me"—this is how Heidegger locates the call, the aphonic call of conscience in *Sein und Zeit* that has concerned us in our reading of Kafka and authority's pull.[7] At any rate, one cannot account for the call that has a hold on me or, disrupting any conscious itinerary, that puts me on hold without my consent, surpassing my initiative or the knowledge I think I have about the way things go as I crawl through the playing fields of Being-in-the-world.

Attentive to that which, defying cognition and eluding memory, stultifies, Lyotard tries time and again to trace the call. There is something that grinds

---

6. For more addiction, see my *Crack Wars: Literature, Addiction, Mania* (Lincoln and London: University of Nebraska Press, 1992).

7. Martin Heidegger, *Sein und Zeit* (Tübingen: Max Niemeyer, 1979). See also Christopher Fynsk, *Heidegger, Thought and Historicity* (Ithaca, N.Y.: Cornell University Press, 1986).

Being, knowledge, memory, and even health, to a level of indifference, something that defies all conceptuality or generalizable principle. He stays close to the ground and keeps his receptors open. When his narrated *Lebenslauf*, his *curriculum vitae*, established in *Peregrinations*, evokes the call on an almost ontological frequency ("there is something like a call," 9), Lyotard claims a lifelong interest in the notion and doctrines of indifference.[8] Something in Being menaces thought, undermines writing, with a quiet, sort of pernicious consistency. In the distant past, Lyotard offers, he himself was committed to the encounter with that to which we remain deaf and sluggish—to the "groundlessness of Being which constantly exerts a fascinating threat over thinking and writing." He writes his M.A. thesis on *Indifference as an Ethical Notion*. A paper investigating a kind of originary stupor that involved the Epicurean *ataraxia*, the Stoic *apatheia*, the extreme Stoic *adiaphora*, the Zen not-thinking, the Taoist nothingness, and so forth, it later on leads to larger considerations of stultifying modalities of Being. I would not hesitate to go as far as grouping his concern with reflective judgment in this category or to mobilize for this thought-numbing area of the work his discussion of Freud's call to let the mind float: "You have to impoverish your mind, clean it out as much as possible, so that you make it capable of anticipating the meaning, the 'What' of the 'It happens . . . '" (18). The poverty leveling of mind does not oppose itself to thought but allows something to arrive, something that we associate with the possibility of meaning.

The advent of the event, moreover, is, as Lyotard contends, itself dependent upon the ability of mind to scale back its holdings, that is to say: "No event is at all accessible if the self does not renounce the glamour of its culture, its wealth, health, knowledge, and memory. . . . Let us make ourselves weak and sick the way Proust did, or let us fall truly in love" (18). The only possible existential glitch here resides in the suggestion that one would be positioned to *make* oneself fall ill or in love; this, no doubt, is said with that smile of wrenching irony for which Jean-François Lyotard was known by his friends. Still, it must be admitted that, in the strict sense, renunciation implies a supplement of will—the *ability*, precisely, to disable, when mind exercises its ability to disable the self-body. That is the only hurdle I see here, and perhaps I am placing it too firmly in this deserted landscape where debility rules. There is a splitting that seems to be at issue, an almost Fichtean split of self according to which one of the selves, the transcendental self, watches the other, more empirical one crash into

8. Jean-François Lyotard, *Peregrinations: Law, Form, Event* (New York: Columbia University Press, 1988).

the wall of necessary failure. It is hardly probable that Lyotard, smile or no smile, would permit such an Idealist formulation to prevail at this time. I will have to suppose that there is no rescued self that survives the crash or that is shown to be firmly cleared to play the weak and sick card.

In order to attune one's being to the event, in order to prime for the advent of meaning, some downsizing has to take place: a thoroughgoing impoverishment, an extreme ascesis, needs to be welcomed and assumed. Yet, because it involves a supplement of will, this degree of ontological deflation still does not sink to the level of being that in "Mainmise" he later on associates with the *mancipium*. Acts of self-depletion are somehow engaged by the subject as it renews the encounter with the limit-experience of deficiency. The depleted condition, which Lyotard eventually reads in terms of the stakes of knowledge, opens the channels in his work to art and politics—inscriptions that run on empty, forfeiting the support of cognition and its corresponding power players.[9] Art and politics are not simply rule-based or governed solely by preexisting contracts or criteria. In a Kantian turn, Lyotard thus argues that both art and politics are exempted from the hegemony of the genre of discourse called cognitive (21). In Kant's terms, such an exemption means that we have no recourse to the sort of judgment he called determinant judgment. Among other things, such cognitive voiding explains why we are essentially bereft—left clueless, off-base, and in a cloud of obscurity.[10]

Reflective judgment implies the ability of the mind to synthesize data, be it sensuous or sociohistorical, without reverting to a predetermined rule. Lyotard writes: "Accordingly, thinking advances through clouds by touching them as enigmatic cases, the reason for which—their 'what they are'—is not given with them, with their 'that they are occurring'" (20). Determinant judgment operates differently. "The problem is the following: a concept being defined, one must find the available cases to be subsumed under it and so doing begin to validate the concept. In other words, understanding possesses a rule of explanation and is trying to select references to which it can be applied. This is a formidable way for wandering through thoughts:

9. My last conversation with Lyotard concerned depletion, his and mine, that is, my struggle with chronic fatigue and the preparations he was making to teach a course at Emory University the following semester on the problem of fatigue.
10. One of the chapters in *Peregrinations* bears the title "Clouds." Lyotard links cloud formations to thought.

it is the way called science" (21). Determinant judgment gives way to the techno-scientific universe, announcing the place of the Heideggerian *Gestell* as the modern way for thinking to be related to Being. It would appear that determinant judgment has won out by securing a type of cognitive base—a calculable grid—that compensates for the backsliding returns and depletions, which were earlier at issue.

In spite of the triumph of determinant judgment in the contemporary world (in the values of programming, forecasting, efficiency, security, computing, and the like), Lyotard shows that "other games or genres of discourse are available in which formulating a rule or pretending to give an explanation is irrelevant, even forbidden" (21). This is particularly the case with aesthetic judgment and taste, which introduce a kind of cognitive humbling, an essential passivity: "No concept, no external finality, no empirical or ethical interest is involved in the reception by the imagination of sensations coming from so-called data. There are only the most humble syntheses. . . . The conceptual rule under which the data could be subsumed must remain inactive" (22). Lyotard in fact ends the first lecture of *Peregrinations*, "Touches," by putting through a kind of ethical call, an ethical call without ethical interest or prescriptive pathos. He says, concluding the lecture, that to "respond to a case without criteria, which is reflective judgment, is itself a case in its turn, an event to which an answer, a mode of linking, will eventually have to be found. This condition may be negative, but it is the principle for all probity in politics as it is in art. I am also obliged to say: as it is in thinking" (27). No predetermination, Lyotard maintains, exempts any thinking from the responsibility of responding to each case. Thinking is responsible to the singularity of each case, being answerable to the unsubstitutable demand placed upon it. It is delusory to give meaning to an event or imagine a meaning for an event by anticipating what that event will be in reference to a prior text. "But it is indeed impossible to avoid this way of thinking completely, because it offers security against the calls or touches of the big X" (27). Traveling through a space between the active and unconscious breaches of mind, the big X marks the spot where sheer receptivity can be located, on the other side of any claim of knowability.

❂ ❂ ❂

The big X has to do with the "something" that may occur—in the case of Cézanne under or on his eyes "if they make themselves receptive enough to it. This 'something' is a quality of chromatism, a color timbre. To achieve this is a matter of a 'passivity' without pathos, which is the opposite of either

the controlled or unconscious activity of the mind" (19). X addresses the uncanny "fact" that "there is" something here and now, regardless of what it is. "It is as if something hidden inside the Montagne Sainte Victoire, say Being, or that entity Kant calls 'the X in general,' was playing in a game against the painter by making 'moves' with chromatic material." One cannot psych out the "X in general" or know what it's up to. On clear days, one can simply acknowledge, follow, or, if your name is Cézanne, somehow paint its disposition. Placing us in the grips of a major double bind, it lords over us like the immovable power play of the *mainmise*.

On the one hand, we strive to let go in order to avoid being hard of hearing when the big X puts out a call: in order to be attuned to the call we are not supposed to know, grasp, or force subsumption on when facing the uncanny fact that it occurs. It hits us as an appeal without precedent, a circumstance without cognitive netting. There is no other hand (which by no means lessens the grip of the double bind). Yet things go on as if there had always been another, perhaps a first hand—this habit turns us over to the shriveled authority of the *manchot* of which Lyotard writes, the missing hand. ("By freeing himself from the tutelage of the other, the *manchot* takes back his hand, takes things back into his own hands. He thinks he is getting over his castration, that the wound may be healing. This dream of being able to get over lack, over what is missing, is the very dream that gives rise to emancipation today," 5.) This missing other hand is the hand played by the supplement of will that we detected earlier, that is, by the action of self-mutilation that permits one to exercise control over a stretch of destiny. Like the crab that loses its claw or the animal tearing off a limb or paw in panic, the *manchot* takes things in hand, albeit in the clutch of a missing hand. The rhetoricity of this moment is impossible, for the *manchot* is shown taking back a hand that no longer is. The inexistent trophy dominates the promissory note of political rhetoric. According to Lyotard, the violence that suppresses castration dominates and blinds the politics of emancipatory struggle today.

Although his thought edges toward the chasms of absolute impoverishment, inscribing mind and taking the body down with it, Lyotard often pulls back from his insight, in the end entrusting his elaboration to a surplus of linguisticity. He shares this tendency with Lacan. Lyotard, for example, has named a hole in being but then recoups by saying there are other games, other discursive genres. Yet he has himself traced a movement where no game plan or map of discursiveness would hold. This indemnifying gesture signals a tension in his articulation, which we have noted in his prescription for making oneself weak or rendering the mind inactive—as if the passivity without pathos that he equally promotes were not possibly coextensive with all the efforts of Being. For what is *mainmise* but an originary condition of oppression, a lower gear in the death drive that in fact tramples the subject-elect prior even to the irreversible alienation of language?

Now all this comes down to the ordeal or trial of the call, to the call of the big X, or Being, or the mountain, or God. On top with Being or God, even the mountain calls. The call is not necessarily of language or entirely without language. It is hard to situate with any certainty. In *Sein und Zeit*, Heidegger had said of the call—the aphonic call of conscience—that it comes from within me and from beyond me. In order to heed the call one has to have emptied oneself, have undergone a personal kenosis (which, to the extent that it empties, drops off the "personal"). In any case, there is nothing on the order of knowledge to guarantee the call or ensure its referential authority (we shall see how the call devoid of knowledge or ascertainable origin becomes the call of the father). Lyotard himself began the essay with such a stamp, miming its necessity by splitting himself off from his own intention. He began in the twilight of unknowing. About the observations he was prepared to unfold, he said of their origin that they "do not come from the place of some presumed knowledge. For I know nothing of what I have to say here. Nothing of this love of knowledge and wisdom that the Greeks instilled in us under the name of philosophy" (1). In this sense, according to the logic of the argument he subsequently develops, Lyotard works through the seduction of woman. According to the biblical fable, she exists in order to make man forget that he does not know (you know, the fable of the apple: "woman's desire is that man forget that he cannot have knowledge," 8). Correspondingly, there is something like a false call that is posited in the fable—a false and therefore also a true call, and primal man has been shown falling prey to the false call, the call to knowledge or to forgetting his castration (already in paradise there was castration!).

○ ○ ○

These calls test man, constitute his trial, firm up his ordeal. ("The letters of the Torah that designate God's asking find their best approximation in the German verb *versuchen*. This word means trial, attempt, tentative, even temptation. Yahweh tries Abraham by asking him for his son," 9–10.) The essential test of childhood, "a great uncertainty concerning childhood," writes Lyotard, involves the binding ("liaison") and the unbinding or disconnection ("déliaison"): "That is to say, concerning the very core of what governs emancipation. This uncertainty concerns the status of the call and of that which calls, which is to say, the status of the father" (7). This goes

very fast but we have already seen that the feminine can pull a fast one, and place a false call ("the evil that speaks in woman"). At the same time the *mainmise* is that of the father, even if he has employed a wayward operator.

> Jesus' response to the question "Who is the greatest in the kingdom of heaven?" quivers like an arrow that has hit its target; it is the little one, the child (Matthew 18:1–5), *parvulus* in the Vulgate. That is why the child must not be "scandalized" [Gr. *skandalisei*: offended, made to stumble] (Matthew 18:6). Using the term *wound*, I said that this scandal or stumbling block (what Freud called seduction) is inherent to childhood insofar as it is subject to the *mancipium* of adults. And *mancipium* must be taken in both senses here: the one that the adult exercises over the child, and the one that their own childhood exercises over them, even while they are exercising it over the child. (7)

Reflecting the double track of *mancipium*, Lyotard understands the terms of "childhood" in two ways: the childhood that is not bound to this time but is "the celestial model of what has no need to be emancipated, having never been subjected to any other *mainmise* than that of the father; and the subject that is inevitably subjected to scandal, to stumbling blocks, and thus to the abjection of what does not belong to the truth of this call" (7). The scandal or stumbling block "is everything that sidetracks this call—violence, exclusion, humiliation, and the seduction (in the original sense) of the innocent child." The one by means of whom the scandal or stumbling block occurs exercises a *mancipium* over the child, thereby misguiding and keeping the child away from his only *manceps*, the father.

Splitting man from the father, Lyotard affirms the disturbing plight that pulls the child from the paternal domain: "This stumbling block and misguidance are necessary. It is necessary to be *bound*, expropriated, appropriated by man rather than the father." Man in this case stands for woman who intercepts the call and runs it through a scrambling device that endangers the man-child. "The woman's desire is that man stand up and rival the Almighty—thus no longer obeying the Almighty's call, no longer being bound to his *mancipium*. Such is the wicked emancipation that the hysteric whispers to her man: you are not castrated. This emancipation is paid for by suffering, labor and death" (8). Woman calls on man to block the call, to disconnect from the divine call-forwarding system in order to come into his own. She disrupts the Edenic paternal power-flow, and throws her man to the winds of time, repetition, and death. Introducing pain into the destinal equation, she levels at the "beyond" of beyond the pleasure principle.

Somehow or other, the only two boys who will not have been led astray by the feminine, which Lyotard collapses into the maternal *mancipium*, are

Isaac and Jesus, whose moms were not entirely women ("Their mothers will have barely been women," 8). This is so because of the effects of maternal time warp: one was with child too late, having been barren, and the other too soon, having been virgin. Sarah welcomes impregnation with a laugh that is to become the name of her child (Isaac: "he laughed"). Lyotard compares the incredulous, vengeful laughter of Sarah to the Virgin's simple faith, framed by a smile. Because of these traits that unwoman them, the Jewess who is on the mat too late and the Christian whose womb conceives too soon are granted a certificate of exemption from the sphere of endangering maternity. These two women, Sarah and Mary, are exempted "from the fate of the mother as seductress. Hence the two sons, Isaac and Jesus, will have been only slightly led astray, or perhaps not at all, by the maternal *mancipium*." The barring of the women—barren or humanly inconceivable—allows for the unintercepted call to come through to these boys. "It is from the father himself that the trial of the binding and unbinding comes to the son." Mother takes her place at the sidelines, steadily transforming herself into the figure of mourning. Always in the grips of a lose-lose situation, mother appears to have the choice between damning herself as invasive seductress or effacing herself under the insistent beat of a death knell. Forgotten and suspended, she remains unforgettable, however, and a bit of a survivor, presiding over the demise of the paternally deposed, if sublimated, son.

Lyotard continues his reading of the fable, though he no longer signals its fabulous contextual hold. Instead he focalizes what he now regards as good emancipation—what amounts to an extreme form of paternal binding. "For the child, good emancipation has to do in both cases with rising to the call of the father, with being able to listen to it. It is not at all a matter of freeing oneself from this voice. For freedom comes, on the contrary, in listening to it" (8). Freedom is signaled, one could say, within the Heideggerian conjunction of *Hören* and *Gehorsam*, of hearing and adhering. Listening is an extreme form of obedience, of opening and giving oneself over to the voice of the other. Paul sketches the switchover from one master transmitter to another when he writes of an abiding enslavement within different registers of address: "For just as you once presented your members as slaves to impurity and to greater and greater iniquity, so now present your members as slaves to righteousness for sanctification" (Romans 6:19). Lyotard comments: "One is emancipated from death only by accepting to be 'enslaved to God,' for 'the advantage you get,' [Paul] continues, 'is sanctification. The end is eternal life'" (Romans 6:22). The enslaved may respond to a different master but the condition of enslavement does not in itself undergo significant modification. Lyotard does not spend much time tracing the slippage from freedom to sanctification but concentrates on the emancipatory drive that may with more or less success satisfy its aims.

⊙ ⊙ ⊙

Jews and Christians have observed a tacit agreement in one area—the vital area that covers the reception of the other. They are similarly disposed at the reception desk of the transcendental intrusion, watchful and ready to take note or direct a command. For Lyotard, the Jewish side of things is unambiguous in terms of receiving the call. On the Jewish side, he writes, "there is no need to comment further upon the listening, which I would wish to call absolute or perfect (in the way one speaks of a musician having perfect pitch), that is, upon the ear that Abraham or Moses lends to the calling of his name" (9). I would like to ask that you lend your ears to this flattering mystification of the Jewish pitch. It grieves me to add a sour note to the assertion, yet how can one's ears, trained on the inaudible, not prick up when provoked by the friendly foreclosiveness of the utterance, "there is no need to comment further"? Affirming Lyotard's own ethics of responsiveness, one must *enchaîner*, one must produce phrases around this silence, even if it should rest on the friendly silence of presumed perfection. The statement calls for something of a midrashic intervention, for it may be wrong to stabilize the calling of the name or what Abraham thought he heard that day (we leave Moses to another treatment, perhaps a psychoanalytical one, as when Lacan, discussing *das Ding*, offers that the burning bush was Moses' Thing). Let us put this call momentarily on hold and proceed.

Lyotard continues: "On this point Jews and Christians are in agreement—emancipation is listening to the true *manceps.*" Both sides of the divide agree upon the essential structure of subjection to a higher force, located in the commanding voice. This is the agreement that modernity disrupts when it tries to imagine and bring about an emancipation without an other. "Such an emancipation can only appear, in terms of the Scriptures, as weakness and impurity, a recurrence of the Edenic scene. The Jews and Christians agree on the impossibility, futility and abjection of an emancipation without *manceps*, without voice."[11]

---

11. There is a sense in which freedom wins out: "But modern emancipation did at least open up an horizon. An horizon, let's say, of freedom. Of a freeing of freedom. Yet as this freedom 'wins out' over itself, as it extends its *mancipium*, its grip, as we approach what I tried to designate, and very poorly, by the name postmodernity, this horizon (historicity) in turn disappears. And it is as if a paganism without any Olympus or Pantheon, without *prudentia*, fear, grace or

Nonetheless, a profound disagreement divides them. It stems, Lyotard offers, from the value that each ascribes to sacrifice. Paul makes virtually no reference to the trial of Abraham, contesting instead the Jews' ritualistic faith that is commemorated in the annual sacrifice, marking the division of the temple into two tabernacles, the second being reserved for the sovereign sacrificer. Paul omits mention, Lyotard points out, of the call that Abraham received—namely, the call of Yahweh, which asks Abraham to offer up his son, or rather submits him to the test of sacrifice but then calls off the test. "There will be no sacrifice of the child. Only a perpetual threat. The threat that Yahweh may forget to send the ram" (10). (Lyotard invites another to speak: "As George Steiner puts it so well in his little book entitled *Comment taire?*, every Jewish son knows that his father might be called to lead him up the hill that is now named *Adonai-Yerae*, that is 'God will provide' [Rabbinic translation], so that he may be sacrificed to Yahweh.[12] Not being sure that God will provide" [10]. For what it's worth, I do not see the earth-shattering insight here; could one not say that every Christian son knows he might be nailed by his father? Is not every father, at least every imaginary father, the foster parent of child Oedipus, out to get him at some level of unconscious deliberation?) The point here is that the bond fastened round the body of Isaac, its "binding," its *liance*, can be undone, "thus marking the precariousness of the binding, almost inviting the people of Israel to forget it, inviting renewed sin and trial, endless rereading and rewriting" (11). God backed off, the supreme Hand desisted. Which is to say: He can always make a comeback. The Christians, on the other hand, went all the way on the issue of sacrifice. Even Jesus was surprised that he was not Isaac and that the game was not called off in the last minute. But just because the game was not called off and the sacrifice played itself out does not mean that this full run amounted to what Lyotard has called a "good emancipation." The transfiguration of suffering, humiliation, and death into passion is *already* emancipation. The flesh was redeemed or pardoned ("graciée"). In this regard, the sacrifice cut both ways.

"Certainly, this confidence in pardoning or remission can give rise to bad emancipation, to appropriation, privilege, and worldly powers. Protestants knew this and so protested" (11). Lyotard ends the elaboration of "Mainmise"

---

debt, a *desperate* paganism, were being reconstituted in the name of something that is in no way testamentary, that is neither a law nor a faith but a fortuitous cosmological rule: development," *Peregrinations*, 9.

12. George Steiner, *Comment taire?* (Geneva: Éditions Cavaliers Seuls, 1986). The title homonymically combines "How to Keep Silent" with "Commentary."

by pointing to a *differend* between the Torah and the Christian testament, which pivots on the question of forgiveness. Hannah Arendt writes in *The Human Condition* that forgiveness is the remission granted for what has been done. "Not a forgetting but a new giving out, the dealing of a new hand. One would have to examine the relationship between this and emancipation" (12). The problem is, can *mainmise* play with a new deck or would such optimism merely set the stage for a new shuffling of *Deckerinnerungen* (screen memories) concerning the unrelenting terrorism of childhood?

There were two test sites for us Westerners, two figures of children who more or less transcended their putdowns. In a sense, however, testing in terms of the Christian reinscription was called off or, more precisely: it was rigged. Indeed, a *differend* has emerged in the church's reappropriation of Christ precisely where it refuses the test. A genuine test has been denied consistently by the church, called off or deemed out of line with the exigencies of erecting an untestable deity. The testing structure is repelled to such an extent that when the issue arises of Christ being put to the test, it becomes a marked scandal. There is the matter of the unavowable Temptation. Unsublatable, the Temptation fades under the worldly scepter of bad emancipation. Even when popular modes of expression try to put the trial back in the Passion—as in the filmic articulation, "The Last Temptation of Christ"—the church sends out its delegation to make street noises and block entry into the body of a tempted, troubled, tested son of God. Christ untested guarantees a certain narrative stability, no doubt—the stability of repression—but it interrupts the disturbing fable of the becoming-god.

I want to stay on this side of the fence and leave the Xians to the sum of transfiguring humiliations, the passions of which so much has been said and what Lyotard sees bolstered, I think, by dialectics, as so many counterfeit test sites. Let us though return to the trial of Abraham, if only to read, in response to Lyotard, the ambiguity of the call that came through on that fateful day. If rising to the call of the father offers a fighting chance for good emancipation, then let us check in on the way that call was placed—or, as the case may be, misplaced and unavoidably dropped. Someone's father took the call, and some kid paid for it . . . . Listen . . . .

"Abraham! Abraham!". . . . .
. . . .
. . . .

The call befalls you and you cannot prevent the "falling" which you are: it throws you. You are thrown (*geworfen*), thrown off from the start, before any "I" can constitute itself or any subject can be thrown together. You are called to come to the world and answer for yourself. In fact "called" is your most proper name, prior to any nomination, any baptism. This is why the call concerns only you. Your being is being-called. But why, why did God call twice? This is a matter that Lyotard does not take up, but it has a bearing, I think, on the way we encounter—or fail to acknowledge—the *mancipium*. For if the oppressive hand weighs so heavily upon us and has left a lasting thumbprint on our being, then it is necessary to recall that there is trouble on the line, and a difficulty in assigning the call with any certitude. Given the static, moreover, that harassed the line and lineage, it remains difficult to determine whether the position of father can be stabilized in this telling and does not itself jump, fall, leap back into childhood's regressive postures. Even God had to double deal, or deal at least with two pressing moments, when placing the call. These two moments have divided God against Himself, effecting once again the weak point of the "big A, *Autre.*" While Lyotard allows for a false call inadvertently to come through in his reading, and has something to say about that which sidetracks the call, he retains a sense of the truth in calling. As if it were ultimately possible to clear the static. God, for his part and party line, stutters—a hapax. Even though He is constantly repeating himself and renewing his threats, I do not believe that in order to make himself clear he has had to stutter the way he does over the name of our ur-patriarch. One version of the story tries to obliterate the repetition of the name, Abraham, but reading closely, I am hearing double.

"Abraham! Abraham!" Why did God have to call out the name twice? Why does God have to say Abraham two times? Or are there two of him? Had God surrendered from the start to the demands placed by the temporal predicament of the addressee, or was He Himself split by the destination of his call? In this double call or the call of the double, Kafka, as if fielding Lyotard's call, situates a parable.

"Abraham! Abraham!" The call came through as a gift that surpassed his initiative, indebting and obliging him before he could undertake any decision. I am not saying that the voice is a phenomenon or a *phoné sémantiké*: perhaps you hear it without hearing. Yet as inaudible and incomprehensible as it may be, it never lets up on calling you, Abraham. . . . .
. . . .

In light of Lyotard's focus on the calling structure that held Abraham in thrall, I can consider this virtually unknown text of Kafka. Titled "Abraham," it begins by splitting the addressee: "There must have been other Abrahams." My perspective, if that is what we can call it, corresponds to that of the child Isaac, switching, at times, also to that of Sarah. "And Sarah laughed," writes Kafka. But mostly I fell for the child Isaac, the one who was benched in the last minute of an ancient homegrown World Series, where the trace of sacrifice, the sacrificial punt, still exists. Isaac, in any case, was benched, pulled off the playing field of a transcendental rumble: Isaac sacked. The story depicts him, if we need to find a cultural diagnosis, as a mostly masochistic, lame loser. "Loser" may still imply too much agency, though. Isaac goes along with the whole being-called story, numbly. Kafka rereads the call that was taken on that fateful day in terms of a terror that was nowhere articulated in the sedimented responses that have accrued to it: the terror of becoming-ridiculous. The fear of becoming-ridiculous accompanies Abraham throughout his trek. For Isaac, there is no avoiding the ridiculousness of his own plight. What could it mean to have to sacrifice your sacrifice, which is to say, the father's sacrifice to which you have been assigned—or rather, to find yourself stripped even of the sliver of will that implicates you in his sacrifice, in the sacrificial act that is not even your own? The grammar of Isaac's failure to sacrifice, that is, to be sacrificed, is even more abject: what could it mean for us today that Isaac's sacrifice was sacrificed, called off? In *The Gift of Death*, Derrida writes that death is the place of one's irreplaceability, unsubstitutability, for "sacrifice supposes the putting to death of the unique in terms of its being unique, irreplaceable, and most precious. It also therefore refers to the impossibility of substitution, the unsubstitutable."[13] The act of his substitution will somehow diminish Isaac even further. His life preserved, it loses all value.

Now we come to Lyotard's assertion of the Jewish perfect pitch as it may be exemplified by Abraham. Let us recall the resolute way in which Lyotard pitches—or rather, ditches—the problem. On the Jewish side, he writes, "there is no need to comment further upon the listening, which I would wish to call absolute or perfect (in the way one speaks of a musician having perfect pitch),

13. Jacques Derrida, *The Gift of Death*, trans. David Wills (Chicago: University of Chicago Press, 1995), 58.

that is, upon the ear that Abraham or Moses lends to the calling of his name" (9). At this point I convoke a counsel of elders, one from the field of literature, the other from the philosophical domain. They have been with us all along. Both are ironists who have reached deeply into abysses. They were fearless when it came to reporting what they had found. Kafka and Kierkegaard, on the trail of the great patriarch, shared an insight into the ridiculousness of Abraham. Kierkegaard's example of foolish faithfulness, which he takes up at length in *Fear and Trembling*, is Abraham: "Abraham believed and did not doubt, he believed in the preposterous."[14] Kafka's parable "Abraham," which ponders the deconstitution of the primal patriarch, evokes Kierkegaard (and Don Quixote).[15] Multiplied and serialized, his several Abrahams are ridiculous creatures—the world would laugh itself to death at the sight of them, a series of miscreants in the procession we have followed. Their performance of insurmountable foolishness inscribes them in an unforgettable saga, dividing while sealing a first letter to Father.

14. Søren Kierkegaard, *Fear and Trembling*, trans. Walter Lowrie (Princeton, N.J.: Princeton University Press, 1981), 35.
15. Franz Kafka, "Abraham," in *Parables and Paradoxes* (New York: Schocken, 1958).

Chapter 7

Was war Aufklärung? /
What Was Enlightenment?

The Turn of the Screwed

"Es ist so bequem, unmündig zu sein"/"It is so comfortable to be immature."[1] Trained on the three monotheistic religions, Lyotard frequently reverts to Abraham on instant replay in order to score a number of crucial theoretical points. In his essay "Emma: Between Philosophy and Psychoanalysis," Emma, as the figure that deals out the wound of sexual difference, gets set up alongside Abraham as his improbable partner and counterpart. What binds the unlikely couple? Both Emma and Abraham are staggered by a mode of address that they integrate only minimally, if at all. Tiny and disabled, they are traumatically called up by a force or voice or prod that cannot properly land in or near them. Yet, the call fatefully diverts them and something happens, jostling them, relating them to the unrelatable. The drama of sheer exposure, the pull of vulnerability overtakes them. The jolt that they receive when picking up the untranslatable call or the call that only ever relays its own untranslatability, is something that resembles the shock of puberty—the rebellious blur bleeding out of the dilemma of impaired comprehension: "what is happening (to me)?" These reflections, linking Emma to Abraham in a no-doubt transgressive yet convincing manner, retrieve a sense of the affective shock that Lyotard is trying to communicate. Neither under the sway of history nor even of anahistory, these affective shocks continue to work themselves into

---

1. Immanuel Kant, *Was ist Aufklärung?* ed. Ehrhard Bahr (Stuttgart: Reclam, 1977), 9, discussing why the majority who are freed from outer constraints (or taken off the leash, "von fremder Leitung freigesprochen [naturaliter majorennes]") prefer to remain minors for the rest of their lives.

our political narratives, though their signals vary in intensity and range. As disjunctive as the extramemorial events may seem—seriously clashing and no doubt incompatible—they nonetheless manage to convey an unaccountable upheaval, at once common yet irretrievably alien. Both Abraham and Emma are terror-riven as they try to field a deracinating call that asks them to stand up in submissive readiness. On one level they are commanded to respond to a call; ready or not, they are made to assume that a call is meant for them. The call rips through them before they are prepared to become who they are, marking an experience of shattering decision. Lyotard designates the moment of faltering self-assumption as the passage through puberty.

It would be wrongheaded to think that one could simply skip over the motif and developmental-historical stopover of puberty when modern politics have depended on teenaged mythologies and fast-tracking disasters. For Lyotard the hysterical aftershock that puberty demarcates in ethics and as political tremor is of consequence. Puberty disturbs a certain level of inherited cognitive tracks, reroutes meaning, and starkly libidinizes relation to world according to the pressures of a newly minted language. "The adolescent does not reinterpret childhood representations. Rather, he interprets 'sexually' what in childhood would have been presented in another language. . . . these traces are affects. Puberty in no way creates them, as it creates only another 'reading' of an affect already there."[2] Drawing puberty onto the political platform of deed and reflection, Lyotard attempts to maintain something of a philosophical claim: "to speak in an intelligible fashion on the subject of the Id-side of the articulable, that is to say of the *Nihil*" (25). In effect, he turns away from an interpretation of drives and scrolls down to the Kantian Id-side of things—even though Kant remains too strongly attached, observes Lyotard, to subjectivist thought, that is, to a philosophy of consciousness. Nonetheless Kant has paved the way of a steep slope on the downside of nothingness, "the Id-side to which I am singularly host and hostage." On the Id-side, Kant allows the particular to be subsumed under the general and to close off singularity. Peril advisory: To the extent that the passage through puberty is a general event, Emma's case cannot be seen as singular, and hysteria must be the most common thing in the world. This is "an aporia lying in wait for all art, including psychoanalytic art, when it wants to make itself into a science: causal regularity crushes

2. Jean-François Lyotard, "Emma: Between Philosophy and Psychoanalysis," trans. Michael Sanders, Richard Brons, and Norah Martin, in *Lyotard: Philosophy, Politics, and the Sublime*, ed. Hugh J. Silverman (New York and London: Routledge, 2002), 36. Subsequent references are cited parenthetically in the text.

the singularity of a case. It would require finding a difference specific to the hysteria of some unique type of being (humanity) in which we all share and that is constituted by late puberty" (37). If I am getting this right, the brand of hysteria ascribable to puberty cuts into the political performance in considerable ways. The excited teen, running high on self-inflationary fuel, and disrupted by an untranslatable address, sparks the scene of action. Puberty's claims announce themselves as each time unique, in full revolt of *what is*, but they are applicable all around, rubbing out the singularity of the runaway teen spirit. What difference would insinuate itself into the most inevitable generality? The nothing and no-man's-land of adolescence is a stretch of being that still needs to be accounted for, even if we lack a grid to tabulate the saturation of the political according to adolescent excitability.

Here Lyotard analyzes "excitation" in speech to get to the question of original repression, for repression controls the event of excitation. *Excitatio*, from *citare*, sets into motion, arousing, capable of bringing forth and awakening. Lyotard, as Michel de Guy has noted, remains one of the radicalizers of Kant, with whom he stays in close contact when revisiting some circumscribed zones of unmarked intensity. Scoping the field of philosophical excitability, he locates what is "stretched to the four corners of Nothing, named by Kant as follows: *ens rationis*, an empty concept without object; *nihil privativum*, an empty object of a concept; *ens imaginarium*, an empty intuition without concept; and the terrible fourth, an empty object without concept, *nihil negativum*, the *Un-ding*, the no-thing" (24). To any philosopher, circuited through Lacan's reading of Freud, this no-thing, "a nullity of object and of concept," identified as the Thing, calls for a rereading and switch in the notion of negativity, even if we are not certain ever to have understood negation. Henceforth the philosopher must examine the a priori conditions of the possibility of an "unconscious judgment." The law issuing from this insight sounds like this: "act always as if the maxim of your will (desire) could never be known, shared, nor communicated . . . not even with yourself. And, for the philosopher, this parody immediately appears inconsistent. How could the 'you' to which the law is directed supposedly address itself, or even have knowledge of this prescription, if it is not allowed to know and share any motive of its deeds?" Configuring the law to accommodate what evades our grasp, what cannot be known—in other words, conforming to the lawyer Franz Kafka's rewrites and stipulations—Lyotard dwells at the limits of philosophical statement and determination, rehearsing that which may well lie beyond the scope of philosophical reach and investigations altogether.

But philosophy has to be prodded if it is to start reasoning with the unreasonable. "The stake is of the same order as that at which Heidegger aimed in

177

The Principal of Reason" (38). In the case study that binds Abraham to Emma, a fateful tremor occurs. Affect, which is not simply physical—though Lyotard relates it to a shuddering staple of puberty—turns up as a "phrase-affect." "The childhood affect (or 'sexual') phrase is noticeable in that it is neither referential nor addressed and is articulated neither according to the axis of its object nor according to that of its addressing." Lyotard is hoping to account for "the 'nothing' of the addressing of the childhood phrase-affect" (39). The childhood phrase-affect, he writes, cannot involve a demand, for a demand "is an expectation of linking." As an affect of *Hilflosigkeit,* be it of pleasure or pain, this "phrase does not spare a moment in linking itself to another phrase. Its sole time is now." The *enchaînement*—or linkage of phrasing—on which his work on the *différend* pivots falls to the side as childhood helplessness in tandem with adolescent panic whizzes by.

Lyotard maneuvers his thought on the major disturbance in development around "a strong alteration"—Freud's designation for the episode of puberty—that occurs when the turnover from childhood to majority gets marked (42). Abram became Abraham just after Yahweh addressed him. Women routinely adopt their husbands' name to mark a traumatic switchover, however sublimated to festivity or cultural expectation. The two affairs of strong alteration, cutting in on each other and binding, match trauma-prints. The calls may come from different transcendental area codes, but they produce a local shakedown. Lyotard states that he does "not confuse God with the shopkeeper. But I say that the Law bursts into pagan affectivity with the same violence as sex (genitality) attacks childhood affectivity" (42). Like Abram, the child Emma is "affectable or susceptible. But, no more than he, she is 'addressable.'" Yahweh demands that Abram listen to him; the shopkeeper demands that Emma receive his invasive address when he faces her as a "you [*toi*], a woman." "His gesture 'says': listen to the difference of the sexes, i.e., to genitality. He places the child all at once in the position of a 'you' in an exchange that she doesn't understand, as well as in the position of a woman in a sexual division which she also doesn't comprehend." Lyotard refrains from pursuing the parallels established here, refusing to convert his argument into a documented form of scholarly laboriousness. Understood. One can fill in the blanks, without risking a watering-down effect or domestication of the partnership he has negotiated between Emma and Abraham, for the drama of sexual difference attaches to the Abram-Abraham story and lets itself be filled out. One could pick up the strand of laughter that pervades the story of Abraham, linking it to the drama of sexual difference and the stall of puberty. No one has forgotten that Sarah is shut out from the scene and, before that, has split her sides in punishable laughter. Ever off the hook,

Abraham, for his part, has fallen on his face laughing, which does not arouse God's wrath. I too refrain from straying into friable ground. Nonetheless, an elaborate pursuit remains a temptation: who would not want to close in on the disruptive burst of laughter that organizes the biblical passage according to destructive markings of sexual difference?[3] Yet, even the Abraham narrative stakes its effectiveness, or one of its sacrificial links, on the return to puberty of the octogenarians. The promised regression to puberty was one reason for Sarah's laughter as her fate began diverging from that of her mate in the endless remake of sexual difference.

Lyotard has brought together Kant, Freud, and a biblical backstory, that of primal father, to bear on the political affect. Who gets to make the call, and how is one responsibly brought up to meet the challenge of its commanding reverberation? The numbed reluctance to take the call, even to hear the call, sustains the affective haze of political torpor and childish indifference. Kant will have tried to pull all humanity out of this comfort zone of childish immaturity. In the famous text, "What Is Enlightenment?" he shows the extent to which one eases off life's demands by remaining immature. Entire cultures and peoples enjoy and hang on to their tethers and don't even ask for a longer leash, a leashless frolic around the political arena and through the vicissitudes of existence. One *chooses immaturity,* one opts for childish beholdenness and the simple binds that obligate us to the external instance, the loom of authority. Lyotard will have tried to demonstrate that the difference between sexes offers a blow, but it remains "only shocking," not more: "it only strikes a blow, in a sense secondary to the *differend* between childhood and adult affect" (44). The aporia that he rides and on which he bases his argument—that we have no access to childhood terror except through adult-distilled narrative, shaky memory spurts, and the like—gives rise, each time anew, to a traumatic tremor that "resides in the untranslatability of childhood susceptibility into adult articulation" (45). When Kant tries to drag the human child, flailing in protest, toward adulthood, he posits a limit between childhood and adulthood, legal minority and majority. The move from an earlier, nearly enslaved state to a more emancipated position cannot be assumed or in any serious way taken for granted:

> Es ist für jeden einzelnen Menschen schwer, sich aus der ihm beinahe zur Natur gewordenen Unmündigkeit herauszuarbeiten. Er hat sie sogar liebge-

---

3. Other aspects of the sexual differend organized around biblical laughter inform part of her doctoral work delivered by Andrea Cooper in seminar at New York University, 2010.

wonnen und ist vorderhand wirklich unfähig, sich seines eigenen Verstandes zu bedienen, weil man ihn niemals den Versuch davon machen ließ.[4]

[Thus it is difficult for any single individual to extricate himself from the minority that has become almost nature to him. He has even grown fond of it and is really unable for the time being to make use of his own understanding, because he was never allowed to make the attempt.][5]

Kant has underscored in different ways the immense difficulty facing those who imagine a world emerging from the shackles and perverse ease of staying behind with the loser crowd of willed underdevelopment, the infantile lull of those refusing to budge from a place of servile adherence.

Maturity seen as self-reliance, a complicity based on understanding and tolerance, belong, for Kant, to the markers of adulthood. He recognizes the obstacle course laid out before any possible emancipatory project or projection, and he shows the extent to which one is embedded in all manner of commands telling us *not to ask questions*, to put up and obey ("Nun höre ich aber von alle Seiten rufen: *räsoniert nicht!* Der Offizier sagt: räsoniert nicht, sondern exerziert! . . . Der Geistliche: räsoniert nicht, sondern glaubt! Hier ist überall Einschränkung der Freiheit," original emphasis).[6] These are the types of called-in restrictions by which humanity, losing dignity and ground, is numbed down and dumbed out. Kant's prognosis stays on the productive side of the negative, bolstered by his understanding of the progressive nature of history.

Letting go of the Enlightenment fictions of a developmental chronicity and oriented becomings, Lyotard focuses on inevitable backslides and temporal whiplashes that yank us out of any reassuring narrative of straightforward development, and throw us back into states of voiceless immaturity. These affective ensembles and economies, latent but powerful, can break in at any moment of the human and post-human growth chart. Raised on Freudian thought, Lyotard puts his finger on the pulse of a switchover to a figure of alteration without the promise of emancipation: puberty marks the spot of a shock spasm from which we may still be reeling.

4. Kant, *Was ist Aufklärung?* 11.
5. Kant, *Practical Philosophy*, trans. and ed. Mary J. Gregor (Cambridge: Cambridge University Press, 1996), 17.
6. "But I hear from all sides the cry: *Do not argue!* The officer says: Do not argue but drill! . . . The clergyman: Do not argue but believe! Everywhere there are restrictions on freedom." Kant, *Practical Philosophy*, 18.

Index

Avital Ronell is University Professor of the Humanities and a professor of German, English, and comparative literature at New York University, where she codirects the Trauma and Violence Transdisciplinary Studies program. She is also Jacques Derrida Professor of Media and Philosophy at the European Graduate School in Switzerland. She is the author of *Dictations: On Haunted Writing*; *The Telephone Book*; *Crack Wars*; *Finitude's Score*; *Stupidity*; *The Test Drive*; and *Fighting Theory*.

The University of Illinois Press
is a founding member of the
Association of American University Presses.

_____

Designed by Jim Proefrock
Composed in 10.25/13 Filosofia
with Avenir, Serifa, and Trade Gothic display
at the University of Illinois Press
Manufactured by Thomson-Shore, Inc.

University of Illinois Press
1325 South Oak Street
Champaign, IL 61820-6903
www.press.uillinois.edu